DATE DUE

DISCARD

1 1 2008

Demco, Inc. 38-293

THE EDUCATION OF NOMADIC PEOPLES

Current Issues, Future Prospects

Edited by

Caroline Dyer

Berghahn Books
New York • Oxford

First published in 2006 by

Berghahn Books
www.berghahnbooks.com

© 2006 Caroline Dyer

Library of Congress Cataloging-in-Publication Data
The education of nomadic peoples : current issues, future prospects / edited by
Caroline Dyer.
    p. cm.
ISBN 1-84545-036-1
    1. Nomads—Education. 2. Nomads—Social life and customs. I. Dyer,
Caroline.

GN387.E34 2006
317.826918—dc22

                                                            2005056784

British Library Cataloguing in Publication Data
A catalogue record for this book is available from the British Library

Printed in the United States on acid-free paper

ISBN1-84545-036-1 hardback

CONTENTS

LIST OF FIGURES

ACKNOWLEDGEMENTS

So many people have helped, both directly and indirectly, to help this volume into print that it would be impossible to mention them all by name. However, particular thanks are due to Aparna Rao, whose network of contacts stretching around the globe provided an invaluable starting point for this collection; sadly, she did not live to see the finished product and we are publishing her chapter posthumously. Thanks also to Marion Berghahn for suggesting a literature review be included and to Saverio Krätli, who happened to have one to hand and readily offered to contribute elements of it! Dawn Chatty has been a supportive sounding board on several occasions and Sheila Aikman made useful comments on the chapters at the draft stage. I owe a huge debt of gratitude to my mother, who fortuitously arrived in India at a particularly difficult time in our research project and reminded us that slow progress is not the same as no progress – just the encouragement that was needed at the time. Archana's unwavering support over the years and Rohan's success at providing displacement activities away from the computer have contributed enormously to my sanity – I thank them both, and dedicate this volume to them.

INTRODUCTION

EDUCATION FOR NOMADIC PEOPLES: AN URGENT CHALLENGE

Caroline Dyer

*E*ducational provision for nomadic peoples is a highly complex, as well as controversial and emotive, issue. For centuries, nomadic peoples educated their children without recourse to non-indigenous sources, passing on from generation to generation the socio-cultural and economic knowledge required to pursue their traditional occupations. But over the last few decades, they have had to contend with rapid changes to their ways of life, often as a consequence of global patterns of development that are highly unsympathetic to spatially mobile groups. To make their way in the contemporary world, nomadic groups are finding that their indigenous modes of education are no longer adequate. All over the world, this has stimulated a search for external educational inputs to support the process of adaptation, both within and beyond pastoralism or hunter-gathering. Yet much of the history of nomads and formal education reflects an incompatibility between the aspirations of service users and the services that are provided, and underlines the often doubtful relevance of formal education to their lives. Success stories are few and far between, yet the need is often strongly felt.

At the same time, from a policy and service provider point of view, the question of educating nomadic peoples has become more pertinent than ever before. Governments around the world have signed up to the international pledge of Education For All (EFA), first mooted in 1990 and re-affirmed in 2000. They are bound by this imperative to consider how to reach out to community groups who have traditionally been excluded from educational provision. The setting of a Millennium Development Goal of Universal Primary Education by 2015 adds further urgency and emphasis.

Nomads have always been one of the hardest groups to reach, not only in practical terms, but also because courses of action on how to educate nomads are closely linked with states' stances on the nature of citizenship. Decisions about whether to draw nomads into education provided by the state or other bodies may be conditioned by perceptions of the contribution nomads make to local and national economies; ecological and infrastructural conditions; dairy, agricultural, forest and cultural policies; the flexibility or rigidity of educational systems; the integrity and sustainability of the nation state; the vision of inclusive development; and so on. The need to take action is evident, urgent and increasingly acknowledged by governments, international development agencies, non-government organisations, and others who are concerned about equity and inclusiveness in education.

Bringing education to nomadic peoples entails immense challenges which go well beyond the immediate and obvious problems of logistics – how to reach out to groups who are always, or often, on the move, and live in sparsely populated and climatically extreme areas. This can be an exciting challenge in which vision and sensitivity are exercised in assisting nomadic groups to re-orientate successfully to often rapidly changing contexts. Educational provision does not have to demand sedentarisation; for it too can be mobile. It does not have to adhere to a rigid model of content and delivery, for it can draw on indigenous knowledge and ways of learning, incorporating both in culturally sensitive interventions that are in tune with nomadic peoples' own visions of their future. Such education might well be provided in a non-formal context, where the groups' cultural values are retained at the centre of educational provision; the best of more formal government programmes would have the same aims in view.

At the opposite end of the spectrum, nomadic peoples' need for externally provided education is driven to a large extent by government policies that, either deliberately or by negligence, are exerting pressures to sedentarise. Sedentary living opens up the possibility of making use of 'mainstream' schools which cater to settled populations. However, the existing model of mass educational provision is rarely sympathetic to nomadic cultures, and children who attend these schools are less likely to value their own cultural heritage, particularly if their traditional learning patterns, or knowledge, find no place in what they do at school. While formal education may open the way to jobs within the wider economy, for which qualifications are a prerequisite, it may be part of a de-stabilising process that exerts pressures to bring the values of the ethnic group into line with the values of the homogenising modern state. In this scenario, 'education' is synonymous with sedentarisation and a delegitimisation of nomadism as an acceptable way of human life.

The chapters in this collection inform, contribute to and extend current debates about the education of nomads. Their critical engagement with the policy and local practices of education (most commonly in the form of formal schooling) are from perspectives that are all informed by extensive periods of time spent with nomadic groups across a wide range of country contexts. Bringing together the contributions of authors who themselves spend frequent and often extended periods of time working with nomadic groups has been an exercise in perseverance and patience over several years. There have, however, always been four important reasons for seeing it through. The first is the need for a book that brings together from around the world accounts of experiences of educating nomadic peoples, and makes them accessible to a wide audience. This volume was originally conceived, ten years ago, because writings about the education of nomads are sparse, and scattered across a range of diverse and not particularly accessible sources. The second is the need to critique the role of education in the context of the wider concerns and issues in nomads' development, and to highlight the role of formal education in shaping, and reflecting, the growth and character of the modern state. This collection thus directs attention towards the relationships between education and power in contemporary society, and how they contribute to marginalisation. A third reason is to draw out from international experience lessons that inform education policy communities and service providers in both formal and non-formal contexts, and help them with complex decision-making. The final, and perhaps most compelling, reason is to use this review of nomadic groups' perceptions and experiences of education to provide critical insights into the nature of education as a concept, and as a practice. Nomadic peoples' experiences can both explicitly and implicitly comment on, critique, and enlarge, our vision of what education both is, and could be. The pages of this book underline an urgent need to do this if we are to understand, and work towards fulfilling, our global commitments to making good quality education accessible to all people, and achieving meaningful Education For All.

The chapters in this volume are loosely thematically grouped, allowing the specifics of particular case studies to be explored, while contributing to a cumulative view of key issues of nomadic education around the world. The ten case study chapters are preceded by two overview chapters. The first of these, Saverio Krätli and Caroline Dyer's 'Education and Development for Nomads: the Issues and the Evidence' is a critical analysis of the literature on education for nomadic groups, drawing on an earlier review Saverio Krätli carried out for the World Bank. This chapter presents and develops the main issues and arguments found in the academic, agency and practitioner literatures, and sets the scene for the chapters exploring specific community and country contexts that follow. It is complemented by Roy Carr-Hill's discussion in the following chapter of 'Educational Services and Nomadic Groups in Djibouti, Eritrea, Ethiopia, Kenya, Tanzania and Uganda', which presents findings from a major African Development Bank funded research project assessing educational provision and challenges for nomadic peoples in these six African countries.

The first three case study chapters explore various aspects of childhood, socialisation of children, and how formal schooling responds to particular groups' cultural traditions. Chapter 3, 'The Acquisition of Manners, Morals and Knowledge: Growing into and out of Bakkarwal Society' by Aparna Rao, opens with a discussion of informal education and the traditional concepts and practices of socialisation of children among the nomadic pastoral Bakkarwal of Jammu and Kashmir in the western Himalayas. It goes on to examine the formal education of Bakkarwal children and the institutions responsible for it over the last roughly twenty years, pointing out how the Indian state's notions of a good and productive citizen are linked to its educational policies towards pastoral nomads. Rao argues that primary curricula must be adjusted to local needs and special capacities, and be more creative and practice oriented. Her conclusion raises a stimulating set of questions about the relevance of schooling systems for not only nomadic, but all children.

Michael de Jongh and Riana Steyn take us to South Africa in chapter 4, with their paper 'Learning to Wander, Wandering Learners: Education and the Peripatetic Karretjie People of the South African Karoo'. The childhoods of Karretjie children entail times of great flux and fragmentation, a ceaseless process of shifting localities and changing relationships with others and where factors such as poverty, domestic disruption and personal uncertainty are the reality of their lives. Their case study demonstates how the Karretjie people lack the necessary mechanisms and resources to secure their educational rights, while the practices of the South African state fail to reflect its enabling policy discourse. De Jongh and Steyn also report on an intervention they developed for improving Karretjie people's access to education, and draw out its implications for both practice and policy, in education and in development more widely.

The final chapter in this group, chapter 5, 'Changes in Education as Hunters and Gatherers Settle: Pitjantjatjara Education in South Australia' by Bill Edwards and Bruce Underwood, is a case study of an Aboriginal nomadic group of hunters and gatherers in South Australia. The enculturation of Pitjantjatjara children provides learning about both local resources and the relationships which determine their rights and obligations in daily life. Edwards and Underwood trace out tensions for this group of sustaining traditional values while at the same time engaging in modern economic and political structures. Their concluding discussion focuses on the significance of appropriate language policy in formal education, and the participation of the Pitjantjatjara in directing the development of their schools, so that their cultural values are honoured, as is their ambition to involve themselves more fully in mainstream Australian society.

Chapter 6 looks at the relationship between culture and poverty. In his 'Cultural Roots of Poverty? Education and Pastoral Livelihood in Turkana and Karamoja', Saverio Krätli proposes that the increasing insecurity of pastoral livelihood has cultural roots, as well as political and economic ones, that can be fruitfully studied by focusing on mainstream culture rather than only on pastoral people. Krätli argues that the link between pastoral poverty and education concerns the nature of the education undergone by pastoralists' fellow citizens at least as much as it concerns the knowledge gap about the 'outside world' amongst the pastoralists themselves; and so poverty eradication among pastoral groups seems conditional upon a radical review of the way pastoralism and pastoralists are represented in mainstream culture. He identifies the arguments used to assert pastoralism's 'inadequacies', and makes a series of suggestions as to how this inaccurate public image can be turned around, and the role formal education can play in doing so.

Reflecting the discussion of development ideology laid out in Krätli's preceding chapter, the following group of four chapters focuses specifically on a theme that underpins the whole collection: nomads' relationships with the state, and in particular, the state as reflected in its key institution of formal schooling. Ismael Abu-Saad's chapter 'Bedouin Arabs in Israel: Education, Political Control and Social Change' takes up the thread from the perspective of the Negev Bedouin Arabs, a traditionally semi-nomadic people living in southern Israel. As a part of the non-Jewish, Palestinian Arab minority in what came to be defined as a Jewish state, the 'outsider' status they share with many other nomadic groups has been exacerbated by state formation, and the nation-state desire to control them. Abu-Saad's chapter explores the important role of conflicting ideologies about land use and service provision, revealing not so much the 'unshared ideology' referred to earlier in this introduction, but a government development ideology that *explicitly excludes* pastoral people. He joins Krätli's call for the radical re-visioning of development ideology, played out through educational institutions, that must take place if nomadic groups are to be able to enjoy the same rights as other citizens of the state.

Chapter 8, by Caroline Dyer and Archana Choksi, reaches a similar conclusion via a very different route, from a case study in India. 'With God's Grace and with Education, We Will Find a Way: Literacy, Education and the Rabaris of Kutch' shows that state failure to engage with the education of nomadic groups is a powerful way of conveying its unspoken, yet clear, development agenda of sedentarisation. Unprecedented pressures on pastoralist livelihoods are provoking among Rabaris a quest for occupational diversification, facilitated by formal educational qualifications. Sedentarisation appears the 'logical' choice for pastoral nomads who seek schooling, since this facilitates accessing a system of formal education that makes no provision for movement. Action research with migrating groups, focusing on provision of adult literacy, confirmed the logistical feasibility of peripatetic teaching, but established that this model lacks legitimacy in the eyes of Rabaris themselves. Reflecting a wider social discourse, Rabaris have come to associate their own traditional occupation with being 'backward' and as having no place in the modernising economy. Rather than adult literacy, their priority is schooling for their children. Dyer and Choksi identify, along with other contributors to this volume, the challenge for the future as being changing government perception that nomads do not fit into the modernising project of a developing country.

The following two chapters in this group describe cases where state actions in providing formal education have had positive outcomes for nomadic groups. In both Iran and Mongolia, state educational provision has had marked ideological inclinations that are potentially unfriendly to nomadic values. But in both cases, nomadic groups have been able to challenge those assumptions and shape the education they receive from state institutions to fit their own cultural values and aspirations. Mohammed Shahbazi's account in chapter 9, 'The Qashqa'i, Formal Education, and the Indigenous Educators', demonstrates how, if state officials in Iran had hoped politically to pacify Qashqa'i youth by altering their culture, the tent school unintentionally *facilitated* enculturation of Qashqa'i youths into the culture and values of their own tribal and nomadic societies. This outcome was diametrically opposed to the ideological agenda for education set by government officials. Shahbazi adds his voice to the call for providers to stop displaying 'expert' attitudes with a 'mission' to recast communities – nomadic pastoralists in this case – into 'better' ones, and instead to work with them to identify what their actual needs are, and how formal education can facilitate meeting those needs. In chapter 10, 'Education and Pastoralism in Mongolia', Demberel and Helen Penn argue that pastoralism has a unique place in the conceptualisation of the state in Mongolia. The chapter draws on the extensive personal experience of Demberel, himself a pastoralist, who occupied very senior positions in the government education sector. In this admittedly unusual context, Demberel and Penn suggest that formal education can be practically organised for pastoralists, and can become valued among pastoralist communities without necessarily conflicting with their cultural and collective identity. However, in Mongolia's current transition economy, the question is whether the kinds of success they describe for Demberel and other pastoralists will continue to be possible in a market economy, where other values strongly prevail.

The final grouping of two chapters focuses on collaborative work with governments to explore ways of addressing challenges of education for nomadic peoples. Dawn Chatty's chapter, 'Boarding Schools for Mobile People: the Harasiis in the Sultanate of Oman' explores why a boarding school in the middle of an extensive tribal area succeeded in the face of the kinds of problems which so often spell defeat. The political underpinning of the thirty-year-old state education system was evident in state messages about Omani citizenship; as was a lack of relevance of the urban and agrarian-based state curriculum for the desert-based communities of Oman. However, the local community wished to take advantage of all that was on offer; and the government was determined to make the desert school a 'flagship'. Harasiis families did not perceive formal schooling as a cultural threat; rather, they regard the institution as providing a special economic opportunity for a select few. This is perfectly acceptable since, as Chatty points out, there was never any idea of universal education among the Harasiis. Chapter 12, 'Adult Literacy and Teacher Education in the Nomadic Education Component of the Nigeria Community Education Programme' by Juliet McCaffery, Kayode Sanni, Chimah Ezeomah and Jason Pennells, reflects on successes and tensions in an education project with the Fulani pastoralist nomads in Adamawa and Taraba States in Nigeria. Their chapter focuses on the two major project components of adult literacy and teacher education. It describes the participatory and pragmatic methodology which draws on the experience, knowledge and skills of the participating communities to enable men and women to develop the literacy and numeracy skills they require for everyday life. The teacher education programme developed a model of building teacher capacity in marginalised communities which addressed, without necessarily resolving, some of the issues inherent in providing education to pastoralist nomadic communities. The conclusion of the chapter reflects on the expectations the project raised, and the sustainability of its inputs, raising issues that have pertinence well beyond the immediate project context.

The volume closes with a brief editor's afterword, highlighting key issues raised by the authors and drawing out from the chapters agendas for future action.

Caroline Dyer
Leeds
February 2005

CHAPTER 1

EDUCATION AND DEVELOPMENT FOR NOMADS: THE ISSUES AND THE EVIDENCE

Saverio Krätli with Caroline Dyer

This chapter is a critical review of the scattered literature that directly, or by implication, sheds light on the complex relationships between the education and development of nomads. It presents, and then problematises from the perspective of nomads, some of the key assertions and assumptions that are made about education in general, education and rural development, and education for pastoral development. Subsequent chapters in this volume offer case studies that illuminate in greater detail some of the key issues we raise here.

Education as Ideological Practice

Education has formally been seen as a fundamental right since its inclusion in the 1948 Universal Declaration of Human Rights. Policy discourse over the years has presented education not only in this light, but also as a means of empowerment – a route by which to overcome social and economic disadvantage. Education is also seen to serve an important purpose in including and integrating or assimilating non-mainstream groups into wider society, and thus in developing and preserving the integrity of the nation state. Since educated citizens are presumed to be more productive than their uneducated peers, school education is seen as necessary to contribute more effectively to national development (which is generally conflated with economic development). All in all, schooling is perceived as a 'social good', and as a universal project in which all should share, and from which all would gain.

In various ways, nomadic populations' schooling record challenges these apparently universal views. Where nomads can be brought into formal education, they are usually, from the point of view of service providers, unsatisfactory clients. In terms of enrolment, attendance, classroom performance, achievement, transition to higher levels of education, and gender balance, their record is consistently disappointing. Educational campaigns may raise some interest at the beginning but are soon deserted. Even the rare literacy achievements are often lost within a few years.

Experiences of providers over the years have thus generated a considerable received wisdom about the difficulties of educating nomads. This chapter seeks to identify some of the background that has led to an often depressing educational scenario. In searching out convincing explanations that challenge this received wisdom and thus ultimately serve to move the debates forward, we draw on a wide body of literature to present alternative points of view. We will argue that education can never be a simple, neutral practice in the way much of the policy literature seems to assume. Rather, it is ideological in nature, and embedded in particular ways of thinking about human development in general, and nomadic development in particular. Every chapter in this volume underlines this point, as each one illustrates how rarely the rationales and ideologies underpinning the actions of service providers (particularly governments) and those of the users of the service (nomads) converge, particularly in perceptions of 'development' and the role of education in its pursuit.

Education for Nomads: the State Imperative

Government provision of education is driven by the requirements of making schooling available to all citizens, in pursuit of liberal humanitarian aims that find expression in national policies and endorsement of the international aim of Education For All (WCEFA, 1990) and now the second Millennium Development Goal (GMR, 2002). Governments that fulfil their responsibilities in such respects are ostensibly offering opportunities to all their citizens to accomplish their full potential as human beings, as well as to assure their survival and lifelong development. An educated citizenry is seen as more likely to uphold the stability and permanence of the nation state, and education thus is an important means by which to enhance the capacity of all citizens to contribute to state building.

Nomads fit poorly into many of these imperatives for a government, and thus present some of the most intrinsically complex and uncomfortable questions as to the nature and aim of educational provision and processes, and of development. The nomadic life-style, and in particular the scattered, low density distribution of pastoral populations, and their varying degrees of mobility, makes assuring access to provision expensive, as well as difficult to organise and manage. Often, when a service provider makes a special effort, such as building extra schools in remote areas or equipping existing schools with boarding facilities, there is a poor response from the targeted recipients. It is, however, assumed that inclusion in formal education is the key for inclusion in development, and more often than not the expectation is that this can only be achieved by assimilating nomads into mainstream society and economy.

Policies and programmes concerning the education of nomads can, then, be grouped around two major rationales, which may work together or against each other. The first rationale is *the full accomplishment of the individual as a human being*, which holds central the notion of education as an individual's basic need and fundamental right, and emphasises inclusion and empowerment. The second rationale concerns national development, and *the integration of nomadic groups into the wider national context*: it thus focuses on the economic and social development of nomads (from the perspective of the state), dealing with concerns such as sedentarisation, modernisation, poverty alleviation, resource management and state building. The ways these rationales are understood, combined and pursued may vary greatly. In whichever combination they are found, however, they are neither neutral, nor dispassionate; rather, they reflect a set of *ideologies* about education, nomads and development. Tensions emerge when these ideologies, once put into practice, reveal themselves to be unshared. Received wisdom about the difficulties of 'providing education' to nomads is based on three major assumptions:

1. The apparently automatic equation that schooling equals progress. Schooling is pursued as a universal project, and there is strong faith in modern schooling as something inherently good, i.e. with value in and of itself.
2. Nomadic pastoralists are placed on a ladder of social evolution that goes from hunter-gatherers to agriculturalists and 'modern' societies.
3. As an indicator of the degree of 'evolution' along such a ladder, mobility becomes a focus. Consequently, pastoralists are categorised according to their – presumed – degree of mobility.

Alternative perspectives on these assumptions render them problematic. To make the first assumption (that schooling is a universal project) is to forget that this project has particular historical and cultural roots. Formal schooling is as least as likely to be a process of reproduction of 'modern' society as it is to be a process of emancipation of humanity – if indeed not more so. No educational process can ever be context free, and thus modern schooling takes place within certain contextual realities which may militate against emancipation: the chapters in this book will illustrate that such realities include political and ideological manipulation, counterproductive practices and damaging results.

The universalising project is equated with 'development' and thus the second assumption – that of the social evolution ladder – gives a sense of urgency to the provision of schooling to nomads. It also, simultaneously, provides many explanations for its failure: attributes of the 'pre-modern' nature of nomads are their lack of effective or 'powerful' knowledge, resistance or incapacity to change, ignorance and superstition, primitive forms of production that require child labour, gender bias against women, and so on. Difficulties that educational service provision encounters are explained away with reference to 'deficit' nomadic culture while any impetus to identify problems within the nature of the provision itself is pre-empted by the underlying assumption that pastoralism is an archaic way of life that will soon disappear.

The third assumption, related to mobility as a measure of lack of social evolution, legitimises the political push for sedentarisation. The framing of mobility as unnecessary and/or irrational behaviour shifts onto nomads the ultimate responsibility for omissions of education provision, for how can the state be expected to provide effective services if nomads move all the time? But to think thus is to obscure the fact that mobility is a livelihood strategy and merely not a lifestyle. As such, it is neither stable nor constantly decreasing, but swings in intensity and changes in nature according to environmental, political and economic conditions (Bonfiglioli, 1988; de Bruijn and van Dijk, 1995). Pastoralists move across a spectrum of mobility *in all directions* (that is becoming at times more or less mobile in various ways) through processes of adjustment to changed life conditions that may last for decades (Toulmin, 1983; de Bruijn and van Dijk, 1995). In practical terms, sparse populations and high labour-demand of dryland herd management strategies are much more real obstacles to the provision of education, in its present form, than mobility.

The emphasis on the universal value of formal education makes it difficult to recognise the cultural specificity and ideological dimension of all educational practices. Although equity in the state's provision of services to its citizens is obviously an important goal in principle, the flags of equity and a child's right to education may veil more or less deliberate practices of cultural assimilation of minority groups into hegemonic societies (e.g. Darnell, 1972). Analysing public service provision to Bedouins in Israel, Meir (1990) points out how the goal of efficiency may open new avenues to political control of the government over nomad groups, and how behind the efforts to ensure education provision there may be the intention to 'sever Bedouin from their nomadic way of life, to sedentarise them, and eventually to control their locational patterns' (Meir, 1990: 771). Similar situations are reported about the Bedouins in the Negev desert (Abu-Saad, this volume), the pastoralists of Kazakstan (De Young and Nadirbekyzy, 1996), Siberia (Habeck, 1997), India (Rao, this volume), and the Roma gypsies in the United Kingdom (Okely, 1997).

Development and Pastoralists: the Sedentarisation and Modernisation Debates

Policies on education for nomads are inevitably embedded in policies for pastoral development (where such policies exist at all, see Dyer and Choksi, this volume). Since changes in the pastoral development paradigm over the years have influenced changes in thinking about educational provision within that context, we first look at major trends in pastoralist development thinking, in order to understand the complexity of education for pastoralists.

From the first efforts in the 1920s to the mid 1980s, pastoral development theories and practices (summarised in Anderson, 1999) rested on the assumption that nomadic pastoralism was an evolutionary *cul de sac*, environmentally destructive, economically irrational, and culturally backward. Seen as a relic from the past in human social evolution, pastoralism was expected ultimately to disappear. It seemed obvious that the initial stage of pastoral development must therefore be a step *away from* pastoralism, first of all towards sedentarisation and alternative modes of production (Hogg, 1988). Thus, until the mid 1980s, encouraging nomads to become sedentary, most probably as farmers, sometimes as fishermen, was a key component of pastoral development thinking. The myth that the development of pastoralism lies in sedentarisation is proving most resistant, and is today still widespread (for an overview of myths and misunderstandings in pastoral development see UNDP-GDI, 2003).

A second factor that militated against nomadic pastoralism was that it was seen as environmentally destructive. Traditional herd management was assumed to be primitive and driven more by cultural than economic factors, representing the antithesis of rational practices advocated by the establishment. Pastoralists were said to be obsessed with the number of animals and with aesthetic issues, at the expense of production/quality. It was theorised that this 'cattle complex' (Herskovits, 1926) led to exceeded carrying capacity, according to an ecological paradigm which held that weak land tenure arrangements, based on traditional common management of grazeland (Hardin's tragedy of the commons, 1968), were resulting in overgrazing, pasture degradation, conflict, drought and famine.

After independence in former colonial countries, and in Africa particularly with the increasing food scarcity in the 1980s, policy makers started to look at the livestock controlled by pastoralists as an important *national* resource (for example Evangelou, 1984; Gefu, 1992). The development of pastoralism was re-conceptualised in terms of modernisation, largely in order to improve productivity: this inclusive approach implied that pastoralists had now a role to play in the economic development of the nation state. Within the new policy aproach, the management of livestock should aim at maximising productivity consistent with modern national and international standards of quality (meat, milk, hide, wool, and other animal products). Pastoralism as a mode of production should be separated from pastoralism as a way of life, and the latter abandoned in order to modernise the former.

From the early 1990s, the orthodox ecological paradigm, already widely questioned within social sciences, was dismissed even by rangeland specialists. Nomadic pastoralism is increasingly recognised as the most efficient and sustainable way of exploiting the natural resources of the drylands (Behnke et al., 1993). These same resources would enable fewer people to make a living exclusively from agriculture or modern ranching. Traditional pastoralism achieves such remarkable performance because of exceptionally high levels of specialisation: efficient tracking of pasture in unpredictable environments requires 'high levels of skilled labour input' (Scoones, 1995: 20). In the context of structurally heterogeneous and discontinuous rangelands productivity, traditional pastoral strategies of flexibility and opportunism are highly rational, and a basis upon which development interventions should be built in highly variable ecosystems (Ellis and Swift, 1988).

The Education of Pastoralists

Situated as a component of shifting priorities in pastoral development, state education has been, and remains, instrumental to a variety of ends, not all of which are necessarily compatible. Whether directly or indirectly, it has been closely associated with efforts to get nomads to abandon pastoralism, or to pursue pastoralism in a manner more in keeping with the modernising imperatives of nation states.

Earlier policy on education for nomads was linked, often explicitly, with the perceived need to encourage nomads to sedentarise. This imperative affected educational policies for nomads either directly, by making education instrumental to sedentarisation, or indirectly, by framing education provision problems as temporary and therefore not requiring a considered, long term response, based on the assumption that they would disappear once nomads settled. In Nigeria's *Blueprint on Nomadic Education* (Federal Ministry of Education, 1987), for example, nomads are categorised according to their stage of sedentarisation – which represents nomadism in terms of deficit, or what it does not yet have: 'the lack of a home of his own and grazing land for his cattle has forced him [the nomad] to be on the move throughout his life' (Alkali, 1991: 56). In a recent study from a participatory perspective one also reads: 'Rural sedentarism in Africa can be discerned as the last stage of the process that occurs over time in the mode of the pastoral production. [...] The three stages towards sedentarisation are nomadic-pastoralism, agro-pastoralism and transhumant-pastoralism' (Woldemichael, 1995: 9). This categorisation runs counter to historical accuracy: pastoralism is a specialisation that developed from agriculture, so there is no evolutionary linearity from nomadic livestock keeping to sedentary farming (see Khazanov, 1984).

Educational provision may thus serve an instrumental purpose in promoting sedentarisation. This can take place in various ways. Where there is (by neglect or deliberately) no alternative provision, nomads have to stay near settlements if they want their children to go to school, leading to a quasi-sedentarisation, or perhaps division of the pastoral family to allow some members to remain nearby so children can attend school, while others continue to migrate. Schools, as a result of their overt or hidden curricula, can inculcate in school-going children the values and world-views of sedentary society, through an articulated or inherent expectation that by introducing them to a sedentary lifestyle, they will absorb it and make it theirs. Nomads are well aware of such strategies (e.g. Shahshahani, 1995) and this has been identified as one of the key reasons why educational provision predicated on the 'myth of sedentarisation' tends to fail (Dall, 1993).

Following the shift in the pastoral development paradigm during the 1980s (Baxter, 1985; Hogg, 1988) some countries abandoned, at least formally, the goal of sedentarisation and transformation of pastoralists into farmers, beginning to focus on how to use education in order to improve pastoralism as such. Nomadic pastoralists should receive formal education because, within their respective countries, they control important 'national' resources (land and livestock), the productivity of which should be improved to match national requirements. Education is seen as an instrument to change nomads' attitudes and beliefs, to introduce 'modern' knowledge and 'better' methods and practices en route to becoming modern livestock producers. In Ethiopia, for example:

> After acquiring knowledge and skills in modern cattle raising and modern farming methods, basic care and nutrition, they will go back to the community where they came from as change agents to improve the living conditions of their people. (Degefe and Kidane, 1997: 36–37)

In Tanzania, the Ministry of Education and Culture emphasises the urgency of educating pastoralists on the need to decrease the size of their herds in order to reduce the pressure on the land. The argument goes on to recommend the application of modern methods of animal husbandry, such as the use of better cattle feeds, preparation of fodder and pasture management, with the goal of improving animal products for wider markets (Bugeke, 1997: 78). In Sudan, the education of nomads is expected to:

> enable them to integrate into the society, to fulfill their civic duties, to gain their rights and privileges, and to increase their productivity [...] develop a national outlook and relate the good aspects of their cultural heritage. (Suleman and Khier, 1997: 67)

Often, the sedentarisation paradigm simply adapted to the shift in pastoral development discourse, managing to survive well after it. One of the first examples of the change from the sedentarisation paradigm is the Nomadic Education Programme in Nigeria. As summarised in Aminu (1991: 51), the programme 'is intended to enable the nomadic population to improve upon their productivity, especially given that they exercise a dominant control of the protein sector of our national nutrition'. As early as 1982, promoters of 'nomadic education' argued that settlement is the 'natural evolution' of nomadism, and therefore not a real issue, while forcing nomads to settle 'before time' would mean the collapse of their culture and system of production, and the consequent loss of their potential contribution to the national economy. On the other hand, they emphasised that although sedentarisation does not have to be a precondition of pastoralists' integration into the market economy at the national level, the immediate and instrumental provision of education could guide and accelerate such a process (Ezeomah et al., 1982; Federal Ministry of Education, 1987).

Despite the shift away from the emphasis on sedentarisation, formal education continues to be intended as an instrument for the transformation of pastoral society, although 'from within', in order to modernise pastoralists 'without uprooting their culture' (Ezeomah, 1983). At worst, this can mean that a stock of essential elements of 'indigenous culture', perhaps identified in consultation with nomads but ultimately chosen by 'experts', is to be blended or incorporated into the nomadic education curriculum with the explicit intent of making the usual schooling more appealing to nomads (Salia-Bao, 1982; Lar, 1991a, b).

With rare exceptions, formal education is used as an instrument for transforming pastoralists into settled farmers, waged labourers, or 'modern' livestock producers. Common to these productivity approaches are accounts of pastoralists' poverty and the assumption that formal education will bring an improvement in their standard of living. Claims that schooling has beneficial effects on pastoral productivity are not, however, well supported by evidence, and indeed few data are available. In Mongolia, the achievement of nearly universal primary education among herders in the 1960s-1980s (with 11.3 percent of GDP spent on education and considerable resources devoted to the livestock sector, see Demberel and Penn, this volume), was accompanied by some increase in livestock productivity. In Kenya, among the Maasai who have increasingly turned to school education during the last 25 years (Sarone, 1986), education does not seem to have affected livestock production, which is being taken over by young non-educated wealthy cattle traders who buy the labour of young non-educated stockless herders (Holland, 1996).

A crucial assumption in approaches that emphasise the role of formal education as a means of introducing changes directed to increase productivity is that it is possible to separate pastoralism as a way of life from pastoralism as a way of production, and to abandon the former in order to improve the latter. This perspective assumes that the individuals will be 'emancipated' through formal education from their traditional way of life as pastoralists, yet maintain the same productive role as herders. In practice, however, this is not usually the case. The reduction of pastoralism to a mere system of production was first theorised and experimented with by the Soviet Committee of the North in Siberia in the 1930s, on the Tungus (Evenki) reindeer nomadic pastoralists. As a consequence of forced collectivisation of livestock and division of labour, only the people in hunting and herding brigades were to work away from the settlements, with one woman each as housekeeper. But rather than staying in the settlements many women followed their husbands, taking with them those children who did not have to stay in boarding schools (Habeck, 1997).

Pastoralism, then, is a mode of perception as well as a mode of production. Awareness of the non-viability of pastoral livelihood strategies in the face of shrinking resources and lowering social status appears to trigger in pastoralists a concern for their own existence and cultural identity rather than an economic concern about the necessity of modernising their production methods. The responses sought to such a concern may have more to do with spirituality than economics (eg. El-Hassan's 1996 discussion of Hamoshkoraib and the Beja pastoralists on the Sudan-Eritrea border). Köhler-Rollefson and Bräunig (1999) warn of the limitations of using a productivity-focused approach within contexts in which livestock is not seen as a mere factor of production, but as an integral part of cultural identity, loaded with ritual and religious meanings which can play key roles in the construction of social capital. Furthermore, all approaches that see formal education as a way to increase productivity, and as a humanitarian goal, fail to consider that increased productivity does not necessarily mean more income for producers, as this is subject to pre-existing relations of exploitation (Kavoori, 1996; Sikana and Kerven, 1991).

The Provision of Educational Services

Mobility, sparse population, harsh environmental conditions and remoteness present technical obstacles to the provision of formal education through systems which are designed for sedentary people in well-connected and densely populated areas. Governments respond to mobility, sparse population and remoteness by introducing various alternatives to the standard education structure – most commonly boarding schools, but there are a few examples of mobile schools and distance education using radio broadcasts.

Boarding Schools

Neither parents nor children like being separated for long periods; parents do not readily give custody of their children to people they do not know, to whom they are not related and whose moral integrity they may doubt (SCF, 2000a; MOEST, 1999; Dyer and Choksi this volume). The success of boarding schools therefore depends on the quality of life within the school, and the capacity to recreate a familiar and friendly environment (see Demberel and Penn, this volume). In some countries, schools in pastoral districts may have a majority of non-pastoral children since they may be subsidised or easier to get into than schools in agricultural areas and, as a result, the prevailing school culture may be anti-pastoralist despite the surroundings (see Habeck, 1997 for Siberia; UNDP-Emergency Unit for Ethiopia, 1996; Närman, 1990 for Kenya; Rybinski, 1980 for Algeria). Where there is legislative capacity to do so, law enforcement may be called on to get children into schools, but this strategy may be counter-productive. In Niger in the 1980s, for example, the government's use of army patrols to bring WoDaaBe pastoralist children to schools and force parents to obey the law on compulsory education simply led to high levels of truanting.

Boarding schools have been discussed in Tibet as the solution to the high rate of drop-out amongst their very sparse population (Bass, 1998). In Qinghai Province, Central China, a basic education project provides additional boarding schools in very remote areas using permanent tent camps (CiC, 2000). Because they are often located in remote pastoral areas, boarding schools are often required to be self-sufficient. Usually self-sufficiency was pursued through farming the fields around the school – work done by the pupils – since learning to become settled farmers was considered an important stage of pastoralists' development. Some recent experiments in school self-sufficiency have, however, been based on animal husbandry rather than farming. The tent-boarding school at YakCho, in Qinghai Province, China, opted for a herd of yaks (one per child) provided by the families and that ensures the main ingredients of the local traditional diet, although 'in order to make the school completely self-sustaining' the project will construct an agricultural polytunnel at the school site (CiC, 2000: 4). Similarly, the School Camel Programme in Samburu, Kenya, establishes herds of ten camels, three of which are provided by the families, in selected schools; and the camels are used as practical learning aids (MOEST, 1999; Sifuna 1987).

Nomadism and Mobile Schools

Tent-schools, schools-on-wheels and various kinds of collapsible schools have been experimented with over at least the past 50 years, for example in Mauritania (Oul Mahand, 1956), Algeria (Blanguernon 1954; Rybinski, 1981), Iran (Hendershot, 1965; Varlet and Massumian, 1975), and Nigeria (Udoh, 1982). Tents are also used as semi-stable structures that are moved seasonally or that simply *can* be moved at low cost if necessary. With the exception of Iran, mobile schools have performed far below expectations. In Nigeria, for example, after almost 20 years since the first attempts were made, today the 'mobile school system is sparingly used due to the enormity of problems that are associated with the model' (Tahir, 1997: 56).

A recent successful mobile pre-school education project in Mongolia uses *gers* (the white tents of the nomads) or even cars as mobile training centres during the summer. These low cost structures can be afforded by local governments or the families involved. Teachers are also nomads, who move with their families and stock together with the group of households involved in pre-school education and are paid by the government for their work as teachers (MOSTEC, 1999; SCF, 2000b).

One successful way of providing mobile education has been by supporting and expanding existing Koranic schools, where they are available. It has been noted, however, in the context of Somalia (Bennaars et al., 1996), that the success and sustainability of Koranic schools is linked to the religious rationale for teaching, which means that teachers work for free, to please God; and a teaching practice that needs a wooden slate as the only resource (see also Chatty, this volume). The introduction of secular subjects would require textbooks and teaching-learning materials from outside the pastoral context, and extra training for the teachers.

Distance Education

Distance education through radio programmes has been used in several countries. The most successful example seems to be the UNESCO adult education project in Mongolia, targeting women of nomad households in the Gobi desert and focusing on basic literacy and practical skills (Robinson, 1997). A second project followed, with national broadcasts and a spectrum of topics well beyond the practical scope of the first one.

Security, Staffing and Language of Instruction

Whatever the mode of education, there are several other issues which affect pastoralists' willingness or ability to make use of these schools. Location of schools is directly related to the question of security for girls, for example. Pastoralists live in remote areas, often close to insecure international borders and conflict-prone regions. Girl children walking long distances to school are prone to risks of sexual attack. In northern Kenya schools in remote centres make good targets for the mass abduction of children, particularly girls, by raiding parties and bandits (Jeremy Swift, personal communication, 2001).

Schools in pastoral areas tend to have high rates of staff turnover. Nomadic populations are affected no less than others by petty government corruption in the manipulation of teaching appointments, but, along with other less powerful social groups, do not have the power to raise and sustain the issue (SCF, 2000a). A school may be seen by local communities as a government enterprise that has little to do with them, so what the government does with it may not appear to be an issue (Semali, 1993; Jama, 1993). Teachers may find their salary is paid erratically, and experience isolation, along with a lack of teaching resources and harsh living conditions, which results in low motivation and high absenteeism. While it is widely recognised that teachers should be from the same pastoral background as the pupils, demand usually outstrips supply; and a pastoral background is not necessarily a guarantee that a teacher will settle in the job rather than trying to move to town (MOEST, 1999).

For minority groups, the language of instruction is also a major issue (see Edwards and Underwood, this volume). If teachers and children are not from the same ethnic group, they are likely to speak different languages and have problems of communication in the classroom. Even if teacher and pupils do share a common language, it is not necessarily the language in which the children are supposed to become literate. Which language – local, national or even international – should be used for the acquisition of literacy is a matter of animated debate. Supporters of teaching literacy in the local language argue that it increases motivation (or minimises exclusion) and school productivity. The argument is however complex, particularly if a local language has no written form, since defining a written form and producing written materials (even just a primer) in a minority language involves very high costs (Vawda and Patrinos, 1999). A recent study amongst San and Khoe in South Africa argues that local languages are part of specific cultural settings and therefore cannot survive independently from the maintenance of the resources, access and modes of production on which such settings depend (Crawhall, 1999). National or international languages, far from being neutral tools of communication, usually have a local history as the language of the colonial administration or of the hegemonic ethnic group. Such local histories provide added meanings and tie the use of those languages to particular social practices and current power relationships (Bloch, 1971; Edwards and Underwood, this volume).

Curriculum Relevance

As the means by which values are transacted in the classroom, the formal curriculum mirrors the developmental intent of service providers; curriculum design is thus much debated. Education systems across the world almost always rely on standard curricula, in which all pupils in the same grade will learn more or less the same things, in more or less the same way. However, pupils' environment and experiences can vary greatly from place to place, and from one way of life to another. Lack of curriculum differentiation has become one of the major explanations for pastoralists' supposed low interest in formal education and the high drop out rate from schools in pastoral areas. It is argued that school curricula are developed by sedentary people for sedentary people, often with an urban bias, and are therefore largely irrelevant to nomads' experience and concerns. Low relevance leads to low interest and is demotivating, and so causes low enrolment figures and high drop out rates. This calls for a differentiation of the curriculum and the designing of special curricula for pastoral areas, relevant to nomads' life. This argument does not sufficiently problematise complex relationships between curricular content, nomads' life and aspirations, and how they are related to participation in schooling. Who is to decide what 'nomads' life' is, and then which parts of it are relevant and should be matched by the curriculum?

The issue of curriculum relevance has, for example, been crucial to the Nigerian national Nomadic Education Programme since the mid 1980s. The two ways by which the Programme tries to achieve relevance are by introducing new topics and adapting standard subjects to match nomads' backgrounds. Social Studies for example includes 'The culture of Nomadic Fulani' and 'The culture of other Nigerians'. Elementary Science has been adapted by adding 'Animal Management' and 'Agricultural science'. Standard subjects like Maths have undergone a 'cultural adjustment' through introducing 'relevant' sets of problems and examples (Federal Ministry of Education, 1987). These changes notwithstanding, the 'relevant' curriculum remains loyal to the goals of sedentarisation and modernisation; one could argue that success in its main aim of making school more appealing to nomads will make its influence more persuasive, and its transforming work on pastoral society more effective:

> The curriculum cultural adjustment will consist of taking into consideration the nature of the prevailing mentality in the Nomadic society to establish the teaching strategies, the subject matter presentation, and material resources adequate to the way in which the subject [i.e. the nomad] perceives the world in order to facilitate the desired changes. (Salia-Bao, 1982: 33–34; see also Lar 1991b)

This approach reflects a simplistic notion of culture as something that can be reduced to a set of essential elements; and it also assumes that pastoralists' interest in basic education for their children results from a desire to learn how to improve livestock production. But this assumption conflicts with pastoralists' own holistic view of pastoralism as a mode of life, not just a mode of production; and overlooks that pastoralists' demand for education appears to be driven more by interest in the opportunities it promises beyond the pastoral economy than a desire to acquire further pastoral specialisation. Because pastoralists are defined only by their productive role, it also assumes that once modernised, people who are now pastoralists will still be livestock producers. But if pastoralism as a way of life becomes unviable, pastoral cultural values and experience of the world might be just as suited to a career as a professional gambler, or a driver, or a lawyer, or even a bandit, as to a 'modern livestock producer'.

Finally, the Nomadic Education Programme approach to curriculum relevance takes a view of modern science as something that is inherently and inevitably superior to local knowledge, so that even at primary level education is supposed to increase pastoralists' performance in their day-to-day tasks. Yet theorists of pastoral development acknowledge the structural limitations of modern science in dealing with the highly unpredictable dryland environment, and call for the support and expansion of more flexible local knowledge and ways of knowing (Scoones, 1995).

The lack of relevance of the standard curriculum appears to be an inadequate explanation for low enrolment and high drop out rates among pastoralists. Mongolia for example, the only country to reach almost 100 percent literacy with about 50 percent of the population being nomadic, achieved this by using a standard curriculum, non-relevant to the pastoral way of life, highly academic and teacher-centred (MOSTEC, 1999; see Demberel and Penn, this volume, for an account of how this worked). The experience of responsive non-formal programmes suggests that attitudes and behaviours and a non-antagonistic cultural environment play a bigger role in meeting the nature of the demand than relevance itself. The 1981–1990 Nomad Education Programme in Somalia, described as successful because of its 'relevant' or contextualised curriculum (Brook and Brook, 1993), was based on non-intrusive 60 day adult education courses with candidates selected by the elders, two for each nomad group. Similarly, the successful tribal education programme in Iran used a standard curriculum, but implemented it with an innovative approach, at the base of which was the conviction that nomads were a cultural resource to be preserved and supported (Hendershot, 1965).

Education as a Social Good

Poverty and Impoverishment

Formal education is expected to make a contribution to the eradication of poverty by opening access to alternative livelihood options. Almost no research has been carried out into the role of education in eliminating poverty among pastoralists, but Holland (1992) working with two groups of Kenyan Maasai found that education is not a precondition for pastoral employment. On the contrary, the increasing commoditisation of cattle and labour is generating new jobs for the non-educated (cattle trading, waged herders). At the same time, the flow of in-migrants from non-pastoral districts, where formal education is more established, provide competition with educated youths from pastoral groups for employment that requires school qualifications.

High levels of social differentiation within pastoral groups, and the changing patterns of pastoralists' own experience of poverty and prosperity, require the definition of poverty to be much more specific. Pastoralists are not automatically the poorest of rural people, although they may qualify as such when the indicators used to determine wealth focus on (monetary) income, 'modernisation' (corrugated tin roofs, permanent houses, latrines, formal education, use of technology), or even food security. In fact, 'pastoralists', far from being a homogeneous category, should be disaggregated not only into 'wealthy' and 'poor', but into various degrees of poverty, distinguishing between the poor who are still socially integrated (that is can still rely on other people's support) and those who in fact have fallen out of pastoral society, although may still identify themselves with it.

Poverty or prosperity also take different meanings when considered at the level of individual (disaggregating by gender), household or homestead: different members (or households) of a prosperous homestead may enjoy prosperity to a very different degree. Studies of local perceptions of poverty and prosperity suggest that they mainly focus on three parameters: labour (a large family with a balanced proportion of boys and girls), livestock, and social network (Broch-Due, 1999). Livestock, and to a lesser degree labour, are highly volatile assets that raids, drought or disease can suddenly wipe out. What makes them stable is the extent of the social network, that is the number of people one can rely on in case of need and the amount of support one can expect from them.

Sometimes ignoring this complexity, education narratives deduce pastoralists' livelihood conditions from characteristics such as the lack of modern clothes or permanent housing, mobility, or the use of child labour, which are part of their life-style and economic organisation. A key figure in the design of the Alternative Basic Education for Karamoja programme (ABEK) in Uganda writes:

> A man owning 1000 heads of cattle, for instance, is still sleeping on hides, wearing a sheet only or a jacket with a sheet wrapped around his waist, or even a jacket with the rest of the body parts below naked. He eats out of a calabash, cannot pay school fees, taxes or hospital bills. (Owiny, 1998: 11)

Pastoralism is a specialisation developed from mixed farming, not the result of a process of farmers' impoverishment. Impoverished pastoralists may go back to farming, and/or become hunters, gatherers, workers, watchmen, food-aid dependents or bandits... and they may try the card of education. Data from recent work in Uganda and Kenya suggest that sending the children to school is a common strategy of impoverished families whose children's labour has become redundant with the loss of the livestock, and whose hopes of going back into business are small and rely entirely on the odd chance of an input of resources from outside the pastoral system. The increase of primary school enrolment in pastoral areas in the 1990s, often attributed to a growing, successful understanding of the value of education, may actually be the indicator of growing impoverishment for pastoral homesteads (Krätli, 2001).

Despite the complexity of interrelations behind decisions concerning one child's school education, one common pattern emerges quite clearly: school is seen and used as an alternative to herding. Those who go to school stop herding and, wherever financially and/or logistically possible, those who stop herding go to school (Dyer and Choksi, 1997).

Additional Knowledge or Trade Off?

From a policy perspective, basic education is no longer seen as an *opportunity* for those children or households who might want it or need it if they have little chance to make a livelihood within the pastoral economy. Rather, formal education is increasingly everybody's *obligation* during school age, independent of considerations about the present or future viability of households' livelihood strategies or need for economic differentiation. This leads to interesting questions about how schools deal with pastoral knowledge. At one end of the spectrum, pastoral expertise is seen as somehow 'natural' to pastoralists rather than learned, a given. The Nigerian ex-minister of education, Aliu B. Fafunwa, for example, writes that one of the objectives of nomadic education is 'the improvement of their [the children's] innate pastoral skills' (Fafunwa, *Foreword* to Tahir 1991: v). A widespread middle ground approach assumes that whatever a child can learn out of school, within a formal education programme it can be learned faster and better, with the improvement of problem-solving skills and even work performance. Over the last decade, following renewed attention to indigenous knowledge in relation to rural development, this position has become controversial. At the other end of the spectrum, therefore, others argue that what is learned at school is not additional to, nor substitutive of pastoral expertise, and see schooling as a trade-off between the gain of new opportunities for income generation outside the pastoral economy and the loss of opportunities for specialisation within the pastoral context (Semali, 1993; Dyer and Choksi, 1997 and this volume).

Virtually no research has focused on the relationship between formal education and traditional pastoral knowledge, apart from an isolated study amongst Maasai schoolboys and non-schooled boys on cognitive processes associated with herd management (Galaty, 1986). Having found that non-schooled boys could perform much more complex classifications and identifications of cattle (from their fathers' herds) than schoolboys, the author argues that to remove children from the context of direct learning and the indirect experience of the pastoral domain does affect their cognitive processes, both in terms of content and organisation.

Literacy and Information

Consistent with an understanding of formal education as additional to existing knowledge is a common conviction that literacy offers the opportunity to expand knowledge by affording access to the immense wealth of written information. Questions of whether written materials in any language are available or accessible to pastoralists aside, this conviction assumes that all knowledge is of the same kind, independent of how it is produced or transmitted, and so written knowledge can simply pile up on oral knowledge. Experience shows that knowledge is tied to social structures and far from being universally commensurable: indeed, where knowledge comes from and how it is produced is crucial to its status as knowledge. Recent work on drought early warning system in Kenya points out how supposedly 'robust' information such as government weekly bulletins on the availability of pasture in specific areas, based on satellite images, are disregarded by the herders in favour of less precise but more 'reliable' word of mouth (Buchanan-Smith and Davies, 1995; also McPeac et al., 2003).

Non-formal Education

Over the last ten years, some governments have turned to innovative partnerships and collaboration with international development agencies (see McCaffery et al., this volume, for Nigeria; and Chatty, this volume, for Oman; and also Mongolia, Senegal, Mali, Uganda and Kenya). The best of these non-formal education programmes focus on providing a service enhancing the life and survival of pastoral societies as such, rather than trying to transform them into something else. The backbone of these alternative programmes is the concept of *responsiveness*. Education provision is understood as a two way process responding to situations on the ground through continuous interaction with the recipients. These programmes recognise that current education systems are by and large unresponsive to the needs and living conditions of children from marginal or disadvantaged communities, as well as to their changing contexts and to the potential of existing community resources for the educational process. Consequently, one main concern, together with providing immediate responsive services, is to try to move formal systems towards more responsive structures:

> Nothing can be gained by trying to get more children to school unless those schools can be improved to the point of usefulness; and one essential mechanism for doing this is to involve children, parents, teachers, communities, and government officials in processes which will shift schooling in a more responsive direction. (SCF, 2000a: 15)

Moving away from the 'technical' focus on production makes room for broad livelihood issues such as resource access, conflict management, political action, communication between the literate and non-literate within the community as well as between local and scientific knowledge. Interaction with recipients raises the awareness that knowledge does not necessarily have to pass through literacy, and provides pressure for taking consequent action. It also helps to understand pastoralists within the context of local and national power relations (ARED and CERFLA, 1998).

Although this new perspective represents a much needed and important change, non-formal education programmes are usually small in scale and have relatively limited impact in national terms. As long as formal schooling continues to be the only route to education-related symbolic values and to higher education, non-formal education programmes will find it difficult to compete. No matter how divergent in principles and goals from mainstream education ideology and practices, if they wish to avoid creating educational ghettoes for the poor, non-formal programmes will need to offer access into the formal education system. This is recognised both by the Alternative Basic Education for Karamoja (ABEK) programme in northern Uganda and the Afar Nomadic Literacy Program in Ethiopia (CAA, 2000), both of which state one objective as providing a bridge to the formal system. From within the formal system and sometimes even by the organisations providing it, non-formal education is often seen as second class education. There is therefore a continuing power issue behind relations between formal and non-formal education, and thus an unresolved tension of legitimacy. Unless this is addressed, even genuinely responsive education programmes may result, in practice, in normalisation processes channelling out-of-school children into unresponsive systems.

Education For All: Contrasting Perceptions of Nomads and Nation State

Unfortunately, the relatively low success rates of education provision in pastoral areas – particularly low school enrolment and high drop out rates – tends to be blamed on the nomads themselves. 'Explanations' include pastoralists' cultural conservatism and resistance to change, the lack of parental schooling or literacy which is generally seen as resulting in a lack of understanding about the need for formal education, and the habit of using child labour within the household economy. Since nomad's apparent lack of interest in formal education is seen as the explanation for poor school success, the issue of education provision to nomadic groups is often framed as a question of *persuading* them to use the service.

An alternative perspective highlights pastoralists' difficulties in *using* formal education as currently provided. Having focused earlier on some hidden agendas of the state with regard to assimilating nomads, we focus here on the distance between educational provision constructed along the lines of liberal humanitarian ideals on one hand, and the requirements of the social and economic organisation of nomadic pastoralists on the other. We argue that the mainstream view of education, created and sustained with reference to apparently universal values, is fundamentally antagonistic to the values and interest of nomadic groups.

The rights-based discourse currently at the core of contemporary educational thinking is geared towards the individual, who is conceptualised as existing freely and independently from wider social structures. However, the basic productive unit of the pastoral economy is not the individual, but the household, or a small cluster of households. Consequently, decisions concerning the schooling of a child are not driven by an idea of individual success or an individual right, but rather by considerations about the household as a productive unit and the balance across all its members of risk, opportunity costs and labour demand. The increasing need for economic differentiation has become part of the division of labour within a carefully managed pastoral household (see Chatty, this volume). Education policies centred on individual development and aiming at 100 percent literacy conflict with this strategy, and lead to persistent misunderstanding of demand.

Children's involvement in household work is a common phenomenon across all levels of livelihood security in nomadic societies. Pastoralism is labour intensive all the year round and this has important implications for the availability of children for schooling, and thus for the design of educational provision. Although child labour is presented in negative terms within mainstream literature, children usually perceive household work as a positive experience, and their parents see in it a process of crucial educational value:

> Children's work is perceived as a process of socialisation, progressively initiating children into work and transmitting skills that will enable them to support themselves and their parents and contribute to the community [...] the most important thing one can do for a child is to teach him or her to work... death can overcome the parents at any time; that's why it is essential to train children young to the work of the parents. (SCF, 2000a: 69)

Contrary to other social groups, nomads consider that leaving a child without work is a sign of parental negligence: 'only parents who did not have their children's best interest at heart would let them grow up without work responsibilities' (SCF, 2000a: 70).

Another important issue concerns how knowledge is instituted within pastoral societies. Research on local/indigenous knowledge among people making a livelihood in highly variable and unpredictable environments, has emphasised the fuzzy nature of local cognitive patterns as a key feature for effective, adaptive and flexible response to unpredictable conditions (van der Ploeg, 1989). The cognitive patterns in use within the school system are, in contrast, based on the formalisation and objectification of knowledge. Although substantial research on this has yet to emerge, it seems likely that school and local cognitive patterns clash; and that such a clash may play a role in presenting formal education as deeply alien to pastoral livelihood – although potentially useful to its economic differentiation.

Towards the Future

As a universal project, formal education has had a very broad goal – the fulfilment of all individuals as human beings – but a narrow field of vision, limited to considerations of the structure and content of the service. Accountancy of the process has also been poor. We suggest that it is now time to reverse the status quo and aim for a broader vision that will lead to more accurate identification of goals.

Analysis of education as a broad phenomenon and a 'discourse' will bring into the field of vision a range of situations and dimensions that, although so far overlooked, appear to influence both the way education is received and its potential for fighting poverty. For example, if nomads' resistance to formal education is a response to a wide range of phenomena which all convey a feeling of cultural antagonism or aggression, interventions focused exclusively at the classroom level, such as making the curriculum more appealing or the timetable more flexible, have little hope of success. To transform education into a more positive and effective process, we need to search out new education contexts, beyond the classroom (for example, development projects, service delivery programmes, pastoral civic society organisations); new dimensions, beyond that of the curriculum; new interactions and agents, beyond teacher-pupil; and new targets, beyond the non-literate.

This kind of broader vision would help to prevent current side-effects of the process of educating nomads such as the brain drain from rural areas to the city and the erosion of local dynamics, loss of institutions for the generation, distribution and reproduction of endogenous knowledge, or the erosion and concentration of social capital. Greater recognition of the dynamic dimension of nomads' culture and livelihood practices might mean that, instead of exposing local people to global dynamics within a centre-periphery framework, bridging institutions can be developed to enable local dynamics to exist locally and also to articulate with national and global dynamics.

Finally, given that formal education has been, and remains, a vehicle for the old negative clichés that inform the image of pastoralism held by the 'outside world' of policy makers, government staff and project personnel, the issue of pastoralism and education can well be described as a 'knowledge gap'. This gap affects both the educated and uneducated, and reflects a 'poor understanding of pastoral systems' by the outside world (due to profound ideological biases as well as poor communication of the available information) coupled with pastoralists' inability to challenge their public image, to 'articulate the rationale of their livelihood and land use system' and to 'question the dominant paradigm driving development policy for pastoral areas' (Hesse and Ochieng Odhiambo, 2001: 4; see also Krätli, this volume). One way to bridge the knowledge gap is by improving communication between all the stakeholders, and refining their understanding of the dynamics of different pastoral systems. This might include facilitating existing and nascent civil society networks, to improve the interface between pastoralists (communities/groups/associations), governments (regional/national) and international institutions; and improving knowledge creation and exchange with regard to resource management and market structures (PCI, 2001). Education in this sense implies re-education of the educated, and is a much more broadly conceived, and shared, project in relation to nomads and education than simply the schooling of pastoralists.

Encouragingly, awareness that formal education is a political issue, and that the wider social and political dimensions of nomads' marginalisation must be recognised, is growing. To narrow power imbalances between pastoralists and the other interest groups over access to resources, 'education' could be aimed at

> building the capacity of pastoral groups to understand, analyse and ultimately contest the overall policy framework regulating their livelihood systems, and the underlying forces that keep them in poverty and on the margins of society. (Hesse and Ochieng Odhiambo, 2001: 8)

Rather than through slow, expensive and general formal education, this seems more likely to be achieved through specifically focused training, targeting key stakeholders in *both* the pastoral set up and the outside world, including formal learning institutions (see also ARED and CERFLA, 1998).

When addressing the issue of the education of nomads, it is too often overlooked that to be a 'nomad' means also to have a cultural identity, to be a Rabari, a Kazhan, a BoDaaDo, a Phala, a Qashqa'i, a Tungus, a Harasiis... This is not a state of wretchedness or the result of exclusion, but an identity to be proud of, a complex and sophisticated – if harsh – way of life. The history of mass education programmes and nomads is the history of the encounter between people who are looking for new ways to affirm the life they identify with in relation to changing living conditions, and people who deeply believe that that way of life is worthless, and that nomads are to be 'redeemed' and 'saved' from it. All too often, the kind of 'knowledge' on which these stances rest remains misleadingly implicit (Bloch, 1998).

Conclusions

This chapter has attempted to make some of the implicit motivations of service providers and users more explicit, and illustrate how the idea of education as a universal project is constantly justified on the basis of beliefs, myths and tradition. Yet universality is itself culturally located – a belief with its own tradition and, we argue, one that we now need to leave behind. We need to link, more successfully, practices of education and issues of nomadic pastoral culture and society, particularly the dynamic relationship between culture, local knowledge, social institutions and poverty. At present, formal education often undermines this nexus, without providing a viable alternative for those who wish to remain in the pastoral livelihood system. An educational system positively effective for nomadic pastoralists would help pastoralists to cope both with pastoral and non-pastoral livelihoods. More effective education in this respect means new processes of teaching and learning which:

- value pastoral livelihood systems as appropriate and technically adapted to their environment;
- equip pastoralists to articulate the rationale of their livelihood systems and challenge with confidence and authority their present public image, as well as adapt in dynamic ways to changes in the pastoral livelihood system resulting from external influences;
- are open and responsive to indigenous or local expert knowledge;
- are intricately linked to wider features of social organisation and institutions;
- recognise that pastoral children may need to be equipped for life in other livelihood systems, but do not assume this is the main objective of their schooling.

If we recognise that pastoral marginalisation results from social and political forces operating within wider society, it should be clear that standard education has little chance of making pastoralists competitive in political representation. Nomads' 'empowerment' within the national context requires a radical change in the culture of mainstream society, since it is this culture that creates conditions of disempowerment in the first place. Such empowerment will not be achieved by education programmes that, because they are designed to change nomads and make them fit in, serve ultimately simply to maintain rather than challenge the existing hegemony. The way forward lies elsewhere.

References

Alkali, H. (1991) 'The Challenges of Educating Pastoral Nomads in Nigeria: Limitations and Options'. In: G. Tahir (ed.) *Education and Pastoralism in Nigeria*. Zaria, Nigeria: Ahmadu Bello University Press.

Aminu, J. (1991) 'The Evolution of Nomadic Education Policy in Nigeria'. In: G. Tahir (ed.) *Education and Pastoralism in Nigeria*. Zaria, Nigeria: Ahmadu Bello University Press.

Anderson, D. (1999) 'Rehabilitation, Resettlement and Restocking. Ideology and Practice in Pastoral Development'. In: D.M. Anderson and V. Broch-Due (eds), *The Poor Are Not Us. Poverty and Pastoralism*. Oxford: James Currey.

ARED and CERFLA (1998) *Bref aperçu sur les travaux de l'ARED/CERFLA en matière d'appui à l'autopromotion par la formation*. Associates in Research and Education for Development Inc. (ARED) and Centre d'Etudes, de Recherche et de Formation en Langues Africaines (CERFLA).

Bass, C. (1998) *Education in Tibet. Policy and Practice since 1950.* London and New York: Tibet Information Network and Zed Books.

Baxter, P. (1985) *From Telling People to Listening to Them: Changes in Approaches to the Development and Welfare of Pastoral Peoples.* Paper presented at the International Symposium on the Africa Horn, Institute of African Research and Sudies, University of Cairo.

Behnke, R.H., I. Scoones and C. Kerven (eds) (1993) *Range Ecology at Disequilibrium: New Models of Natural Variability and Pastoral Adaptation in African Savannas.* London: Overseas Development Institute.

Bennaars, G.A., H.A. Seif and D. Mwangi (1996) *Mid-Decade Review of Progress Towards Education for All.* Nairobi: The Somalia Case Study.

Blanguernon, C. (1954) 'The Schools for Nomads in the Hoggar', *Fundamental and Adult Education* 6 (1): 8–14.

Bloch, M. (1971) 'Why Do Malagasy Cows Speak French?', *Kung! The magazine of the LSE Anthropological Society.*

——— (1998) *How We Think They Think. Anthropological Approaches to Cognition, Memory, and Literacy.* Boulder, CO: Westview Press.

Bonfiglioli, A.M. (1988) *Dudal. Histoire de famille et histoire de tropeau chez un groupe de WoDaaBe du Niger.* Paris: Cambridge University Press et Editions de la Maison des sciences de l'homme.

Broch-Due, V. (1999) 'Poverty and the Pastoralist: Deconstructing Myths, Reconstructing Realities'. In: D.M. Anderson and V. Broch-Due (eds) *The Poor Are Not Us. Poverty and Pastoralism.* Oxford: James Currey.

Brook, D.L. and G.A. Brook (1993) 'Social Studies for Somali Nomads'. *The Social Studies* 84 (1): 5–9, Helen Dwight Reid Educational Foundation.

Buchanan-Smith, M. and S. Davies (1995) *Famine Early Warning and Response: the Missing Link.* London: IT Publications.

Bugeke, C.J. (1997) 'Nomadic Education in Tanzania'. In: C. Ezeomah (ed.) *The Education of Nomadic Populations in Africa* Volume I. Breda: UNESCO.

CAA – Community Aid Abroad and Oxfam Australia (2000) *Learning for self-determination. The Ethiopian Afar Nomadic Literacy Program.* http://www.caa.org.au/world/education/reports/afar.htm.

CiC – Children in Crisis (2000) *China Progress Report, June 2000.* CiC.

Crawhall, N. (1999) 'Going to a Better Life: Perpectives on the Future of Language in Education for San and Khoe South Africans'. *International Journal of Educational Development* 19 (4–5): 323–335.

Dall, F. (1993) *Education and the United Nations Convention on the Rights of the Child: The Challenge of Implementation.* Innocenti Occasional Papers, Child Rights Series No. 4, International Child Development Centre. Florence: UNICEF.

Darnell, F. (ed.) (1972) *Education in the North: Selected Papers of the 1st International Conference on Cross-Cultural Education in the Circumpolar Nations and Related Articles Montreal, 18–21 August, 1969.*

de Bruijn, M. and H. van Dijk (1995) *Arid Ways. Cultural Understandings of Insecurity in Fulbe Society, Central Mali.* Amsterdam: Thela Publishers.

Degefe, S. and G. Kidane (1997) 'Nomadic Education in Ethiopia'. In: Ezeomah, C. (ed.) *The Education of Nomadic Populations in Africa* Volume I. Breda: UNESCO.

De Young, A. and B. Nadirbekyzy (1996) *Redefining Schooling and Community in Post-Soviet Kazakstan: Tokash Bokin and the School at Aikkanar*. Report. University of Kentucky and Kazakh State Academy of Management.

Dyer, C. and A. Choksi (1997) 'The Demand for Education among the Rabaris of Kutch, West India'. *Nomadic Peoples* 1 (2): 77–97.

El-Hassan, I.S. (1996) 'What If Pastoralists Chose Not to be Pastoralists? The Pursuit of Education and Settled Life by the Hadendawa of the Red Sea Hills, Sudan'. In: A. Ahmed and H. Ati (eds) *Managing Scarcity. Human Adaptation in East African Drylands*. Proceedings of a Regional Workshop held on 24–26 August 1995, Addis Ababa, Ethiopia, Organization for Social Science Research in Eastern and Southern Africa (OSSREA) and Centre for Development Studies (CDS), University of Bergen, Addis Ababa.

Ellis, J.E. and D.M. Swift (1988) 'Stability of African Ecosystems: Alternate Paradigms and Implications for Development'. *Journal of Range Management* 41 (6): 450–59.

Evangelou, P. (1984) *Livestock Development in Kenya's Maasailand. Pastoralists' Transition to a Market Economy*. Boulder, CO and London: Westview Press.

Ezeomah, C. (1983) *The Education of Nomadic People: The Fulani of Northern Nigeria*, Stoke-on-Trent, United Kindom: Nafferton Books and Deanhouse Centre.

———— K. Salia-Bao and S. Udoh (eds) (1982) *The Problems of Educating Nomads in Nigeria. Proceedings of the First Annual Conference on the Education of Nomads in Nigeria*. University of Jos, 5–6 February 1982, Jos, Nigeria.

Federal Ministry of Education (FME) and Youth Development (1987) *Blueprint on Nomadic Education*. Lagos: Nigeria Government Printers.

Galaty, J.G. (1986) *Cattle, Classification and Education: Aspects of Maasai Practical Cognition*. Paper presented in the Session on the Semantics of Animal Symbolism at the World Archaeological Congress, Southampton, England 1–7 September 1986.

Gefu, J. (1992) *Pastoralist Perspectives in Nigeria. The Fulbe of Udubo Grazing Reserve*. Research Report No. 89. Uppsala: The Scandinavia Institute of African Studies.

GMR (2002) *EFA Global Monitoring Report. Education For All: is the world on track?* Paris: UNESCO.

Habeck, J.O. (1997) *Sedentarisation of Nomads in the Evenki Autonomous District (Siberia)*. Paper presented at the 35th ICANAS (International Congress of Asian and North African Studies) in Budapest, 7–12 July 1997.

Hardin, G. (1968) 'The Tragedy of the Commons'. *Science* 162: 1243–48.

Hendershot, C. (1965) *Report on the Tribal Schools of Fars Province. White tents in the Mountains*. Washington D.C.: United States Agency for International Development (USAID).

Herskovits, M. (1926) 'The Cattle Complex in East Africa'. *American Anthropologist* 28: 230–72; 361–80; 494–528; 630–64.

Hesse, C. and Ochieng Odhiambo, M. (2001) *Concept Note. Reinforcement of pastoral civil society in East Africa. A programme of capacity building and participatory action-research*. London and Nairobi: IIED and RECONCILE. www.eldis.org/fulltext/conceptdoc.pdf

Hogg, R. (1988) 'Changing Perceptions of Pastoral Development: A Case Study from Turkana District, Kenya'. In: D. Brokensha and P. Little (eds) *Anthropology of Development and Change in East Africa*. Boulder, CO: Westview Press.

Holland, K. (1992) The Diversification of a Pastoral Society: Education and Employment among the Maasai of Narok District, Kenya. Ph.D. Thesis. Montreal: McGill University.

—— (1996) *The Maasai on the Horns of a Dilemma. Development and Education*. Nairobi: Gideon S. Were Press.

Jama, M.A. (1993) *Strategies on Nomadic Education Delivery. State of the Art Review*. Document 1103, Education Unit. Mogadishu: UNICEF-Somalia.

Kavoori, P.S. (1996) *Pastoralism in Expansion: The Transhuming Sheep Herders of Western Rajasthan*. Ph.D. Thesis. Den Haag: The Hague Institute of Social Studies.

Khazanov, A. M. (1984) *Nomads and the Outside World*. Cambridge and New York: Cambridge University Press.

Köhler-Rollefson, I. and J. Bräunig (1999) *Anthropological Veterinary Medicine: the Need for Indigenizing the Curriculum*. Proceeding of the 9th International Conference of the Association of Institutions of Tropical Veterinary Medicine, Harare, 1998.

Krätli, S. (2001). *Educating Nomadic Herders Out of Poverty? Culture, education and pastoral livelihood in Turkana and Karamoja*. World Bank's Learning and Research Program on Culture and Poverty. Brighton, United Kingdom: Institute of Development Studies, University of Sussex.

Lar, M. (1991a) 'Effective Approach to Curriculum Development for Nomadic Education'. In: G. Tahir (ed.) *Education and Pastoralism in Nigeria*. Zaria, Nigeria: Ahmadu Bello University Press.

—— (1991b) 'Developing a Relevant Curriculum for Nomadic Children in Nigeria'. In: S. Udoh, G. Akpa and K. Gang (eds) *Towards a Functional Primary Education for Nigeria*. Jos, Nigeria: Ehindero.

McPeac J.G., C.B. Barret, P.D. Little and G. Gebru (2003). 'Assessing the Value of Climate Forecast Information for Pastoralists: Evidence from Southern Ethiopia and Northern Kenya'. *World Development* 31 (9): 1477–94.

Meir, A. (1990) 'Provision of Public Services to Post-Nomadic Bedouin Society in Israel'. *The Service Industries Journal* 10 (4): 768–85.

MOEST – Ministry of Education, Science and Technology (1999) *Report on Formal and Non-Formal Education in Parts of Samburu, Turkana, Marsabit and Moyale Districts*. Nairobi: MOEST and Canadian International Development Agency (CIDA).

MOSTEC, Education Division (1999). *EFA 2000 Assessment Country Report: Mongolia*, Ulaanbaatar: Ministry of Science, Technology, Education and Culture (MOSTEC), Mongolia.

Närman, A. (1990) 'Pastoral Peoples and the Provisions of Educational Facilities. A Case Study from Kenya'. *Nomadic Peoples* 25–27: 108–21.

Okely, J. (1997) 'Non Territorial Culture as the Rationale for Assimilation of Gypsy Children'. *Childhood: a Global Journal of Child Research* 4 (1): 63–80.

Oul Mahand, C. (1956) 'Ecoles de campement au nomades de la Mauritanie'. *L'Education Africaine* 44 (34): 40–41. Published in English in: *Fundamental and Adult Education* 8 (3): 131–32.

Owiny, C.D. (1998) *Report on Oxfam-funded Participatory Education Workshops held in Dodoth County, Kotido District, Uganda, 19 October–5 November 1998.* Kampala: Oxfam Uganda.

—— (1999) *Report on Oxfam-funded Study on Education in Pastoralists Communities in Uganda. 21–30 September 1999.* Kotido, Uganda: Kotido Agro-Pastoral Development Programme.

PCI – Pastoral Communication Initiative (2001) *The Horn of Africa Pastoralist Communication Initiative.* A Collaboration between the United Nations, the Institute of Development Studies (U.K.) and DFID. Addis Ababa: UNEUE. http://www.ids.ac.uk/ids/particip/research/pci.html

Robinson, B. 1997. *In the Green Desert: Non-Formal Distance Education Project for Women of the Gobi Desert, Mongolia. Education for All, Making it Work* (Project). Paris: UNESCO.

Rybinski, A. (1980) 'La scolarisation des pasteurs nomades en Algerie indépendante – réalisations et insuffisances'. *Africana Bulletin* 29: 45–63.

Rybinski, A. (1981) 'Expériences françaises en matière de l'éducation des pasteurs nomades'. *Africana Bulletin* 30: 159–76.

Salia-Bao, K. (1982) 'Nomadic Culture and Curriculum Development'. In: C. Ezeomah et al. (eds) *The Problems of Educating Nomads in Nigeria. Proceedings of the First Annual Conference on the Education of Nomads in Nigeria. University of Jos, 5–6 February 1982.* Jos, Nigeria: University of Jos.

Sarone, O.S. (1986) *Pastoralists and Education: School Participation and Social Change among the Maasai,* Ph.D. Thesis. Montreal: McGill University.

SCF – Save the Children Fund (2000a). *Towards Responsive Schools: Supporting Better Schooling for Disadvantaged Children. Case Studies from Save the Children.* Education Paper No. 38. London: Department for International Development.

SCF – Save the Children Fund (2000b) *Pre-education for Nomadic Children in Mongolia. A Video.* Ulaanbaatar: SCF Mongolia.

Scoones I. (1995) 'New Directions in Pastoral Development in Africa'. In: I. Scoones (ed.) *Living with Uncertainty: New Directions in Pastoral Development in Africa.* London: Intermediate Technology Publications Ltd.

Semali, L. (1993) *The Social and Political Context of Literacy Education for Pastoral Societies: The Case of the Maasai of Tanzania.* Paper presented at the 43rd Annual Meeting of the National Reading Conference (Charleston, SC, December 1–4, 1993).

Shahshahani, S. (1995) 'Tribal Schools of Iran: Sedentarisation through Education'. *Nomadic Peoples* 36–37: 145–56.

Sifuna, D.N. (1987) *Pastoral Communities and Education in Kenya. A Historical Perspective.* Nairobi: Kenyatta University, Department of Educational Foundations, Staff seminar, 14 January 1987.

Sikana, P. and C. Kerven (1991) *The Impact of Commercialisation on the Role of Labour in African Pastoral Societies.* London: Overseas Development Institute. http://www.odi.org.uk/pdn/papers/31c.pdf

Suleman, S.A. and M.M. Khier (1997) 'Nomadic Education in the Sudan'. In: C. Ezeomah (ed.) *The Education of Nomadic Populations in Africa* Volume I. Breda: UNESCO.

Tahir, G. (1991) *Education and Pastoralism in Nigeria.* Zaria, Nigeria: Ahmadu Bello University Press.

Tahir, G. (1997) 'Nomadic Education in Nigeria'. In: C. Ezeomah (ed.) *The Education of Nomadic Populations in Africa* Volume I. Breda: UNESCO.

Toulmin, C. (1983) *Herders and Farmers or Farmers-Herders and Herder-Farmers?* Pastoral Network Paper 15d. London: Overseas Development Institute.

Udoh, S.U. (1982) 'The Problem of Administering Mobile Schools'. In: C. Ezeomah (ed.) *The Problems of Educating Nomads in Nigeria. Proceedings of the First Annual Conference on the Education of Nomads in Nigeria. University of Jos, 5–6 February 1982,* Jos, Nigeria: University of Jos.

UNDP-Emergencies Unit for Ethiopia (1996) *Report on Afar Region of Ethiopia, January 1996, Situation Report on Region 2 (Afar National Regional State.)* United Nations Development Programme Emergiencies Unit for Ethiopia.

UNDP-GDI (2003) *Pastoralism and Mobility in the Drylands.* GDI Challenge Paper Series, The Global Drylands Imperative (GDI), Drylands Development Centre, Nairobi, Kenya: United Nations Development Programme.

van der Ploeg, J.D. (1989) 'Knowledge Systems, Methaphor and Interface: The Case of Potatoes in the Peruvian Highlands'. In: N. Long (ed.) *Encounters at the Interface: a Perspective of Social Discontinuities in Rural Development.* Wagenings Sociologische Studien 27. Wageningen, The Netherlands: Wageningen Agricultural University.

Varlet, H. and J. Massoumian (1975) 'Education for Tribal Populations in Iran'. *Prospects* 5 (2): 275–281.

Vawda, A.Y. and A. Patrinos (1999) 'Producing Educational Materials in Local Languages: Costs from Guatemala and Senegal'. *International Journal of Educational Development* 19: 287–99.

WCEFA (1990) *The World Conference on Education For All: meeting basic learning needs – a vision for the 1990s. Background document.* New York: Inter-Agency Commission for the World Conference on Education For All.

Woldemichael, B. (1995) *Education for the Pastoral Communities of Eritrea: a Research Study.* Asmara: The Ministry of Education, Eritrea and Rädda Barnen, Swedish Save the Children.

CHAPTER 2

EDUCATIONAL SERVICES AND NOMADIC GROUPS IN DJIBOUTI, ERITREA, ETHIOPIA, KENYA, TANZANIA AND UGANDA

Roy Carr-Hill

Nomadic Groups and Education for All

Introduction

The level of participation of nomadic groups in formal education is known to be low. Many attempts have been made to establish education services that would meet their learning needs, but they have often failed. These failures have been variously ascribed to the weakness of the school network given the scattered populations involved, or to the inability of nomadic education programmes to respond to the nomads' mobile way of life, or to irrelevance of the content to their traditional culture, and to their need to retain flexibility to deal with changing and often adverse circumstances, such as droughts, above all other needs.

Nomadic groups pose a serious challenge to the national and international target of Education For All by 2015. In the context of a renewed commitment to 'Education For All' at the Dakar Conference in 2000, this chapter reports on a 6–country study in Djibouti, Eritrea, Ethiopia, Kenya, Tanzania and Uganda of current provision of education to nomadic groups, and how nomadic groups react to existing services. It was carried out jointly by UNESCO (ICBA in Addis Ababa and IIEP in Paris) and UNICEF, and funded by the African Development Bank. The purpose of this study was to document and advance the agencies' understanding of this situation in more detail, to increase the awareness of governments of the problems of nomadic communities and facilitate the development of policies and programmes on basic education for nomads and particularly the girls, in order to promote their social and economic progress and human development.

The Background Literature

Krätli and Dyer have thoroughly reviewed the background literature in the opening chapter of this volume; the purpose here is to highlight only those specific issues that are important for this study in the Horn of Africa. Some see the failure as a pastoralist 'problem', arguing that pastoralists are quite prepared for their children to be educated but that they have tended to shun schooling because the provision is inappropriate in terms of relevance, siting of schools, etc.; and that for governments to provide appropriate provision would be inordinately expensive (conversation with senior official in the Eritrean Ministry of Education). Others take the view that, inasmuch as the education system is aligned with modernity, then most formal education programmes will be confrontational to nomadic culture and to what nomadic children need and want to know for their way of life. This contested view of pastoralism and the social and environmental context were crucial for understanding the debates in these six countries.

A Pastoralist Problem

For some, 'conventional approaches are largely felt to be unworkable in subsistence pastoral conditions' (Gorham, 1978: 1); others point to the 'irrelevance of an imported western model of schooling and its incompatibility with prevailing social and cultural values and practices' (Sarone, 1984: 16). This emphasis on explanations means that there are few attempts to describe in detail the educational initiatives that have been attempted to reduce disparities between nomadic groups and their more settled colleagues. Gorham's (1978) report on what had been tried, where and how – ranging from the boarding schools of Kenya to the tent schools of Iran – remains a useful, if dated account. The introductory chapter to this volume is similarly large in scope, although there is only limited material on what has been tried and what works – and why.

More surprisingly, there does not appear to be any attempt to locate the debate within the context of the calls at the Dakar Conference for 'Education For All' so as to 'broaden the means and scope of education' (WDEFA 1990: Article 5) and 'develop more tailored and imaginative approaches'. A search through all the country submissions to the World Education Conference at Dakar, Senegal in 2000 showed that there were very few specific intiatives indeed and, where nomadic groups were mentioned, they were seen as part of a general rural problem.

'Friends of Pastoralism'

This literature almost always begins from the starting point that pastoralism is at a crossroads and in crisis (Galaty et al., 1981; UNICEF/UNSO, 1992). A variation on this theme is to present pastoralists as skilful and rational users of a variable natural resource base who are struggling to maintain their livelihood in the face of external ignorance and prejudice (Baxter and Hogg, 1990; Behnke *et al.*, 1993; Scoones, 1995). The phenomenon of pastoralism losing ground (both literally and metaphorically) as national economies become more oriented to agriculture, services and tourism, as urban populations increase as a proportion of national population, and settled peasant farmers encroach upon the land that pastoralists need between dryland grazing seasons, is seen as a global phenomenon.

The key proposition, however, is that state-provided[1] education is inherently antagonistic towards pastoralism (Krätli, 2000) and that it is, by implication, partly responsible for the crisis in pastoralism. However, the general literature on pastoralism (Salzman and Galaty, 1990; UNICEF/UNSO, 1992; Anderson and Broch-Due, 1999) is limited in its analysis of the effects of education – whether positive or negative – and its impact on the viability of pastoralism and the well being of pastoralists. Given that the levels of enrolment are usually very low, it is difficult to argue that education can be seen as responsible for a crisis in pastoralism, in the same way that it is a mistake for 'mainstream explanations for the failure of educational provision in pastoral areas ... [to] blame the recipients' (Krätli, 2000: 24).

What Happens on the Ground

In fact, as Frantz (1990) argues, pastoralism is not a pure idealised form but a living culture and economy encompassing practices that might seem on the surface to be inherently antagonistic to the pursuit of pastoralism. For example, sedentarisation – whilst the complete opposite of pastoralism – is not a new feature of pastoral societies (Salzman, 1990; see also Mohammed, 1998) nor is it necessarily negative, representing a state of being inherently in conflict with pastoralism. Salzman and Galaty (1990) reject the notion of idealised conceptual poles separating pastoralists on the one hand and agriculturalists and town dwellers on the other.

Thus, better off pastoralists may settle because they have the resources and inclination to invest in other assets as well as animals, whereas those who are poorer may be driven to settlements and towns by drought, excessive stock theft or other personal circumstances. They live and often work with the intention of rebuilding their herds and

> would often resist any suggestion that they are, themselves, anything but pastoralists. Here pastoralism as a commitment to a way of life or a value orientation must be distinguished from a strict definition of pastoralism as an actual practice. (Salzman and Galaty, 1990: 18)

What is clear from the literature is that the specific context of each nomadic community is an important determinant of what is possible and of their likely responses to what is provided. This study examines some evidence from scattered communities in these six countries.

Study Design and Methodology

Six country teams were formed, coordinated by UNICEF country offices. An international technical support team coordinated by IIEP devised several instruments for collecting background information from national authorities and interview and questionnaire instruments for collecting information in the field from both providers and from nomadic groups[2]. These were considered and revised jointly with the country teams. Care was taken in the conceptualisation and design of the study to maximise the quality of the research. All efforts were made to ensure that the research tools were geared to measure what was being investigated. There is obviously a limit to the extent to which tightly-constructed questionnaire items could measure the respondents' views, strategies and expectations, especially when used in a cross-national context covering a wide range of different groups. A semi-structured interview schedule may have been a more suitable and accurate instrument for this purpose. On the other hand, there has to be a balance between comparability and meaning.

There was also a limit to the extent to which the findings for a small sample investigated in each site could be generalisable to the respective nomadic pastoralist cluster, or indeed to the general population of nomadic pastoralists in the country. This was particularly difficult for nomadic groups among refugee populations, where it was almost impossible to distinguish between those individuals from urban areas and those from rural areas, and among those who were originally from nomadic groups.

A wide range of sites and institutions were visited and a wide range of people interviewed. The fieldwork posed a number of logistical and theoretical problems. As is inevitable with a research study, there are aspects that one would like to have changed in the design and implementation of the study, if one were able to start again. The teams also encountered several practical difficulties that illustrate not only the difficulties encountered when carrying out this kind of research, but also those that would be faced by the needs assessment exercise that need to be carried out on a systematic basis by countries if the Education for All (EFA) goals are to be achieved. For example, some teams had to spend several days travelling to access nomadic and pastoralist groups. Some of the sites were a long way from regional and district headquarters. In Uganda, the researchers had to make special arrangements with airlines in order to be picked up in the Karamoja region.

The Background and Context in the Six Countries

Definition: Who are the Nomads?

In each of the six countries studied, a significant proportion of the population – at least ten percent – are considered to be nomads or pastoralists. For many of their citizens, nomadism and pastoralism were normal ways of life until very recently; for example, in Djibouti, *all* of the current population had parents or grandparents who had been nomadic. Those currently considered to belong to nomadic communities are a mix of 'pure' pastoralists, agro-pastoralists and transhumant pastoralists. Correspondingly, there is a varied pattern of movement, sometimes constrained by the encroachment of settled farmers, sometimes by clashes with other pastoral groups; but in some cases, parts of the groups are still moving several hundred kilometres with their herd.

A lot of ink has been spilt about the definition of nomadism. Livestock is at the centre of the nomadic economy but, in practice, we found that the six country studies covered a wide variety including some 'pure' pastoralists, a majority called agro-pastoralists, some preferring the term transhumant pastoralists, and some nomadic fishermen. Nevertheless, nearly all nomads consider cattle as a sign of prosperity and security because matrimonial and social alliances depend on it. Mobility is seen as a key feature because they move with their cattle to find water and grassroots, according to the climate. In Djibouti, because everyone who is in the countryside is either a nomad or a nomad who is beginning to settle, the research team's definition explicitly excluded a reference to mobility because their nomadic populations '*are less and less mobile but continue to have a nomadic lifestyle*' which they defined as non-sedentary, living off livestock, in easily-moved tents. The Tanzanian team also talked about new types of nomads including not only fishing communities but also small-scale mining groups, tea harvesters and sugar cane cutters. They have many of the characteristics of nomadic peoples such as the absence of a fixed domicile (Ezeomah, 1990), moving between areas and temporary employment. Clearly, this latter definition has resonance in developed as well as developing countries

One common feature in the reports was the relative difficulty in counting the population of nomads. This was partly because of the lack of recent censuses and partly because any household surveys that had been conducted almost by definition excluded nomads. Whatever the data source, there was also a problem in agreeing on which groups counted as being 'nomadic'.

Issues of Poverty: Definitions and Indicators for Each Country

People define and experience poverty in different ways – lack of land, unemployment, inability to educate children, etc. – but most define poverty as the inability to meet basic needs. Using standard official definitions based on income, poverty is widespread throughout the region (see Human Development Report, 2000), and other indicators would give a similar picture. The issue here then is the *relative* poverty of nomadic groups both in definitional and statistical terms.

In Djibouti, an estimate based on a 1996 household survey (EDAM, 1996) suggests that, among the rural population, 86 percent live in relative poverty and 45 percent in absolute poverty. Note, however, that because of the high levels of urbanisation, the numerical majority of the poor are in the capital. Nomads in rural areas depend on remittances from family that lives in towns. One estimate made in 1989 suggested that one needed at least 100 Djiboutian francs per person per day to live on, of which 74 came from relatives working in towns. The nomad economy has become marginalised.

The average per capita income of pastoralists in Eritrea is estimated to be US$100 per year, compared to the national GDP per capita of US$200, and most barely cover 60 percent of their families' needs in a normal year. The Welfare Monitoring Survey (World Bank, 1996) suggested a long list of possible causes of poverty with rurality heading the list (70 percent), followed by insufficient food aid (69 percent) and needing food aid (50 percent) even in what are considered the good years.

In Kenya, the percentage of people currently living below the poverty line in 1997 was estimated to have increased to 52 percent in 2001 (PRSP 2001: 20). Overall poverty was higher in most ASAL Provinces. The Northeastern province was not included in the 1997 survey due to insecurity and El Niño rains, but later assessments show that the poverty level in the province is over 90 percent.

In Uganda, the presentation was in terms of the UNDP Human Development Index. The 1998 values for Uganda were 0.4046, while the value for Kotido was 0.1781; the corresponding income index values were 0.2098 and 0.0946.

Pastoralist areas have the highest rates of poverty and the least access to basic social services, for reasons that included intermittent drought, insecurity, lack of communication infrastructure, lack of income generating activities, lack of market for livestock, and poor integration into the national social and political economies. Several of the national reports referred to a cycle of poverty. Poor access to markets and lack of high-grade stock account for low sales and hence no cash income. Lack of capital in turn leads nomadic pastoralists to poor farming practices and destruction of the natural environment. This reduces the potential of the fragile ecology leading to pastoralists having to move even further with their herds, weakening both their access to markets and the quality of their stock.

Sources of Income of the Various Groups

Pastoralism is, nevertheless, seen as the best mechanism for survival in the lowlands that are prone to drought, famine, insecurity, and so on. Moreover, because livestock provides nomads not only with wealth but also prestige and social status, nomads tend to give equal emphasis to the number of animals as to their economic significance and the availability of grazing resources. But there had been substantial changes in the pattern of income-generation activities in the six countries, including regular (i.e. similar to other rural poor) subsistence farming, attempts to improve livestock management and diversification away from agriculture. In nearly all groups, many had taken up subsistence farming. However, the potential for crop production in nomadic areas tends to be limited due to low rainfall and is practised only on a small scale, for example, along river valleys and on the highlands.

The economy is therefore based essentially on the herd and the sale of its products: milk and butter, leather and wool. Animals are sold when necessary, but this is usually regretted (e.g. in Djibouti and Ethiopia). The Kenyan government recognises that pastoralism can be the most efficient means of economic production in the fragile ecology where nomads operate. Their Poverty Reduction Strategy Programme (PRSP) for example states that, in 1998, export of hides and skins was the fourth largest national income earner for the country. But attempts to improve breeds in herds raises the issue of increased inputs and requirements of better and increased husbandry and effective marketing.

In some areas, irrigation from perennial water sources is used to grow horticultural products for the export market. Dryland agriculture is geared towards food consumption and is concentrated near homesteads. Women, therefore, play a major role here.

Policies concerning the disadvantaged often mention nomadic or pastoralist groups as one of the targets. But poverty programmes appear to have left behind nomadic groups, as if the only possible exit strategy from poverty is to settle. This may be true but it needs very careful planning with the pastoralists themselves; and that does not appear to have been the practice to date.

Conflict and Its Impact on Nomadic Groups

The policies of the various governments towards security are a central factor in the sub-region, often being confrontational and militarist. Governments have done very little to genuinely involve the local people, those who understand and can articulate the praxis of the principles and practices of the lifestyle of the sub-region. Instead, governments have tended to depend on military operations, declarations of states of emergency, and so on. Large investments to maintain security in many parts of the sub-region have yielded little success. Conflicts that are socio-culturally based cannot be solved by use of guns and force but need an approach involving dialogue and attitude change by the initiative of local community elders of the warring factions. But the PRSPs in these countries do not even mention the issue of insecurity; and there is no provision in budgets for community dialogue.

Education: Access, Participation and Provision

Access

Network of Schools Available

The population density in many African countries, especially in areas with substantial numbers of nomads has always been – and remains – low. Not unsurprisingly, despite very considerable efforts since Independence, the school network is correspondingly thin.

The main reasons given in Eritrea for children not attending school were that there were no schools available, the distance to school was excessive and there were no boarding facilities. In the Northeastern Province of Kenya, schools are scattered and far apart in most of the arid parts of the district: for example, Ilivet Primary School is 550 km from the district headquarters and the roads are in bad condition. Another example of a coverage problem was cited in Uganda. Out of 63 inhabited islands in Kalangala, only six have primary schools. Children on the other 57 islands cannot afford the costs of water transport, estimated to be ten times that of land transport. Unsurprisingly, school attendance outside the towns was very low.

Financial Barriers

Assuming that there are schools available, the principal impediment to the scolarisation of the children of the poor in many parts of rural Africa is probably the level of fees imposed by the school system. These often represent a significant fraction of family income even for only one child. The Ethiopian study reports that one reason pastoralists do not send their children to the schools is they cannot afford to pay for their food and lodging in the towns where the schools are located. However, even where fees are not charged (Djibouti and Tanzania), or the parents could in principle anyway afford to send their children to school, there are a number of other interrelated problems. It is well known that there is a wide range of tasks that both boys and girls in rural areas are expected to carry out, so that sending them to school imposes a significant additional non-cash burden on the families.

Cultural inhibitions and activities (such as livestock tending) that school-age children are engaged in play a significant role in keeping pastoralists' children out of school. This is particularly important in terms of the participation of girls; and there have been a number of attempts to encourage girls to school, which we shall discuss later.

Participation Rates

Of the 40,000 pupils enrolled in elementary level in Djibouti, just over 9,000 are enrolled outside the capital. The national Gross Enrolment Rate (GER) is very low (about one-third of the numbers of children of school-going age are enrolled in school) and even lower (about one-fifth) outside the capital.

The GERs are even lower in rural areas with 14.9 percent for boys and 7.9 percent for girls. Drop out rates are also higher outside Djibouti capital.

Of the 262,000 enrolled in school in Eritrea, in the three study districts (Gash Barka, NRS, SRS), less than a quarter (60,000) are enrolled. The disparity in educational opportunities among the six administrative zones, as measured by the deviation of GER from the national average of 52 percent, ranges from as low as 41 percent below for Southern Red Sea Zone to as high as 26 percent above for Maekel Zone (essentially in the capital Asmara). Similarly, the three nomadic regions have a very low Net Enrolment Ratio (NER) as compared to the national average.

In the three study areas the GER is 21 percent for Shieb, 14 percent for Forto and 12 percent for the Raihaita, Afambo and Aitos areas, compared to 29 percent, 37 percent and 11 percent for the corresponding regions. The GERs were 7.6 percent less for Shieb, 22 percent less for the Forto area and only 1 percent more for Raihaita, Afambo and Aitos nomads, showing that the nomadic areas are underprivileged in terms of educational opportunities. The situation is most serious for the Hidarib nomadic population. Female students account for between 21 percent and 23 percent of the students in the three areas and their GERs are correspondingly even lower at 10 percent, 14 percent and 5 percent, respectively.

There are nearly 13 million children of school-going age in Ethiopia and 1.25 million of them are in the three study regions (Afar, Borena and Somali). The national GER is just over 57 percent but the GERs in most of the study areas are much lower: 12 percent in Afar, 30 percent in Debub Omo and 11 percent in Somali, with the GERs for girls much lower still. Women and girls hardly ever attend school even if they are enrolled. The NER (relative to the 7–14 year-old population) is very small indeed; less than 1 percent in the Afar Region; and Afar children themselves are only a minority of those enrolled.

There are 6.7 million children of school-going age (6–13) in Kenya, with about 660,000 in the nomadic areas. The twelve pastoral districts have comparatively low GERs, with a majority of children of primary school age not enrolled in schools. In 2000, the national primary school gross enrolment rate (GER relative to the 6–14-year-old population) was 87.6 percent (88.1 percent male, 87.1 percent female): the GERs in Garissa, Wajir, Mandera, Turkana and Marsabit are 12.9 percent, 19.3 percent, 22.2 percent, 32.2 percent and 41.3 percent, respectively. The majority of the population in these districts are nomadic pastoralists. The lowest of these low GERs are found in the predominantly Muslim Northeast Province districts of Garissa, Wajir, Ijara and Mandera, where a large proportion of children are out of school. This may indicate possible conflict between Islamic faith and formal, western-type education. For example, the GER for Garissa (12.9 percent) indicates that 87 percent of the children are outside the formal educational system either in child labour, herding or idling at home, or combining these activities with a parallel education system such as *madrassa*.

There is the same story for net enrolment rates (NER). The data appear to show that NER in districts where nomads co-exist with sedentarised communities is high but very low where nomadic pastoralists are a majority. At the same time the disparities between boys' and girls' enrolment are large among nomads. In recent years, there have been increases in enrolment in some ASAL districts, most of which are UNICEF focus districts – such as Marsabit, Narok, Turkana, West Pokot, Wajir and Kuria – where a lot of sensitisation and awareness-raising activities had been carried out. However, NER has decreased in the districts of Marakwet and Wajir. This could be attributed to insecurity arising from cattle rustling and ethnic clashes.

In 2000 in Tanzania, there were nearly 900,000 pupils in primary school, with only 74,000 admitted to Form 1 (the first grade of secondary) compared to 473,000 leavers from Standard 7 (the end of primary). The classroom teacher-pupil national average ratio is high in Tanzania with 1 teacher for 72 pupils, but the enrolment in nomadic areas is low compared to non-nomadic areas.

There were varied reports from the study areas. In Bagamoyo, there seemed to be no difference between the enrolment rates in wards with predominantly nomadic populations and others, although attendance was low in the nomadic areas. In contrast, in a ward in Mbulu, where the Hadzabe lived in villages 10 km and 8 km from the school, the comparative GERs of children of settled families and of nomadic families were 112 percent and 8 percent, respectively.

In Uganda, there are 6.8 million children in primary school. In the five study areas, there are just over 460,000 pupils – with the majority in Mbarara – and 7,450 teachers. Universal Primary Education was introduced three years ago and has been successful at attracting students to school but the capacity to train teachers has been limited. As a result, the pupil-teacher ratio has worsened over the last three years in all except two of the 45 districts. All these augur badly for quality primary education.

Provision of Basic Education

Facilities

In recognition of the distances and the problem of coverage, many of the countries are providing boarding facilities or hostels and some of these are specifically aimed at nomadic groups. Where the school is some way from the home, but has no boarding facilities, an important factor is whether or not lunch is provided at school. In a number of cases, this will be through the World Food Programme; in others the school organises lunches and charges the parents; and in yet others, parents and community themselves organise the lunches. Each of these systems is difficult to sustain – for example, the Uganda team reported that, after a number of months, the children only came to school if the food had been delivered and otherwise stayed away – but are frequently cited as a determining factor.

A wide range of other approaches has been tried in Kenya including a bursary fund, preference in the supply of equipment and textbooks, recruitment and training of pre-service teachers in ASAL. A quota system for admission into national secondary schools ensures that children from disadvantaged areas such as ASAL benefit from quality secondary education.

Quality of Education

It seems obvious that parents will be less willing to send their children to a poor quality school, although there are suggestions in the literature that once groups have decided to send their children to school – especially boarding school where parents are unlikely to know what is going on – they are less concerned about the quality.

Most reports found that existing schools are inadequately equipped and staffed; a critical shortage of textbooks; and that the teachers do not seem to have either the capacity or the equipment to prepare handouts. This imposes a severe problem on the teaching-learning process. In the nomadic pastoralist-dominated districts, the drop out and repetition rates tend to be higher and the transition rates from primary to secondary lower than the national average.

Alternative Provision

One argument is that schooling has failed among the nomads because schools retained the colonial authority structure. They are hierarchical, authoritarian and bureaucratic rather than participant and democratic. There have been a number of government attempts to introduce non-formal programmes for both children and adults, some of them running for several years (SCF, 2000). For example, in Kenya, there have been pilot projects for out-of-school children (in Baringo, Garissa, Madera and Wagir, among others); and COBET (Complementary Basic Education in Tanzania) and COPE (Complementary Opportunities for Primary Education) in Uganda are similar schemes targeting out-of-school children.

Equally, there is a range of non-formal programmes organised by NGOs. Some of these are more or less specifically targeting nomadic children such as ABEK (Alternative Basic Education for the Karamoja) and CHANCE (Child-Friendly Alternative Non-formal Community Education) in different parts of Uganda.

Views of the Nomadic Groups Themselves

Given the nature of nomadic society – on the move with their assets and their animals – and their settlement in isolated areas, far from infrastructures, it is not surprising that the lowest enrolment rates are among these communities.

To have children at school, communities need to be settled near schools and risk scarce pasture for livestock, or move with their children, taking them out of school, thereby rendering the institutions under-utilised or even temporarily closed during some seasons. Nevertheless, some parents still decided to send their children to schools. That decision made, however, they faced practical issues of access. For example, there was a lack of housing for students who remain behind and absence of middle schools in the area in Eritrea; a shortage of staff, lack of money to pay school levies for textbooks, support staff, etc.; and lack of lunch provision in Uganda.

As part of preparation for the PRSP in Uganda, a survey was carried out where respondents were asked what the factors affecting school attendance were. Nationally, ill-health was the most frequently cited factor (by 64 percent) followed by inability to pay fees (52 percent) and buy uniforms (42 percent), with the rainy season, insecurity, harvest time, housework and distance all being mentioned by fewer than 30 percent of respondents. In the nomadic districts, ill-health was also seen as very important except by respondents in Kotido (32 percent); respondents were much more likely to cite fees in Kotido (92 percent), but much less likely in Kalangala or Nakasongola (26 percent and 29 percent, respectively); while those in Adjumani were much more concerned (66 percent) about uniforms than the rest. In Kotido and Moroto, harvest time, housework and insecurity were cited at least twice as often as the national average; whilst those in Adjumani emphasised distance and insecurity, those in Mbarara were concerned with housework.

In most of the interviews in the study in the different countries, a wide range of factors outside the control of the educational system was cited. These were mainly broader issues associated with poverty, such as: lack of livestock; harsh climate coupled with recurrent drought (Eritrea and Kenya); lack of water and health facilities for both human and livestock; poor infrastructure (e.g. road networks); poor market for livestock; and insecurity due to conflicts over land and livestock.

Is Education Useful for Us?

With respect to adult education, the groups interviewed said that they need adult education in order to gain literacy partly in order to read notices and instructions – indeed that was often a reason for sending at least one child to school – but also in order to be able to read religious texts. They were also concerned to acquire numeracy and skills for business and animal management (see also Okech, 2000). Participation in government adult education programmes is also low, although the figures reported at the national level sometimes look optimistic.

All the communities studied in the six countries have their own traditions of education, which remain intact to the present day. Their knowledge and values are basically passed on orally to the younger generation. Nomadic communities' views and expectations of schooling vary according to specific contexts and groups.

Discussion of Findings

It is important to emphasise the diversity of pastoralist groups, the variety of their contexts, and the varied attitudes of parents to education (for example, in herding situations, boys and not girls are kept away from school). Second, the range of providers varies between countries and, within any one country, between districts and, within a district, between the district headquarters and more remote areas. Third, while there is a wide variety of alternatives available, it is also important to recognise that many of the alternatives are not specific to nomadic groups.

Demand, Participation and Provision
Educational Demand
Nomadic communities' views and expectations of education and schooling vary according to specific groups and circumstances. The research teams encountered many examples where nomadic parents would approach the education system strategically in that they sent one or two of their children to school as one possible avenue for ensuring an economically independent future for the family. Whilst a similar attitude amongst sedentary rural populations usually leads to the boys being sent to school, in some cases, the reverse was true among nomadic groups, as the boys' herding functions were seen as more valuable for the family economy.

Participation in Education
Enrolment rates in the first level of formal education, in districts with large proportions of nomads, which are reported by the Central Statistical Offices, are nearly always lower than the national average. Participation rates among girls are particularly low, and this constitutes a major challenge for attaining Education For All. In most cases, the enrolment rates in the specific sites where the research was carried out and where nomads were presumed to be concentrated were lower still.

Enrolment in pre-primary or in secondary is almost non-existent. Participation in government adult education programmes is also low, although the figures reported at the national level sometimes look optimistic. Participation in NGO programmes is enthusiastic but limited.

Educational Policies and Provision
There is scant mention of nomadic communities in the educational policy documents of most countries. This does not mean, however, that they are being ignored. It simply means that, in general, they are seen as being on a par with other marginalised groups.

Although the communities studied have their own, intact, traditions of education, curricula have rarely been adapted to accommodate these; instead it is presumed that the national standard will be taught in all government schools, although the practice sometimes varies. In contrast, there are several examples of the school calendar and timetable being changed in order to accommodate pastoralist herding functions, although the scale of the adaptation often appears to be insufficient.

There are isolated examples of government boarding schools that do appear to have enrolled and retained children from nomadic groups, but they are expensive either in terms of state subsidy or financial accessibility.

Teacher recruitment and allocation is nearly always centrally driven and it appears to be a matter of luck rather than design if the teacher can speak the local language. Teachers rarely receive any specific training for teaching children from nomadic groups, and are sometimes less than enthusiastic about teaching them.

School feeding programmes have been introduced nearly universally but have encountered the usual problems of distribution and supply. In nearly every district studied, examples were cited of children withdrawing from school when the food did not arrive. Whilst there appears to be short-term effects on enrolment and also possibly on performance, these are not sustainable and long-running programmes may induce a dependency syndrome.

Do Nomadic Groups Require a Specific and Particular Policy Response?

Educationally, pastoralists appear to be just an extreme example of the problem of enrolling children from poor rural populations. In terms of school access, enrolment, attendance, classroom performance, achievement, continuity to higher classes and parity between boys and girls, they regularly score at the bottom of the ladder (MOEST, 1999: 17; Berstecher and Carr-Hill, 1990). On the other hand, they have otherwise sophisticated cultural structures that guide their lives. Some argue that formal education programmes as traditionally provided appear to oppose nomadic culture at all levels, both in their principles and goals (Krätli 2001), undermining the young person's sense of identity and their independence. In particular, while schooling may provide opportunities for income generation *outside* the pastoral economy, children lose the opportunity of specialisation *within* the pastoral context (Dyer and Choksi, 1997).

Parents of both boys and girls cited as reasons for not sending their children to school: food shortage at home and in school; long distances to school; and, for boys, child labour/petty trade (for girls looking after younger children); and additionally for girls, pregnancy and early marriage. Most of these reasons are also typically given by all parents in rural areas as reasons why they do not send or maintain their children at school.

There are, however, some important differences from subsistence farmers, in terms of their approach to the participation of their children in the school system. In particular:

- in some cases, it is more likely that nomadic groups will send their girls rather than their boys – at least to the first grades of primary school – because it is the boys who are involved with herding;
- pastoralists who are livestock wealthy are more likely to keep their children away from school than those who have smaller herds because they need more children to look after the herds.

Whilst most of the governments have developed a Poverty Reduction Strategy Programme (PRSP) or another similarly comprehensive strategy to alleviate poverty, the particular situation of nomadic groups and the problems of confronting culture have rarely been articulated. For example, the Pastoralist Thematic Group in Kenya laments that:

> During the year 2000/2001, the government of Kenya spent 4.8 billion on relief. This huge figure can be interpreted as being 'the cost of doing nothing' to address the long term structural development challenges in ASAL.

Most of the governments are moving ahead with decentralisation and policies for empowering local community governments that are democratically elected. While laudable in principle, in practice these require extensive capacity-building and presume a population with at least a basic level of education. The Ethiopian report remarks that 'unless concerted effort is made to increase and improve educational provision the result will be increased deprivation, alienation and non-participation'.

In contrast, the increasing diversification of economic activities, remarked upon by many, would fit with the way in which many curricula are being developed. Indeed, the (not evaluated) success stories appear to be linked to 'integrated' programmes including employment and income-generating opportunities. While the opportunity for their children to access school is an issue, it is not necessarily the most important.

Conclusion: What is the Extent of the Problem for EFA?

It is important to assess the participation rates for nomadic groups relative to the respective national situation. The countries are very different in size ranging from 620,000 in Djibouti to 65 million in Ethiopia. The number of children of school-going age accordingly varies substantially from 72,000 in Djibouti to an estimated figure of approximately 26 million in Ethiopia. In terms of national enrolment rates, the countries can be divided roughly into two groups: those with national GERs between 50 percent and 60 percent (Djibouti, Eritrea and Ethiopia); and those with GERs over 75 percent (Kenya, Tanzania and Uganda) (see Tables 2.1 and 2.2 below).

Table 2.1. *National Figures for Participation in Primary School (000s)*

	Pop. (000s)	% of nomads	SGA	No. of SGA children (000s)	No. in school (000s)	GER
Djibouti	620	16	6–12	72	36	50
Eritrea	3,600	28	7–11	502	262	52
Ethiopia	65,000	13	7–14	(E)25,617	14,704	57
Kenya	30,000	25	6–14	6,700	5,900	88
Tanzania	32,000	19	7–13	(E)5,650	4,370	77
Uganda	21,000	5	6–14	8,000	6,800	85

Notes: SGA = School-going age; GER = Gross Enrolment Rate; (E) = Estimated

Table 2.2. *Estimates for Nomadic Groups*

	No. and % of nomads		SGA	No. of SGA children (000s)	No. in school (000s)	GER
Djibouti	100	16	6–12	63	7	11
Eritrea	1,000	28	7–11	194	60	31
Ethiopia	7,000	11	7–15	(E) 2,759	298	(E) 11
Kenya	7,500	25	6–14	1,675	660	39
Tanzania	6,000	19	7–13	1,000		
Uganda	1,030	5	6–14	(E) 393	(E) 150	(E) 38

Notes: SGA = School-going age; GER = Gross Enrolment Rate; (E) = Estimated

It is noticeable that, in each of the countries, the Gross Enrolment Rates are substantially lower for the nomadic groups than the overall national enrolment rates. Indeed, if we were to compare the GERs for nomadic groups with those for the sedentary population, we would see that the GER for the nomadic groups is always less than half the value for the non-nomadic group. In discussing policies, there are therefore (at least) four issues to consider.

First, *the size of the target population* as policies that are obviously appropriate for several million children may not be seen as viable for much smaller populations. For example, the provision of own language textbooks is easy when the target population is large, and much more problematic when it is small. Similarly, geographical distribution is not such an important issue when the target population is large; it matters when it is small; and so on.

Second, it is important to compare *the relative overall enrolment rates* among both the parent and nomad populations. Where there is very low enrolment among the general population then perhaps provision should be part of provision for the poor, because there is no particular reason to separate out nomads (or any other group); but where there is high overall enrolment then perhaps there needs to be special provision because the nomadic groups are reacting differently to the services provided by the State.

Third, *the proportion of nomads in the national or regional/provincial population* is a crucial factor. In countries where the nomadic groups are a substantial proportion of the population – for example, in Eritrea, Kenya and Tanzania – provision has to be part of the mainstream system; but in countries where nomadic groups are a minority then provision should be special or at least geographically specific.

Fourth, *the extent to which the national government is concerned or not with nation building and/or social inclusion.* Governments that only give lip-service to social inclusion – certainly the majority among over-developed industrialised countries and probably the majority of developing countries – will ignore these issues; other governments, where the democratic polity is powerful, are more likely to pay attention to the concerns of these groups.

Attaining EFA was always going to be difficult. Trying to include geographically dispersed, mobile sub-populations who see no reason to participate in Western style school systems just makes it more complicated.

Notes

1. The rather clumsy qualification 'state-provided' is used because we also want to differentiate between formal education (usually school) and a variety of non-formal alternatives.
2. We are grateful to Jason Pennells for providing us with the materials he used in a similar study in Nigeria.

References

Anderson, D.M. and V. Broch-Due (eds) (1999) *The Poor Are Not Us. Poverty and Pastoralism*. Oxford: James Currey.

Baxter, P. and R. Hogg (1990) *Property, Poverty and People: Changing Rights in Property and Problems of Pastoral Development*. Manchester: University of Manchester, Department of Social Anthropology and International Development.

Behnke, R., I. Scoones and C. Kerven (eds) (1993) *Range Ecology at Disequilibrium: New Models of Natural Variability and Pastoral Adaptation in African Savannas*. London: Overseas Development Institute.

Berstecher, D. and R. Carr-Hill (1990) *Primary Education and Economic Recession in the Developing World since 1980*. Background paper for Jomtien (Thailand) Conference. Paris: UNESCO.

Dyer, C. and A. Choksi (1997) 'The Demand for Education among the Rabaris of Kutch, West India'. *Nomadic Peoples* 1 (2): 77–97.

Djibouti Ministère du Commerce et du Tourisme (1996) *Enquête djiboutienne auprès des ménages-indicateurs sociaux (EDAM-IS)*. Djibouti: Direction générale de la statistique.

Ezeomah, C. (1990) *Educating Nomads for Self-actualisation and Development.* UNESCO: International Bureau of Education, Geneva.

Frantz, C. (1990) 'West African Pastoralism: Transformation and Resilience'. In: P.C. Salzman and J.G. Galaty (eds) *Nomads in a Changing World.* Series Minor XXXIII. Naples: Instituto Universitario Orientale.

Galaty, J., D. Aronson and P. Salzman (eds) (1981) *The Future of Pastoral Peoples. Proceedings of the Conference in Nairobi.* Ottawa: International Development Research Center.

Gorham, A. (1978) *The Design and Management of Pastoral Development. The Provision of Education in Pastoral Areas.* ODI, Pastoral Network Paper 6b. London: Overseas Development Institute.

Krätli, S. (2001) 'Educational Provision to Nomadic Pastoralists: A Literature Review. Prepared for World Bank'. University of Sussex: Institute of Development Studies.

MOEST – Ministry of Education, Science and Technology (1999) *Report on Formal and Non-Formal Education in Parts of Samburu, Tukana, Marsabit and Moyale Districts.* Nairobi: MOEST and CIDA – Canadian International Development Agency.

Mohammed , A.M.I. (1998) 'Basic Issues of Pastoral Crises in the Western Lowlands. "Discussion and Recommendation with Emphasis on Education"' dissertation for M.Sc. in Agricultural Economics, University of Reading, U.K.

Okech, A. (2000) *Needs Assessment Survey for Functional Adult Literacy in Karamoja Uganda 2000.* Prepared by Anthony Okech, for the Ministry of Gender, Labour and Social Development, in collaboration with the World Food Programme in Uganda, Kampala.

PRSP (2001) *Poverty Reduction Strategy Paper (2001–2004),* R.O.K MOSP. June *2001* Prepared By The People And Government Of Kenya. Nairobi: Nairobi Government Printer.

Salzman, P. (ed.) (1980) *When Nomads Settle: Processes of Sedentarization as Adaptation and Response.* Praeger: New York.

Salzman, P. and J.G. Galaty (1990) *Nomads in a Changing World.* Series Minor XXXIII. Naples: Instituto Universitario Orientale.

Sarone, O.S. (1984) *Development and Education for Pastoralists: Maasai Responses in East Africa.* CDA Discussion Papers No 19. McGill University: Centre for Developing Area Studies.

SCF – Save the Children Fund, (2000) *Towards Responsive Schools: Supporting Better Schooling for Disadvantaged Children. Case Studies from Save the Children.* Education Paper No. 38. London: Department for International Development.

Scoones, I. (ed.) (1995) *Living with Uncertainty: New Directions in Pastoral Development in Africa.* London: Intermediate Technology Publications.

UNDP (2000) *Human Development Report 2000.* New York: UNDP.

UNICEF/UNSO (1992) *Pastoralists at a Crossroads: Survival and Development Issues in African Pastoralism.* Nairobi: UNICEF/UNSO.

WDEFA (1990) *World Declaration on Education for All.* Paris: UNESCO.

World Bank (1996) *Population and Human Resources Division: Eastern Africa, Poverty Assessment Patterns of Poverty in Eritrea.* Washington D.C.: World Bank.

CHAPTER 3

THE ACQUISITION OF MANNERS, MORALS AND KNOWLEDGE: GROWING INTO AND OUT OF BAKKARWAL SOCIETY

Aparna Rao

Introduction

The first part of this chapter discusses the context of informal education and the traditional concepts and practices of socialisation among the nomadic pastoral Bakkarwal of Jammu and Kashmir in the western Himalayas. It shows that knowledge is not just 'a thing', but also 'a relationship' (see Barth, 2002: 2). Both context and content are thus gender and age specific and prepare Bakkarwal girls and boys for their future lives. The chapter goes on to examine the formal education of Bakkarwal children and the institutions responsible for it over the last roughly 20 years. It discusses the extent to which the state's notions of a good and productive citizen are linked to its educational policies towards pastoral nomads (see Krätli with Dyer, this volume). It further argues that primary curricula must be adjusted to local needs and special capacities, and for all children – nomadic and sedentary, rural and urban – they must be more creative and practice oriented. The data presented are drawn from fieldwork in the mid 1980s, and then again from the late 1990s until 2002, and cover the period immediately preceding and during the years of violent turmoil in this region.

Growing into Bakkarwal Society

The transmission of knowledge takes place over the entire human life span, but it is especially during childhood and the years just preceding adulthood that culture-specific elements tend to be imbibed more intensely through various forms of informal and formal education. These phases of life are universally recognised as those in which education and the principal inculcation of norms and values take place. I begin by contextualising and discussing some of these norms and values among the Bakkarwal.

The Context of Childhood

The Bakkarwal (for details see Rao, 1998a) are an increasingly stratified, patrilineal, Sunni Muslim community of nomadic pastoralists who spend the entire year within the boundaries of Jammu and Kashmir, east of the Indo-Pakistan ceasefire line. They are culturally close both to the transhumant Gujar of the Kashmir Valley (Casimir and Rao, 1985), and to the semi-sedentary Gujar of Azad Kashmir, west of the ceasefire line. In the 1980s, the Bakkarwal population was estimated at roughly 16,000 individuals, organised in 39 patrilineal and preferentially endogamous units, known as *zat* or *khel* (Rao, 1988). These units consist of patrilineal groupings of families whose ancestors migrated into their present areas in the late nineteenth and early twentieth centuries from the valleys of Allai and Kunhar in present day Pakistan (Rao, 1999).

Throughout the year Bakkarwal life is physically hard. Until the early 1990s almost all Bakkarwal migrated twice annually between semi-alpine and alpine summer pastures above the Vale of Kashmir and winter grazing and browsing areas in the colline belt that stretches eastwards from Poonch to Kathua (Casimir, 1991; Casimir and Rao, 1985, 1998). Even today entire families cross very high mountain passes during the five-month spring and autumn migration, looking for appropriate grazing on the arduous journey back and forth, facing storms and other inclement weather and a variety of other natural hazards (Kango and Dhar, 1981; Khatana, 1992; Rao, 2002). Migration also involves considerable mental tension, since to be a pastoral nomad means facing possibly unhelpful farmers, competing herdsmen of various communities, frequently tyrannical forest officials, and if one is poor, exploitative and wealthy fellow Bakkarwal. But Bakkarwal life is also greatly enjoyable, especially in the summer months, when the herds can be grazed in the high mountain pastures full of lush grass and flowing streams (see Rao, 2000 for the connotations of high altitude). Except during migration, settlement sizes are small (one to nine tents or huts), and very rarely do several generations live together. Young children are hence largely socialised within small family units.

Access to herds, pasture, water and labour is obtained, managed and lost by individual households. Herd animals can, for example, be acquired through male inheritance (anticipatory or otherwise) and female dowry among the wealthy (Rao, 1990); at weddings as part of bridewealth or as gifts brought by guests to the young couple; as dower to a divorcée; or as part of the salary of a hired shepherd. Access to pasture obtains through inheritance, marriage, employment, exchange, borrowing, purchase, lease or usurpation. While access to water is generally unrestricted in the summer area with its ubiquitous streams, in winter, water rights with their concomitant salt-lick areas are mainly leased from the state or from peasants. Grazing areas are not held in common by more than a two-generational extended family, nor are there any joint herding units.

Though women and older girls help extensively in herd-related activities during the day, herding is basically a male job. There is no prescribed lower age limit, and children start helping from the age of six or seven years, especially in the lambing and kidding periods. By the time he is about fifteen, a boy is expected to start taking on regular herding responsibilities under his father's or elder brother's supervision. There is no upper age or status limit, but as they grow older, men increasingly hand over specific tasks to their sons, though they keep the basic management in their hands until they are too old and infirm to do so. Wealthy men invariably employ shepherds (Rao, 1995) for the routine herding, but supervise them both directly and indirectly through their sons. A man without sons is hence in something of a predicament (Casimir and Rao, 1995).

Table 3.1: Phases of the Human Life Cycle

	Bakkerwali			English Terms
AGE	**General**	**Men**	**Female**	**Male/Female**
Birth – 4 years	B	jatak	jatak	
	A			infant
4 – 6/7 years	L	nikko	nikki	
	A			child
6/7 – 10 years	K	badero	badera	
				juvenile
10 – puberty		lura	betki	
Puberty – 1st. Child	JAWAN	gado	gadi	adolescent
1st Child – Old Age	no term	no term	no term	
Old Age		budo*	budi**	adult

* or *bujurg* for males of well-being; ** for woman this begins at menopause

Just as the year is divided into months and seasons, so also is human life conceived of as divided into stages or phases. Bakkarwali language does not distinguish between the terms 'life cycle' and 'life', both being known as *jindagi*, and divided into seven major phases (Table 3.1). A girl or boy in one of the first three phases is generally termed a child (*balak*), and though

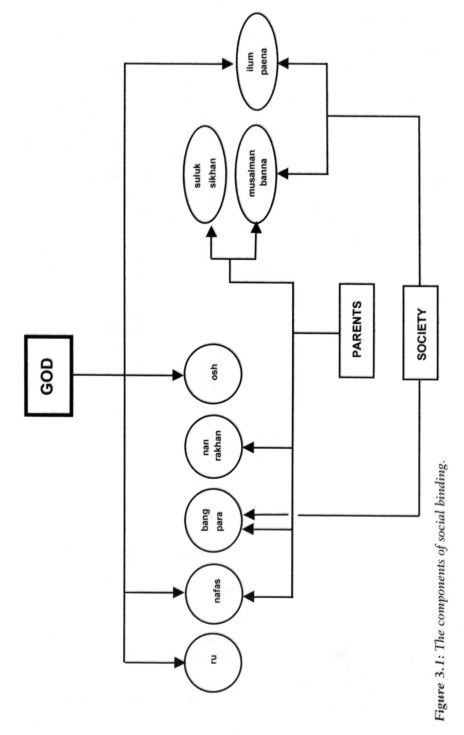

Figure 3.1: The components of social binding.

gender is differentiated from birth, terminological gender differentiation begins at about four years of age. From roughly the end of the juvenile period until one has a couple of children oneself, one is classified as *jawan*. No specific classificatory term appears to exist after this, until one reaches old age. The first four phases, extending from birth to puberty, are considered to be those of childhood, and the first four years of life are said to constitute roughly the first of these four phases. Figure 3.1 illustrates the various steps in the social and biological transition of an infant into human and ultimately adult society. Elsewhere (Rao, 1990, 1998a) I have dealt in some detail with the first five of these; here I shall deal with the latter three, placed in the right-hand side of the diagram.

Manners and Morals

A key notion in the concept of being well bred in northern India and large parts of Pakistan is that of *adab* (see Metcalf, 1984). Something of these notions of etiquette and behaviour are reflected in the Bakkarwal concept of *suluk* (see Fig. 3.1). The learning of basic *suluk* begins in early childhood, first in passive fashion, and in a more active way when *osh* (personhood, see Fig. 3.1) increases. Its basic elements relate to dress and body postures, and are gender-specific in their details. Elements of *suluk* beyond these basics depend on one's *osh*, and hence on a variety of other factors such as whom one mixes with socially. Being properly clad is part of being well mannered and well behaved, although as it is also related to purchasing power, really good *suluk* is attributed only to the wealthy, and then again especially to wealthy men. Another important aspect of *suluk* concerns the hair and head covering. Among most South Asians long hair is a sign of female beauty and sexuality; and head coverings in South Asia as elsewhere have much to do with honour. At six months an infant receives its first haircut; no gender differentiation is made at this stage, but after she is about two years old, a little girl's hair is never cut; boys and men are expected to shave their heads regularly. Long before the first haircut, around one week after its birth, every infant gets a tiny cap (*topi*). A child retains this first type of cap until it is about four or five years old; only the size increases with the months. After this, however, a gender-based difference marks the caps of both boys and girls. Caps among the Bakkarwal exemplify a number of complex meanings (for details see Rao, 1998a) and are explicitly associated both with Bakkarwal tradition and Islamic prescriptions.

As opposed to head coverings, body postures are associated with what I shall term secular social morals, summed up in the concept of *uthan bethan*. Literally translated as 'getting up and sitting down', this concept encompasses a complex range of norms and values impinging on social responsibility, sexual control, the domestic space and well-being.

Well-being can be, and is, demonstrated through physical and social expanse, and families who have demonstrated their well-being through wealth and good pastures spend the summers at higher altitudes where there is little crowding (Casmir, 2003; Rao, 1992, 2003). In this nomad society, which is *per se* physically an open one, the quality and amount of space are hierarchised; wealthy men have the most legitimate space of their own, poorer men less, women little, and children none at all.

As they grow older, gender differentiation expressed in body postures, in ways of 'getting up and sitting down', prepares boys and girls for their future social roles. Simultaneously, from their earliest years, children of both sexes are left to develop a certain physical autonomy. A child below the age of seven or eight is rarely chastised, because it is considered to be too young to understand and possess enough *osh* (personhood) to be aware of its actions. As in many Middle Eastern and South Asian societies, here too increasing cultural competence is expected of a child from the age of about seven onwards. The juvenile period between about six or seven and ten years is in many ways critical. It is at this stage that the basic amounts of *nafas* (selfhood) and *osh* (personhood) should stabilise, and in keeping with this, the child must increasingly be involved in the daily tasks of a herding household.

The Daily Routines of Play and Work

In the early stages of childhood here as in most other societies, work and play are intertwined. Toys are unknown, but when out herding, children weave toy tents from grass, and play games individually and in twos, rather than in groups. It must be remembered that throughout the year Bakkarwal camps (*dera*) are small and children are not usually allowed to wander off on their own, for example, to other camps. A child's world thus consists primarily of its own camp and this camp's members and hence its access to social knowledge (*khabar*) is very limited.

Until they are about eight, most children tend to play more than they work; this is especially true of boys, who are anyway considered more immature than girls. In the process of playing and helping with work, all children learn to recognise the right plants and trees, and practise how to handle the forests and negotiate the mountain slopes. By about nine or ten, they must know the names and uses of trees, some of which are collected as fuel, others as construction material for the winter huts, and yet others as fodder for the different herd animals. Milking and churning are arduous but essential tasks; while the latter is done only by the housewife, older children may milk if their mothers are sick, and younger children help their mothers by holding each animal being milked. Herding is basically a man's job, and only males go to the highest pastures (Rao, 1992, 2003). If there are no sons, shepherds are hired by the well-to-do; in less wealthy families little girls herd near home from the age of six or seven until about the age of ten; after this they may also go to graze during the day, but only if accompanied by their fathers or siblings. Boys start herding when they are a little older, since as children they are considered less responsible than their sisters. As they grow older the mixed work and play groups split according to gender, with girls increasingly helping their mothers with domestic tasks, and boys spending more time herding. Girls with younger siblings spend more time caring for them and practising their future role as mothers.

In Bakkarwali usage both small children and animals are tended (*palna*). Tending has many components, but one main goal – survival. After all the necessary precautions have been taken a child is expected to survive. It is around the age of ten that the foundation is laid for the capacity which develops variously in different persons to fend for themselves and be responsible. There is now no more need for elaborate care and tending. From now on until they reach puberty a girl and a boy are termed *betki* (lit. 'little daughter') and *lara/lura* respectively, and this change of terminology marks the entrance into the next phase of the life cycle.

A Prelude to Puberty

Whereas a child below about ten is still considered fairly vulnerable (*najuk*), a pubertal boy and girl are thought of as basically sturdy, strength being one of the elements circumscribed by the term *jawan*. They have crossed one set of dangers which threatened mainly their physical life; they will face a second set when they are around sixteen or seventeen, and they must be prepared for this confrontation. These dangers are more social than physical, though they too stem from their own *nafas* and *osh*, which must at this stage be manipulated through socialisation. While this manipulation is required for both girls and boys, it is generally felt that 'girls are less of a problem on the whole than boys – if one is a little careful, they give less trouble. They also grow up much more quickly'. Mixing with the right persons is crucial at this stage, since it is explained that a good (*nek*) person teaches others good things simply by his/her presence, and establishes harmony even in strained situations; by being with such a person even an enemy is turned into a friend (lit. 'good person': *uske naldushman ato to sajjan banto*). Similarly by keeping bad company one 'goes bad'.

Gender differentiation in socialisation is publicly marked in this phase by male circumcision, there being no female counterpart to it, which takes place between the ages of six and twelve. This act finally confirms the boy as a Muslim (*musalman banna*; see Fig. 3.1), but it also affects him physiologically and prepares him gradually for puberty. In Bakkarwali there is no term specifically designating the period preceding sexual maturity or full adulthood. However, 'certain things' are said to 'happen' in the ages 'between ten or eleven and sixteen or seventeen', and these culminate in 'a boy and a girl becoming *jawan*'. Girls and boys are now terminologically distinguished from those younger and older and are known respectively as *gadri* and *gadro*. Physically much happens now, I was told: a boy's chest (*sina*) expands and a girl's breasts (*chuchi*) first develop, though they really grow only after marriage; wisps of hair appear on their bodies and on a boy's face. Both boys and girls grow in height and weight, since both increase in strength (*takat*). Now, it is said, the levels of blood in a girl and semen in a boy start to 'rise'.

To help his 'strength ripen' a boy must now start accompanying the family's animals to the high pastures. For older men, this later becomes a romantic and idealised phase of life, yet it is in many ways ambivalent, above all, perhaps, because it is in this phase that the social binding of a person is to be successfully completed. Errors at this last stage may have devastating effects on all. This ambivalence is built into the term *jawani* which is associated – as far as I could gather, exclusively in men – with what may be described as a carefree disposition. Romance and adventure are part of it, but so too are thoughtlessness and the lack of a sense of proportion. The general increase in 'heat' in boys and girls in this phase of life leads to a 'rise' in the levels of body fluids, and this in turn to the physical strength achieved in the years to follow. But this rise is also associated with the development of certain undesirable wishes, and hence special care must be taken to achieve and maintain a highly sensitive equilibrium between 'hot' and 'cold'. If a girl's parents are not careful enough, a pretty girl could grow so 'hot' as to become too aware of her own beauty, and a sturdy boy overly conscious of his own strength.

With the onset of menarche, a girl attains a new social status and participates in new productive activities. From this day she is classified as among those who should possess modesty and the sense of shame and modesty (*laj*). If necessary, she may now milk and churn, except during her monthly period, but until she herself marries and becomes a mother she may no longer go to the highest pastures, nor may she be present at the birth of a baby, since she herself is no longer 'pure'. A girl who has reached menarche may no longer be careless about wearing her cap. From now on it would be a real shame (*sharam*) to be seen with bare head (*sir nango*) – it would indicate that she does not have the emotion of *laj*. A young girl now openly acquires the label of *aibdar*, imperfect, since her innate imperfection is now obvious to all, and yet she is simultaneously considered weak (*najuk*) and vulnerable. A girl must be engaged before she reaches menarche and becomes nubile. In principle the earlier the better, for her and for all others, since the chances of her becoming sexually dangerous to herself and to others must be minimised. Both ideally, and as far as I could gather in reality, a girl is a virgin (*kuari*) until her first marriage.

The Acquisition of Knowledge and Information

A child's acquisition of traditional practical knowledge is ascribed to its God-given *osh* (personhood), but no specific term is used for this knowledge, which, like '… each tradition of knowledge [is] characterized by distinct and … stringent criteria of validity … in some kind of systematic relation to the uses to which [it] … is put' (Barth, 2002: 10). Its specificities depend on the child's community, its place of residence and various other factors which all go to build its innate temper and disposition (*mijaj*). It is a part of life, to be taken for granted in adulthood. But there are other kinds of knowledge – specialised knowledge (*ilum*) – which are acquired only by a few and thus highly valued, although perhaps of little concrete use in everyday life. The term *ilum* (see Figure 3.1) was traditionally applied to knowledge of a religious nature, whose acquisition is in principle a strenuous and lengthy process. Access to it is not for all, nor is it meant for all. Unlike among some religious leaders for whom until very recently the term *ilum* comprised religious knowledge alone, among the Bakkarwal *ilum* has for many years also applied to knowledge acquired through schooling. As opposed to religious *ilum*, schooling, which for the Bakkarwal is primarily state-managed, is allegedly destined for all, and yet the acquisition of this 'secular' *ilum* does not always appear to fit into recognisable cultural patterns. To begin with, it is not always very clear what the benefits of this *ilum* are; many of its features appear to clash unreasonably with time-honoured usage, and finally, those dispensing it are viewed as humans who take, rather than give.

Growing out of Society

From casual conversations in the early and mid 1980s it appeared, however, that most Bakkarwal parents favoured schooling. Of 24 men and women asked more pointedly, 19 favoured schooling for sons and twelve for daughters (see Table 3.2). When asked why they favoured schooling, fathers mostly replied in terms of the future economic well-being of their sons; the mothers also mentioned future wealth and prestige, but most also linked this to their own security in old age. Fathers who wanted to send their daughters to school cited a variety of reasons, all of which related to imbibing the culture of what they considered domesticity in the dominant culture; while they mentioned economic criteria only once, the mothers' arguments for schooling girls basically mirrored the fathers' economic arguments concerning their sons. The arguments forwarded by the eight parents not in favour of schooling their daughters tended to underline their fear of the child's learning evil ways. The two mothers who opposed their sons' schooling reasoned in terms of their health. Especially intelligent children (with lots of *osh*) are prone to attract the evil eye (*ak*). In 1984 Shafi died due to *ak*, 'since he could write', his mother told me. Mothers felt that schooling also led intelligent children to think too much, to reflect (*fikur*) and worry about things. Although it is good if a child understands and grasps (*samajh*) what he is told and taught, because he then considers (*fikur*) his actions, thinks about (*soch*) them, and develops a sense of responsibility (lit. cares about someone, *is ko uska fikur e*), too much (*much*) pondering is bad, since it 'cools' one down and can lead to sickness, early ageing and even death.

Table 3.2: Responses of Twelve Mothers and Fathers Each, Concerning the Schooling of Their Children

	In Favour of Schooling		Against Schooling		No Opinion	
	Sons	Daughters	Sons	Daughters	Sons	Daughters
Mothers	9	5	2	5	1	2
Fathers	10	7	2	3	0	2

Although this is a very small sample of parents, schooling had a place in Bakkarwal ideology in the early and mid 1980s. To see to what extent this corresponded with practice, I considered a sample of 297 Bakkarwal men and boys and 231 women and girls between the ages of 7 and 45 years, obtained from the records of the official Census of 1981, and found that 57 (19.19 percent) and 6 (2.59 percent) respectively were classified as literate. The issue of how to define literacy and effects of literacy are being increasingly debated in India (see e.g. Basu et al., 2000). At the time a literate person was implicitly defined as someone above five years of age who was able to read and write (personal communication, Census Office, Delhi). Table 3.3 sets out details concerning the males. A comparison of these census data with the opinions of parents set out above indicates a fairly great discrepancy between ideology and praxis. Several intertwined factors appear to be inimical to the schooling of Bakkarwal children.

Table 3.3: Break-down of 297 Males According to Age, Incidence and Percentage of Literacy, as Given in a Sample Population of the Census 1981

Age group (in years)	N	Literate	Percentage
7–10	86	13	15.11
11–19	85	23	27.05
20+	126	21	16.66

Social Stratification and Access to Knowledge

As already stated, even in the 1980s Bakkarwal society was increasingly stratified. In this high altitude pastoral setting, as in most high-risk contexts '... rapid acquisition of adaptive information ...' (Spencer, 1993: 47) was crucial to survival. Those who acquired information (*khabar*) more rapidly than others could also consolidate and eventually enhance their well-being more rapidly, and perhaps for a longer period of time, than those who were slower at doing so. Both information and the access to it were usually transmitted across the generations, so that the son of a man who had access to a great deal of information was likely to have more access than the son of a man who had little access. In other words, there existed an intergenerational hierarchisation of information processing which led to a social, economic and ultimately, political hierarchy in the capacity to make choices and take decisions.

For analytical purposes *khabar* could be classified according to three spheres to which it pertained: the private, the public and the alien (i.e. beyond that of the group or community), whereby partial overlapping between two or more spheres was inevitable. The Bakkarwal conceived of these spheres in a hierarchical fashion, the alien (*pablik*, or *ukumati* when relating more specifically to government matters) increasingly being accorded the greatest formal value. This was largely because access to information in the alien sphere could imply – and in its turn lead to – becoming known as the representative of a group of families. This in turn could lead to obtaining more information in the public sphere (of one's own community), and this again to more options. But to gain access to the alien sphere one must first have access to and enough information about the other two (*karelu*: private, household, domestic, and *biradari/kaumi*: public at two different levels within the community). The objective veracity of information may or may not be important: as Khana put it, 'a man like X knows about everything, he knows your value, he knows the value of your questions which people like me don't fully realise. I just say what I think – he says what should be said'.

Whether relating to the *ukumati*, community, or private spheres, veracity of information is of course of great importance, since it can afford or suppress access to crucial resources. It is essential to be aware in time of the availability of medicines for goats and sheep, of weather conditions in particular areas, of the current rates of silver jewellery, of wages for shepherds or going rates of interest within the community. When relating to the *pablik* sphere, however, objective veracity was fairly unimportant in the 1980s, since the information was rarely verifiable for most. While the importance of objective veracity was contextual, the manner in which it was displayed was always of significance, since once could impress others, obtain their following and through them create still larger networks – as a kind of mediator or patron – to improve one's situation further. It was thus important to be perceived to have access to what was considered to be information. One such obviously visible source of information in the 1980s was a school for one's children in the close vicinity of one's camp – on one's own territory (Rao, 2003). A school was perceived as both a source and a result of successful access to socio-political knowledge and information.

Most families whose sons attended – and continued attending – school had fairly large herds and employed hired shepherds; in other words, only families with a certain degree of wealth sent their children to school. As one man commented, 'We want our children to be educated instead of tending animals (lit. going with the animals, *mal ke nal jana*). We can afford servants for that – each of us here has three or four servants.' Often, these families were also no longer entirely dependent on their flocks of small stock; most also had cattle and / or some agricultural land, though of mediocre quality. A few of these families felt that sufficient diversification, i.e. a combination of land, cattle and small stock, or alternatively of land, cattle plus enough schooling, could lead a boy out of the constraints of a pastoral economy. Schooling, they also felt, could lead to political influence, and this was said to be borne out by members of the Khatana *zat*, who had diversified the most, increasingly attended school and become increasingly wealthy and influential.

However, it would be simplistic and incorrect to conclude that children from poorer families did not attend school simply because of poverty. Indeed, it is too often simply assumed that because children are an economic asset, poverty in itself, or even the child's role in economic activities, leads to children not being schooled. As the first part of this chapter showed, not every work performed by children in any society can necessarily be classified as 'child labour', but rather 'a standard process of socialisation' (Lieten, 2000: 2037). Among the Bakkarwal it was the shortage of schooling facilities and the monopolisation of existing facilities by the wealthy and powerful that went a long way in preventing the children of the less wealthy from receiving formal education. 'In summer we can't send our children to school at C – that's Hajji A's school', said Shafi, referring to the mobile (*gashti*) school situated in Hajji A's territory. Nine-year-old Hamid's parents were very poor, but he had studied up to Class 2. He studied 'with whoever agrees to take him [as a student] – we give milk to some Kashmiri or Punjabi, who teaches a little – all private. None of the other children here ever went to school, but we'll admit all of them if a teacher is available', said Hamid's mother.

Mobile Schools and Special Hostels

> *'An egg a day is more important than mother's love ...'*
> The Director of a Gujar Hostel, Srinagar (1980)

Reminiscent of centuries of racist European discourse and treatment of Gypsy children (Liégeois, 1987), the children of many nomadic or ex-nomadic communities in India, such as the Bhil in western Rajasthan and the Konchi Korava of Karnataka, are still taken away from their parents and kept in residential schools 'away from the influence of their parents and society ...' (Gurumurthy, 1996: 110, cf. also Ruhela, 1997; Rao and Casimir, 2003a, 2003b). In Jammu and Kashmir the Government had deliberated over the 'problem' of schooling posed by the nomadic population as early as 1916:

> Owing to their nomadic habits, it is difficult to arrange any educational institution for them. Even if moving schools could be arranged, the scattered nature of [their] ... dwellings on the uplands would probably render any such arrangement inefficacious. The only plan which I can see is to encourage the children of such as spend the winter months in the lowlands of the State to come to the ordinary schools during that time. (Sharp, 1916: 46)

Those were the years of feudal-cum-colonial rule in Jammu and Kashmir – years in which British missionaries were putting in 'manly, self-sacrificing service' to '... develop the bodies, the character and the souls ...' of sedentary and urban Kashmiris, '... an otherwise feeble people ...' (Baden-Powell, 1930). Shortly hereafter, the perhaps less 'feeble' nomadic Bakkarwal were declared a 'Criminal Tribe' (Anon. 1926; Banerji, 1928, C.S., 1914). Some 60 years later, in 1976, the government of Jammu and Kashmir introduced the concept of mobile schools for the young children of nomadic pastoralists. But even in the mid 1980s, their functioning was highly debatable. Sadiq, the adolescent son of an important Bakkarwal leader had studied up to Class 5 in a mobile school, before moving to a sedentary school in their winter area, where he studied up to Class 7. He felt that

> Now [i.e. 1983] the mobile schools hardly run. Formerly they were better. The teachers used to be Jammu Gujar, or Hindus. Now they are mostly Bakkarwal, and anyway they don't come for more than one month ... The Bakkarwal are the worst – they fill up the attendance registers at home.

Indeed, the few Bakkarwal who at that time fulfilled the qualifications to teach were appointed as teachers in these mobile schools. All came from wealthy and influential families, and it was widely felt that 'the very few educated help only their own families'. Gujar teachers in these schools had even less empathy with Bakkarwal children. As HK, a teacher from a sedentarised Gujar family of the Rajouri region expressed it (in 1985):

> It is frustrating to teach the Bakkarwal children because they have no perseverance and do not concentrate. They are 95 percent illiterate – as against 5 percent Gujar illiteracy. Among the Banihara [a community allied to the Gujar; for details see Rao and Casimir, 1985; Rao, 2002] it would be 50 percent illiteracy.

The percentages cited by HK are extremely doubtful, but reflect the attitude of those who are no longer nomadic towards those who still are. 'Reliance on internal teaching staff [to] encourage internal cultural and ethnic solidarity and joint perception of child development ...' (Meir and Barnea, 1987: 34) cannot always be presumed. The following example recorded on 15 July 1983 in the sub-alpine summer pasture of L. was fairly typical for the situation in the 1980s, and illustrates the problems faced by both children and their teachers:

> This year we had a teacher for the first time – a Gujar from Rajouri – one BK. In *phagan* [mid-February to mid-March] he went back from ... where we were in winter to his home in Rajouri, and he never came back. Anyway he came only every fourth day or so and didn't teach all the children. He was a Government employee and got his salary, but he taught only those who gave him good milk, or a lamb or a kid. He also ate with us. He used to ask the children to assemble in school, but often they waited the whole day and he never turned up. In T. [the winter region of this family] there are other schools for local children, but for nomads (*khanabadosh*) there was only this one.

It so happened that BK suddenly appeared shortly after this conversation. He told me that he was coming after an absence of three months (they claimed five months). He was a sedentary Gujar from Rajouri and had passed his BA. Since he was subsequently unemployed, he – like many other Gujar youth – took on this job for want of anything better.

> Before getting a job in a normal school the condition for us Gujar is that we must work for at least three years in a mobile school. I still have six months to go. I didn't come all these months as I was looking for a transfer, but it didn't come through, although a relative of mine [then minister] is well placed. I report for duty off and on and then go off. What to do – it's a hard way to earn one's living. I first reported in 1981 in J. [an alpine pasture area nearby]. Mobile schools have been there for the past forty years or so, but they haven't helped ... I get no TA/DA [travel or daily allowances] – only CA [current allowance], nor does the Government provide books, blackboards, etc., for these children.

BK did seem to understand the specific problems faced by Bakkarwal children, but was clearly keen to get out of his posting as quickly as possible.

The Years of Violence

As the editor of this volume so rightly observes in her introduction, education everywhere, whether formal or informal, is a form of ideological practice. When the state is involved, she notes that this practice often consists of promoting sedentarisation. So also in Jammu and Kashmir, where until the late 1980s the little schooling offered to nomadic pastoralists by the state was implicitly – though not explicitly, given the feeble attempts to provide mobile schools – meant ultimately to 'help them' abandon migration in the general process of 'modernising'. Simultaneously, however, education was implicitly supposed to turn the Bakkarwal into better, migrating livestock producers, with higher rates of productivity for pastoral produce whose importance and value it was exclusively the state's prerogative to decide upon, in the framework of its notions of 'development'. Hence, for example, to push their efforts at improving livestock, government sheep breeding programmes, which were initiated to improve wool quality and quantity, focused on herders who had attended primary school or were at least literate. There were no such programmes to improve the productivity of the *Kaghani* goats, which were the major component of Bakkarwal herds and were locally prized for the quality and quantity of their meat. On the contrary, all attempts were made to dissuade the Bakkarwal from keeping goats – notwithstanding the increasing and acute shortage of meat in Jammu and Kashmir.

But all official notions of 'development' and 'modernity' were dealt a severe blow and came to an entire standstill after 1990 when armed violence broke out in the region. Caught between a variety of militia fighting for the region's separation from India and innumerable Indian military personnel, herding and migration have become even more arduous than they were, and migration patterns and socio-economic conditions have changed drastically for the Bakkarwal (for some details see Rao, 1995, 2002, 2003). Access to pasture at all times of the year often has to be negotiated, not just with officials of the government's forest and wildlife departments as was the case earlier, but also with ubiquitous militia men and Indian security personnel. Safe passage often consists of bribing one's way through a series of zones under the control of varying armed units. Many of the poor and middle-income herders whose winter and summer pastures have been cordoned off by the Indian army since 1994 have had to sell their herds and are reduced to the status of manual labourers outside the pastoral system. In some places, in the late 1990s, various militia men began intervening in pasture disputes (e.g. Swami, 2001); so too did the Indian army. More recently, especially in their winter areas, many Bakkarwal men, women and children, have been brutally massacred by Islamist terrorists on simple suspicion of collaborating with the Indian army; in other areas, Indian troops have persecuted Bakkarwal on suspicion of harbouring such terrorists.

The wealthier have tried to minimise difficulties during migration by transporting herds by truck as far as roads are available. Those who cannot afford this continue to face severe harassment, lose their choice animals, and sometimes even their lives. For a variety of reasons therefore the wealthiest herd-owners and their families have increasingly curtailed their migration. But to survive, their flocks have to migrate. These are entrusted to hired shepherds or poor relatives, who as servants rather than as owners, are less liable to blackmail by the ubiquitous armed units. This in its turn, has impinged on sociopolitical stratification within the community, for now the well-being of the rich and their flocks depends largely on the rapid access that these poorer migrating herders have to adaptive information, independently of the sedentarised rich.

Until the late 1990s such information was not available to the poor via the schooling system. In general primary education in Jammu and Kashmir was dismal during the entire decade, and only one out of fourteen districts was covered in 1994 by the government's National Literacy Mission. In rural areas the gap was increasingly filled by schools that were funded and organised by the RSS backed Vidya Bharati Educational Society (cf. Sarkar, 1996) or the Jama't-e Islami of Jammu and Kashmir, both of which preach and teach obscurantist and reactionary ideologies ('Hindu' and 'Muslim' respectively) of hate and intolerance.

No new mobile schools were created after 1987, and those which existed at least on paper, became entirely dysfunctional. Indeed, even their official numbers were decreasing: while 306 such schools existed in 2001[1], according to government records, by 2002 the number had dropped to 298, with 7,000 boys and girls officially registered and a high 'drop-out rate' (DRI 2001; Bachloo 2002). Simultaneously, however, the children of some of the rich and now nearly sedentarised families had started sending their children to non-mobile schools, and by 2001 roughly 127,000 Gujar and Bakkarwal children were enrolled in sedentary state-run schools (personal communication, Director of the Gujar-Bakkarwal hostel, Srinagar, 2001).

When mobile schools were first started they were planned to provide children with primary education, following which they were qualified to attend mainstream, non-mobile schools. To facilitate middle and high-school level studies, and also to help those children attend primary school whose parents migrated to areas where mobile schools were not viable, hostels meant specifically for Gujar and Bakkarwal children were set up in the early 1980s. By 2001 there were 13 such hostels – one for girls in Jammu and 12 for boys in the districts of Anantnag, Baramulla, Budgam, Kupwara, Pulwama, Srinagar (with a capacity of 50 boys each), Rajouri, Poonch (125 boys each), Doda, Jammu, Kathua, Udhampur (100 boys each). However, from the early 1990s until at least 2002, the hostels in Anantnag, Baramulla Doda, Kupwara and Pulwama were taken over and occupied by Indian security personnel, and hence could not be used by children (Bachloo, 2002). Very many government school buildings throughout rural Jammu and Kashmir were also occupied by Indian security personnel to live in and store their belongings. Simultaneously, there were numerous violent attempts by Islamist organisations which are active in the winter area of the Bakkarwal to prevent children from attending the few functioning schools (e.g. Swami, 2003). Teachers and parents were threatened, and children often forced to work as informers and porters. Obviously, under such circumstances, formal state education in general was extremely difficult; for pastoral nomadic children it was well nigh impossible.

Partly to try and deal with this situation, a co-educational school-cum-hostel was started in Jammu by the Gurjar-Desh Charitable Trust. Another reason for founding it was to provide employment to Gujar (and Bakkarwal) teachers who constitute only 2–3 percent of all teachers in Jammu and Kashmir, although there is an official reservation of ten percent for them (personal communication from the Director, Gujar-Bakkarwal hostel, Srinagar, in 2001). However, this school, which has excellent modern facilities has hardly any Bakkarwal students, nor does its curriculum even faintly reflect any component of Bakkarwal lifestyle.

According to community leaders, some 70 percent of Bakkarwal boys have by now studied up to Class I or II. Very few girls have been to school, and even those who have stop after Class II. While such high dropout rates must be prevented, the larger issue facing educationalists concerns the future of a child once it has finished school – what can a child really do after schooling with what it has learned in school? The possibilities are extremely limited. Like most parents in South Asia, Bakkarwal parents also want their sons to 'earn salaries', 'to get steady government jobs'. In reality, however, 'those who have studied get no jobs'. Simultaneously, children who have been to school even for a few years have next to no knowledge about herd management, nor do they usually wish to be herders. Most children who were in school or had attended school for some years did not even appear to know what they really wished to do later in life. Indeed, they appeared never to have thought about this and told me that I was the first person to have put this question to them. Many felt that the herding profession (*pesha*) had no future, since it was 'backward' (*pasmanda*), but nor could they think of any alternatives, even for themselves.

Issues of Backwardness and Modernity: the Content of Education

Backwardness (*pichrapan*) is an important word in the political and educational discourse of most states, and so also of modern India. Through school textbooks children are told that: 'After (national) independence it was felt that the greatest obstacle for our citizens was represented by the backwardness of our rural citizens' (NCERT, 1989: 13, translation mine). Illiteracy is linked to lack of knowledge, while not attending schools which are at least officially secular is projected as synonymous with being ignorant. Illiteracy and ignorance explain the backwardness of rural society (NCERT, 1989: 14). This model applies particularly to women, who are 'in a backward state' (NCERT, 1989: 15). As for the Bakkarwal:

> They are backward ... and amongst the backward (in the State of Jammu and Kashmir) they are perhaps at the bottom of the ladder ... This backwardness is all-round, but it is particularly marked in scanty educational advancement, and unhealthy living conditions. Economically, some of them may be considered as fairly well off in comparison with other backward communities; at least this conclusion is reached by having a look at them in political, administration and urban hierarchy in the State, where some of them have good positions. (Soc. Welf., 1969: 1)

On the one hand, these 'backward' herdsmen are simultaneously frozen into a picturebook romanticism: 'The shepherd grazing his sheep in Kashmir's snow-clad mountains and valleys ... [is] a picture of an Indian' – (KB, 1989). On the other hand, there is a clear message that the Government and its agencies are actively attempting to change this Indian, by 'removing [his/her] backwardness'. Thus to 'improve the state of the Bakkarwal' the Government undertook measures ' ... for their settlement, educational advancement, economic uplift and improvement in the living and working conditions' (Soc. Welf., 1969: 2). Paraphrasing Nandy and Visvanathan (1990: 145), the removal of 'backwardness' – or 'development' as the process is usually termed – is a short-hand expression for attending to the overall needs of the poor, (still) nomadic, unhealthy and 'scantily educated' Bakkarwal. The ideal agencies entrusted with this process are those of the Government and its (especially urban or urbanised) representatives. It must be remembered that this entire process is based on the premises that nomads are pernicious to 'modernisation' and also to the image of a modern nation – irrespective of the actual contributions they may make to local and national economies.

Although official Indian state policy on education conceives of schooling as a system that '... should ... develop ... potentialities [and] ... the growth of the individual' (DNP, 1979), in reality, schools as Ivan Illich observed so long ago, ... change the meaning of "knowledge" from a term that designates ... life experience into one that designates ... marketable entitlements ...' (Illich, 1974: 9). Schools everywhere also

> ... act as agents of both cultural and ideological hegemony through the process of selective tradition ... The dominant culture in the school is passed off as the 'tradition', or 'the significant past' and thus legitimized as *the culture* that is common to all. The selection process ensures that certain meanings and practices are chosen for emphasis while others are excluded. (Scrase, 1990: 25)

In South Asia such selection naturally tends to lead to the assertion of the values of the dominant sections of society. By accepting these values even superficially, one gains access to power networks of the dominant society, beyond one's community, thus enhancing one's status within it. Since in hierarchical societies this access is largely predetermined, schooling today often tends to reinforce old power structures, albeit in new forms – much as it did in the early colonial period. Indeed, I suggest, schooling could at least to begin with even decrease the autonomy of those who are lower in the community's hierarchy, because they are now doubly 'proved' to be 'ignorant', hence incapable of correct decision making and therefore 'backward'.

Bakkarwal children who had attended schools for longer periods spoke with contempt about their community: 'You'll find out very soon that the Bakkarwal are a shameless people (*belehaz kaum*)', the eighteen-year-old Mohammad Yusuf told me when I first met him. He was studying in the 9th class and staying in a Gujar-Bakkarwal hostel. On a visit to his parents with whom I was spending a few days, he insisted that his mother – who was 'forward' enough to serve tea in cups, rather than in more common tumblers or bowls – use saucers with these cups, and told her: 'otherwise sister [referring to me] will think you're as backward (*pasmanda*) like the other Bakkarwal women.' Similarly, Ghulam Nabi who had studied up to Class 10 informed me:

> I'm not backward like the others here. I let my hair grow and don't wear a turban. I've told my mother so often not to let my sisters wear caps, to dress properly. But our women are all backward. Many of our rich men are not so backward. My late uncle Hajji I., was one of the richest Bakkarwal.

Fatima, who had gone to school for six years, also felt that the 'Bakkarwal are a bad (*buri*) community.' She was astonished that I had no problems eating

Bakkarwal food, because she had problems ever since she went to school. 'I can't eat at their homes, I get sick, they are so dirty ... Every day I have to take care how and what my mother cooks, to see that she does it the right way'. Indeed Fatima's mother also had problems with her daughter: 'she thinks she knows everything better simply because she can read and write! She has even stopped mixing with the other girls here', she told me.

In 2001 the Indian government introduced an amendment to the national constitution (93rd Amendment Act, 2002) to make free and compulsory elementary education for the age group six to fourteen years a fundamental right (for details see, for example, Godbole, 2001). The following year, the government of Jammu and Kashmir also decided to provide primary schools '... at a distance of every kilometre with minimum of two teachers ... similarly, a middle school every 3 kms with a minimum of six teachers' and to achieve universal elementary education by 2007 (ZEO, 2002). In 2003 the government of Jammu and Kashmir also decided that the medium of instruction in all schools will henceforth be English. Already every Bakkarwal at least theoretically requires a minimum of three languages to communicate – Bakkarwali within the community; the locally dominant language(s) in various times of the year (e.g. Kashmiri, Dogri, Punchi, Pahari) to communicate with peasants, traders, etc.; and Urdu, which is the official language of administration in Jammu and Kashmir. Linguistic flexibility is connected with the extent of contact with the outside world, and hence while younger men tend to be bi-lingual in some form, women are rarely so.

Access to knowledge and information through schooling is thus translated for a child in terms of a multiplicity of dominant discourses – adult, high status, majority communities, etc. The introduction of English as a medium of instruction can, at least to begin with, only add to the list of these discourses that a Bakkarwal child must cope with even before s/he learns any alphabet. And his/her parents can hardly 'participate' in the process of learning referred to as 'people's participation' in the Free and Compulsory Education Bill drafted by the government of India in 2004 (see also Balagopalan, 2004)[2].

In his oft-cited work on the Kashmir conflict Ganguly (1998) suggests that one reason for the current turmoil is the political mobilisation of Kashmiri Muslim youth who were exposed to modern forms of education. The link between education and rebelliousness is as true today as it was in 1536 when someone opined 'Some say povertie is the cause that men come to be theves, murderers, rebels, bit I thynke ... Education is a greate cause of these ...' (Anon. 1536). Indeed, those Bakkarwal who have begun resisting traditional community leaders and their exploitative ways (and are said to have recently appealed to Islamist terrorist organisations for help) do come from middle-income families with access to schooling. But it is not yet clear whether they contest the dominant value system or its incompatibility with community-specific educational values and ideals. The question Judith

Brown (1975) asked so many years ago for Kpelle children remains unanswered for Bakkarwal children: is it possible for a child who does not belong to the dominant stratum of a society to undergo existing forms of schooling and simultaneously retain its identity and heritage? Much more research is required to understand what happens to 'private experience', when these children '... recognise themselves in the public objectivity of an already constituted discourse ...' (Bourdieu, 1977: 170).

Conclusion

The first part of this chapter discussed the context of informal education and the traditional concepts and practices of socialisation. The second part has been devoted to an examination of the formal education of Bakkarwal children and of the institutions responsible for this. The data presented suggest that in the states of South Asia, the entire formal schooling system transmits the dominant culture, passed off as either 'modernisation' or as 'tradition', both of which are assumed to be of equal relevance and significance to all loyal citizens. As everywhere, to create such citizens, certain elements of belief, practice and ideology are selected from a vast and varied repertoire, while others are rejected. This selection tends to lead to the assertion of the values of the dominant sections of society. By accepting these values even superficially, one gains access to power networks of the dominant society, beyond one's community, thus enhancing one's status within the latter and often assuming the role of power broker. Since in hierarchical societies this access is largely predetermined, schooling in contemporary South Asia tends, by and large, to reinforce old power structures, albeit in superficially new forms.

Based on rigid perceptions of 'development', assumptions of sedentarisation have everywhere largely determined educational facilities for migrating families. On the other hand, Dyer and Choksi (1997: 320) report that the Kutchi Rabari 'wanted government to provide boarding schools for their children', and Chaudhuri (2000: 55f.) notes that for the Chang Pa increasingly moving to Leh, education and health facilities are the prime motives. But at least primary education, I suggest, should not automatically imply sedentarisation, and in this sense the mobile schools of Jammu and Kashmir are an innovative step in the right direction.

The larger problem is that formal education such as it exists today throughout South Asia almost inevitably means that children not only acquire no knowledge and interest in their community's traditional occupations, but also look down upon these and hence also on family members practising them. But no state can, even with affirmative action programmes, provide jobs for all, and the existing contents of education alone are also not of much use in finding employment. It is beyond doubt that primary schooling must become a fundamental right, and it must be made compulsory; but educational norms and values must also change. Primary curricula must be adjusted to local needs and special capacities, and for all children – nomadic and sedentary, rural and urban – they must be more creative and practice oriented. Education must, in sum, be perceived as 'a process of pleasurable instruction' (Spencer, 1928: 83).

Too little attention has been paid to the link between postcolonial educational institutions and the manner in which 'development is practised and imagined by governments and international agencies' (Simpson, 1999: 4; see also e.g. Faust and Nagar, 2001 for a recent discussion of some interesting issues). 'The State cannot create ideas', commented Archer (1932: 4), it usually continues with ideas that have been handed down from previous regimes. What is the nature of the education actually imparted? Where, how and by whom is knowledge disseminated? What are the contents of the role models that are projected; how far are the educational norms and values imparted compatible with those of the communities to which the children belong? What are the concrete employment opportunities for those who are schooled, where, and why? These are some of the crucial questions that must be asked and answered.

Notes

1. Their break-down by district is as follows:

In Winter areas	Rajouri 61	Poonch 36	Jammu 29	Kathua 19
In Winter/Summer areas	Doda 45	Udhampur 38		
In Summer areas	Baramulla 25	Anantnag 17	Kupwara 14	Pulwama 11
		Budgam 8	Srinagar 3	

2. Menon (2003: 1748) is critical of the change in the illustrations in textbooks, where apples and cherries have replaced mangos in what she refers to as the 'total rejection of local materials'. Menon is perfectly correct in critiquing this approach for large parts of India, but since for Bakkarwal and other children in Jammu and Kashmir apples are infinitely more familiar than mangoes, this well illustrates the pressing need for local participation in the compilation of basic reading materials.

References

Anon. (1536) 'A Remedy for Sedition'. In: I.L. Plunket and R.J. Mitchell (1934), p. 12 *Ye Good Olde Dayes*. London: Methuen.

Anon. (1926) *'Appendix I to Notes'. Newspaper Cutting from 'Kashmir', Lahore, 7th April,1926*, London: India Office Records, File No. 264 of 1923 [R/2 Crown Rep's Records Indian States Pt. 1 – Kashmir]. R/2 [1067/90].

Archer, R.L. (1932) *Contributions to the History of Education*. (Vol. V. *Secondary Education in the Nineteenth Century*). Cambridge: Cambridge University Press.

Bachloo, A. (2002) 'Mobile Schools in Disarray as Nomadic Tribe Kids Drop-out High', *Kashmir Times* 14 December, 2002.

Baden-Powell, Lord (1930) 'Foreword'. In: E.D. Tyndale-Biscoe *Fifty Years against the Stream. The Story of a School in Kashmir 1880–1930*. Mysore: Wesleyan Mission Press.

Balagopalan, S. (2004) 'Free and Compulsory Education Bill, 2004', *Economic and Political Weekly* XXXIX(32): 3587–591.

Banerji, Sir A. (1928) '*Extract from the Jammu and Kashmir Government Gazette, Jammu, Thursday the 15th Bhadon 1985. Appendix II to Notes*', London: India Office Records, File No. 264 of 1923 [R/2 Crown Rep's Records Indian States Pt. 1– Kashmir]. R/2 [1067/90].

Barth, F. (2002) 'An Anthropology of Knowledge'. *Current Anthropology* 43 (1): 1–18.

Basu, K., J. Foster and S. Subramanian (2000) 'Isolated and Proximate Illiteracy and Why These Concepts Matter in Measuring Literacy and Designing Education Programmes'. Working Paper No. 00-W02 Department of Economics. Nashville: Vanderbilt University.

Brown, J. (1975) 'The Archaic Illusion: a Re-examination of Lévi-Strauss' View of the Developing Child'. In: Williams, T.P. (ed.) *Psychological Anthropology*. Paris: Mouton Publishers, pp. 103–108.

Bourdieu, P. (1977) *Outline of a Theory of Practice*. Cambridge: Cambridge University Press.

Casimir, M. (1991) *Flocks and Food: a Biocultural Approach to the Study of Pastoral Foodways*. Cologne: Böhlau Verlag.

—————— (2003) 'Pastoral Nomadism in a West Himalayan Valley: Sustainability and Herd Management'. In: A. Rao and M.J. Casimir (eds) *Nomadism in South Asia. Oxford in India, Readings in Sociology and Social Anthropology*. Delhi: Oxford University Press, pp. 81–103.

—————— and A. Rao (1985) 'Vertical Control in the Western Himalayas: Some Notes on the Pastoral Ecology of the Nomadic Bakrwal of Jammu and Kashmir', *Mountain Research and Development* 5 (2): 221–32.

—————— and A. Rao (1995) 'Prestige, Possessions and Progeny: Cultural Goals and Reproductive Success among the Bakkarwal', *Human Nature* 6 (3): 241–72.

—————— and —————— (1998) 'Sustainable Herd Management and the Tragedy of No Man's Land: An Analysis of West Himalayan Pastures Using Remote Sensing Techniques', *Human Ecology* 26 (1): 113–34.

Chaudhuri, Ajit (2000) 'Change in Changthang: to Stay or to Leave?' *Economic and Political Weekly* XXXV(1/2): 52–56.

C.S. (1914) 'Notification dated, Srinagar, 29th October 1931 and signed by Hari Kishan Kaul, Prime Minister'. Jammu: Jammu Archives, C.S. Old Records, File No. 221/A- 9 of 1914.

DNP (1979) *Draft National Policy on Education 1979*. Delhi: Government of India, Ministry of Education and Social Welfare.

DRI (2001) 'Dropout Rate Increasing in Mobile Schools', *Kashmir Times*, 13 August, 2001.

Dyer, C. and A. Choksi (1997) 'The Demand for Education among the Rabaris of Kutch, West India', *Nomadic Peoples* (ns) 1 (2): 77–97.

Faust, D. and R. Nagar (2001) 'Politics of Development in Postcolonial India: English-Medium Education and Social Fracturing'. *Economic and Political Weekly* July 28–August 3: 2878–883.

Ganguly, S. (1998, 1st edn. 1997) *The Crisis in Kashmir. Portents of War, Hopes of Peace*. Cambridge: Cambridge University Press.

Godbole, M. (2001) 'Elementary Education as a Fundamental Right'. *Economic and Political Weekly* XXXVI (50): 4609–613.

Gurumurthy, K.G. (1996) *Cross-cultural Research and Other Anthropological Essays*. Delhi: Reliance Publishing House.

Illich, I. (1974) *After Deschooling, What?* London: The Writers' and Readers' Publishing Cooperative.

Kango, G.H. and Bansi Dhar (1981). *Nomadic Routes in Jammu and Kashmir (Part I)*. Srinagar: Directorate of Soil Conservation, Government of Jammu and Kashmir.

KB (1989) 'Bhartiyata'. Chapter 6 in *Kishor Bharati*, Part II, for Class VII. Delhi: Delhi Education Department.

Khatana, Ram P. (1992) *Tribal Migration in Himalayan Frontiers. Study of Gujjar akkarwal Transhumance Economy*. Gurgaon: Vintage Books.

Liégeois, J-P (1987) 'Governments and Gypsies: from Rejection to Assimilation'. In: A. Rao (ed.) *The Other Nomads. Peripatetic Minorities in Cross-cultural Perspective*. Cologne/Vienna: Böhlau Verlag, pp. 357–71.

Lieten, G.K. (2000). 'Children, Work and Education, Part I'. *Economic and Political Weekly* XXXV (24): 2037ff.

Meir, A. and Dov Barnea (1987) 'The Educational System of the Israeli Negev Bedouin'. *Nomadic Peoples* 24: 23–35.

Menon, U. (2003) 'Where have the Mangoes Gone?'. *Economic and Political Weekly* XXXVIII (18): 1747–49.

Metcalf, B.D. (1984) (ed.) *Moral Conduct and Authority. The Place of Adab in South Asian Islam*. Berkeley: University of California Press.

Nandy, A. and S. Visvanathan (1990) 'Modern Medicine and Its Non-Modern Critics: a Study in Discourse'. In: F.A. Marglin and S.A. Marglin (eds) *Dominating Knowledge. Development, Culture, and Resistance*. Oxford: Clarendon Press, pp. 145–84.

NCERT (1989, 1st edn. 1988). *Hamara Nagarik Jivan*. (A Textbook for Class VI.) Delhi: NCERT.

Rao, A. (1988) 'Levels and Boundaries in Native Models: Social Groupings among the Bakkarwal of the Western Himalayas', *Contributions to Indian Sociology* 22 (2): 195–227.

——— (1990) 'Reflections on Self and Person in a Pastoral Community in Kashmir'. *Social Analysis. Journal of Social and Cultural Practice* (Special Issue, ed. Werbner, P.) 28: 11–25.

——— (1992) 'The Constraints of Nature or of Culture? Pastoral Resources and Territorial Behaviour in the Western Himalayas'. In: M.J. Casimir and A. Rao (eds) *Mobility and Territoriality: Social and Spatial Boundaries among Foragers, Fishers, Pastoralists and Peripatetics*. Oxford: Berg Publications, pp. 91–134.

——— (1995) 'From Bondsmen to Middlemen: Hired Shepherds and Pastoral Politics', *Anthropos* 90 (1–3): 149–67.

——— (1998a) *Autonomy: Life Cycle, Gender, and Status among Himalayan Pastoralists*. Oxford/New York: Berghahn Books.

——— (1998b) 'Prestations and Progeny: the Consolidation of Well-being among the Bakkarwal of Jammu and Kashmir (Western Himalayas)'. In: T. Schweizer and D. White (eds) *Kinship, Networks and Exchange*. Cambridge: Cambridge University Press, pp. 210–33.

—— (1999) 'The Many Sources of Identity: an Example of Changing Affiliations in Rural Jammu and Kashmir', *Ethnic and Racial Studies* 22 (1): 56–91.

—— (2000) 'Blood, Milk, and Mountains: Marriage Practice and Concepts of Predictability among the Bakkarwal of Jammu and Kashmir'. In: M. Böck and A. Rao (eds.) *Culture, Creation, and Procreation: Concepts of Kinship in South Asian Practice*. Oxford/New York: Berghahn Books, pp. 101–34.

—— (2002) 'Pastoral Nomads, the State and a National Park: the Case Of Dachigam, Kashmir', *Nomadic Peoples* (ns) 6 (2): 72–98.

—— (2003) 'Access to Pasture: Concepts, Constraints, and Practice in the Kashmir Himalayas'. In, A. Rao and M.J. Casimir (eds) *Nomadism in South Asia. Oxford in India, Readings in Sociology and Social Anthropology*. Delhi: Oxford University Press, pp. 174–212.

—— and M. Casimir (1985) 'Pastoral Niches in the Western Himalayas (Jammu and Kashmir)'. *Himalaya Research Bulletin* 5 (1): 28–42.

—— and —— (2003a) 'Movement of Peoples: Nomads in India'. In: V. Das (ed.) *The Oxford India Companion to Sociology and Social Anthropology*. Delhi: Oxford University Press, pp. 219–61.

—— and —— (2003b) 'Nomadism in South Asia: an Introduction'. In: A. Rao and M. Casimir (eds.) *Nomadism in South Asia. Oxford in India, Readings in Sociology and Social Anthropology*. Delhi: Oxford University Press, pp. 1–42.

Ruhela, S.P. (1997) *Children of Indian Nomads. Studies in Enculturation and Socialization*. Delhi: Regency Publications.

Sarkar, T. (1996) 'Educating the Children of the Hindu Rashtra: Notes on RSS Schools'. In: P. Bidwai, H. Mukhia and A. Vanaik (eds) *Religion, Religiosity and Communalism*. Delhi: Manohar, pp. 237–47.

Scrase, T.J. (1990) 'Cultural Hegemony and the Dialectics of Educational Reform in India'. *International Journal of Indian Studies* 1: 23–40.

Sharp, H. (1916) *A Note on Education in the State of Jammu and Kashmir*. Calcutta: Government of India.

Simpson, A. (1999) 'The Labours of Learning: Education in the Postcolony'. *Social Analysis* 43 (1): 4ff.

Skinner, D. (1990) 'Nepalese Children's Construction of Identities in and around Formal Schooling'. *Himalayan Research Bulletin* X(2/3): 8–17.

Soc. Welf. (1969) *Report of Socio-Economic Survey of Gujjars and Bakerwals in Jammu and Kashmir State*. Delhi: Government of India, Department of Social Welfare.

Spencer, C. (1993) 'Human Agency, Biased Transmission, and the Cultural Evolution of Chiefly Authority'. *Journal of Anthropological Archaeology* 12: 41–74.

Spencer, H. (1928, 1ˢᵗ edn. 1911) *Essays on Education and Kindred Subjects*. London: J.M. Dent and Sons.

Swami, P. (2001) 'Disturbed Doda'. *Frontline* 18 (17), 18 August, 2001.

—— (2003) 'Cloaks and Daggers'. *Frontline*, 17 January, 2003.

ZEO (2002) 'ZEO's Conference begins Legislation to make Elementary Education Compulsory'. *Kashmir Times*, Srinagar/Jammu, 15 May, 2002.

CHAPTER 4

Learning to Wander, Wandering Learners: Education and the Peripatetic Karretjie People of the South African Karoo

Michael de Jongh and Riana Steyn

Introduction

The nexus of sociocultural singularity i.e. peripateticism, development, education, ideology, policy and practice is the crux of this chapter. The case material of the itinerant Karretjie People presented here touches directly on the core issues raised by Krätli and Dyer in their introductory chapter – that education is not merely an impartial enterprise, it is ideological, and this finds expression in policy and appropriate praxis – or, as in the context at hand, a lack thereof.

South Africans are justifiably proud of their new constitution which is arguably one of the best in the world. Article 10 of the Bill of Rights, which is enshrined in this constitution, affirms that 'everyone has inherent dignity and the right to have their dignity respected and protected'. In a speech the then Minister of Education Kader Asmal referred to this article and commented that

> (t)he prison of illiteracy is an immediate affront to this right, because language is a vital compass for intellectual navigation, for meaningful movement, within a constitutional order. The State issues its instructions – and confers its benefits – in written regulations, statutes and correspondence. Illiteracy, placing citizens outside this world of law, forcing citizens to depend upon third party translators, is almost a form of serfdom. (Asmal 2000)

In a speech to parliament in a similar vein, the minister provided statistics which, in broad terms, give some idea of the extent of the problem: in South

Africa 3.5 million adults over the age of 16 have never attended school; another 2.5 million adults have had some schooling but were ill-taught or lack practice and so have lost their prior ability to read or write. In other words, there are six million South Africans who are barred from the written word, from the whole universe of creativity and humanity that books hold; and also, logically, from the ordinary, everyday empowerment that the written language gives – in jobs, travel, and even constitutionally.

Disturbing as such figures and their implications are, they do not include reference to children, or to the discrepant *de jure* and *de facto* roles that language plays in certain regions in South Africa today. Couched in general terms they also, obviously, do not reveal the particular dire circumstances of specific communities, nor are they sensitive to the context of some of the truly poorest of the poor South Africans in the central rural areas of the country – the epitome of this country's different 'geographies of poverty'.

This chapter concerns itself with one such 'invisible' community, the peripatetic Karretjie People of the Great Karoo, that great expanse of arid scrubland and flat topped hills which comprises much of South Africa's central plateau (Fig. 4.2). These wanderers call themselves *Karretjiemense* – (donkey) Cart People – with reference to the donkey-drawn conveyance which carries them and all their worldly possessions when they move between temporary overnight camps. The bond connecting these people is derived from a common origin and a specialised skill, sheep-shearing, which necessitates continuous spatial mobility. This service which they provide to the farming community of the region, and the implied mobility, is made possible by the donkey cart which also enables them to exploit tenuous resources and to adapt to changing circumstances. Karoo-wide they number

Figure 4.1 *Karretjie People on the way to their next shearing assignment.*

thousands, are unilingually Afrikaans-speaking and are for a considerable part of the year without predictable income.

The Karretjie People, amongst whom we started working more than 12 years ago, were then, and are still today, only to a slightly lesser extent, to all intents and purposes illiterate, neither adults nor children ever having had the benefit of schooling or even access to a school. In other words, the distressing statistics which the minister cites encompasses communities country-wide with high illiteracy rates, but clearly does not identify a small community like the Karretjie People which is almost completely illiterate because of their history and distinctive lifestyle but also because, to outsiders, policy-makers included, they are inconspicuous at best and inconsequential or aberrant at worst.

Karretjie Niche

The Karretjie People are for the most part descendent from the gathering-hunting /Xam-speaking San and/or the nomadic-pastoral KhoeKhoen (mainly Griqua and Korana), that is, of the earliest inhabitants of the Karoo.

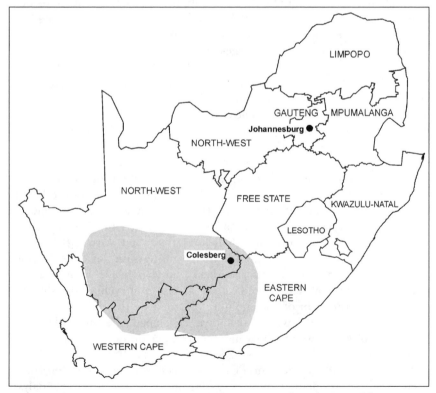

Figure 4.2 *Approximate Location of the Karoo within the Republic of South Africa.*

Archaeological evidence, the historical record, local folklore and oral tradition not only confirm the early presence of these forebears, but also the changing nature of their interaction with the more recently arrived pioneer white farming community from the south. The first sporadic contacts in the eighteenth century were followed by extended periods of conflict, intermittent times of peace, increased competition for resources and eventually the powerful impact of a burgeoning agricultural economy and commercialisation in the rapidly developing towns.

The competition for resources, at least initially, centred around two main issues. First, the farmers hunted the game in the hunting grounds that the /Xam for generations had regarded as their own. When the /Xam then began slaughtering the more easily accessible domesticated stock of the farmers, they themselves became the hunted. Second, the farmers in the areas of the Griqua and Korana were in competition for the same grazing lands for their stock.

Eventually though, the lifestyles of both the /Xam and the Griqua and Korana were transformed. In the case of the /Xam for example, they changed from nomadic hunters to become so-called 'tame Bushmen' farm labourers. They retained, at least initially, their mobility, first on foot, later with the help of pack animals and eventually, within a few decades, they had adopted the donkey cart as mode of transport, constructing their carts from materials salvaged from derelict horse carriages and motor cars.

Those of the /Xam who were not hunted or had not succumbed to some foreign disease like the smallpox epidemics in the eighteenth and nineteenth century (affecting both the /Xam and the Griqua), sought refuge in alternative (there was for example a mass migration of the Griqua in the middle of the nineteenth century) or remote areas or in the case of small pockets of /Xam, in rock shelters. Finally though, those who survived and remained in the region, ended up squatting near towns or were drawn into the agricultural economy to become labourers on white-owned sheep farms. Like their parents and grandparents many of the present Karretjie People were born on a farm and in spite of their present itinerant existence, a number of them have a history of having lived at least semi-permanently on a farm. It was on the farms that their forefathers first learned the skill of shearing. This they perfected, and when wool farming as an enterprise expanded, the need increased for workers who were available, in numbers and in teams, at a particular point in the agricultural cycle of the shearing season. With the help of the mobility afforded by the donkey cart, the Karretjie People, as they were now known, developed a flexible and floating lifestyle in order to exploit shearing opportunities on farms spread far and wide (De Jongh and Steyn, 1998: 236–37; De Jongh, 2002).

In our study of the Karretjie People, the *karretjie* (cart) cum overnight shelter and a co-residential, income sharing entity, is used as unit of analysis due to the complexity of flexibility and fluidity caused by fission and fusion of household composition. The arrangement of *karretjie* units at a particular outspan (a piece of neutral land next to a secondary or tertiary road) and the mobility patterns of different units, are determined by a number of internal and external factors. Internal factors are mostly associated with interpersonal relationships. External factors primarily relate to economic and social imperatives (see De Jongh, 2004).

Seasonal sheep-shearing is a niche livelihood, and for decades if not generations, a delicate balance, though weighted on the side of the farmers, was maintained between the demand for shearing and the 'supply' of shearers on the road. But this balance was lost in the second half of the twentieth century, resulting in a significant increase in the number of Karretjie People in the Great Karoo. In fact in the last few decades of that century the growth rate in the number of Karretjie People outstripped demand for their services as sheep-shearers. A number of factors seem to have played a role in this trend. One was land consolidation, with new owners needing fewer workers for the larger property than the total employed on the originally separate farms. A second factor was a period of economic stagnation caused by drought and fluctuating world wool prices among other things. More recently, game farming has started to make inroads in the region, resulting in the wool-bearing Merino sheep disappearing from the veld (De Jongh, 2002).

To further exacerbate a situation where a surfeit of Karretjie shearers already meant that they competed against each other for contracts, they also had to compete against teams of unionised shearers from beyond the Great Karoo. The advent of such sheep-shearers, and the increasing disinclination of farmers to allow Karretjie families to set up temporary camps on their land, tended to erode the bonds of familiarity between these local shearers and the farmers. Previously Karretjie teams that returned to the same farms season after season were in a position to negotiate terms of employment – even though the farmers were in an overwhelmingly more advantageous bargaining position – as well as obtain loans to tide them over in periods of difficulty. Farmers also extended assistance in times of illness, taking sick family members to the doctor or hospital in the nearest village, and in some instances and more recently, taking an interest in the education of the Karretjie children. Although these relationships have not died out entirely, they have begun to wither. Even though the shearers may still be fortunate enough to be employed, their wives, children and other dependants have to be left in the corridors of land between the public roads and the boundary fences of the farmers, as the farmers have taken to fetching only the shearing team, sometimes from outspans far removed from the shearing activity (De Jongh, 2002).

Given such developments and in spite of the fact that the Karretjie People regard the peripatetic philosophy and lifestyle as core values, a significant number of them sooner or later reach a stage when they contemplate or are forced to consider a different, usually sedentary, way of life. The rational decision-making which results in a radical change from an itinerant to a sedentary lifestyle only takes place, however, in the context of the limited options which their asymmetrical structural position within the wider community imposes upon them. Illiterate, and possessing a limited range of skills, the Karretjie People are ill-equipped to take advantage of opportunities even if the regional system had allowed them access to a wider purview of alternatives. The reality is that the incidence of a more drastic and irrevocable decision to forsake the itinerant lifestyle completely in order to settle in town has recently become increasingly apparent (De Jongh, 2002, 2004).

Poverty, Policy and Peripatetic Shearers as Potential Learners

Despite democratisation South Africa is still, literally, a country of poor people. Impoverishment in this country also has, figuratively speaking, many faces and should be contemplated from different perspectives. Poverty in South Africa is not only pervasive and endemic, relative and absolute, but also structural, generational, gendered, geographical and stratified. Poverty is geographical in the sense that South Africa may be regarded as consisting of three types of poverty areas: the urban areas and their squatter sprawl, the *platteland* (rural South Africa, literally 'flat land') with its small towns and almost exclusively white-owned farming land, and the erstwhile 'homelands' (reserves or bantustans) originally set aside for occupation by different black ethnic groups.

Poverty in some rural areas in particular tends to be less visible than in others. This relates to the stratified nature of poverty and there seems to be an inverse relationship between the level, or degree and extent of poverty and its visibility. Hence people living in shacks in the informal urban settlements are more conspicuous because of their proximity to the main concentrations of the population, but also because their numbers are statistically significant. The state is hence inclined to direct more of its efforts for mitigating poverty, and development in general and educational initiatives specifically, toward them, even though they are in many respects better off than the rural poor. Two sectors, or poverty levels, of the rural population *have* also been receiving formal attention, though not to the same extent. Thus people living on white-owned farms and in the former homelands may eventually benefit from tenure reform and, in some cases, land redistribution and to a lesser extent housing and educational provision (De Jongh, 2002).

The South African Karoo in many ways typifies the second (*platteland*) of the above mentioned three types of geographical areas. The large sheep farms are owned by whites: farm labourers, and certainly itinerant shearers, still generally have no share in the agricultural economy of the area. The landowners are in fact 'lords of the manor' who not only dictate the presence and activities of people on their property but also direct much of the pattern of life in the area at large. Harsh and inhospitable as the Karoo may seem, every day the setting sun transforms the harshness of the region into the softer hues of early evening. This seems to further accentuate the ostensible empty quietness of the vast plains and rugged hills of a region symbolised by its gentle and genteel pulse of pastoral life. Often, however, this is but a veneer which disguises the reality of hardship of large numbers of the 'invisible' people who eke out an existence in the Karoo.

To residents of the area the Karretjie People are invisible in the sense of being a familiar and conventional sight, much like the natural environment, and in the sense that they are also total strangers, even though they may be tolerated as part of the human environment. This is because of a lack of real interest in them as people together with a lack of social intercourse and interpersonal relations, other than categorical relations with them, in spite of their still being, to many farmers, indispensable shearers (De Jongh, 1997: 93 and 2004: 175).

As is the case for people in the broader context of the Karoo and other rural areas, poverty for the Karretjie People is experienced by all the members of the family but some individuals bear more of the brunt of it than others. Privation, particularly at certain times, is experienced by women especially, and children may be neglected during times when either or both parents are absent or exert themselves to gain unpredictable access to resources. *Karretjie* units which travel alone, without the benefit of the supportive network of other units in a caravan on the road or as a small community at an outspan, small families in general and single parent households, are even more vulnerable. The absence of the shearers, the timing (or lack thereof) of pregnancy and birth, and childcare arrangements in seasons of stress, all stretch resourcefulness to the limits (Chambers et al., 1981: 231–33). Given the arid Karoo environment and the sparse vegetation, obtaining water and wood for fuel is a constant struggle. Depending on the location of an outspan and disposition of possible neighbouring farmers or town dwellers, women and children for example spend an inordinate amount of time collecting wood and fetching water. Most of the rest of the day is taken up by domestic responsibilities, those at the outspan often having to stand in for absentee members of other *karretjie* units. Only when, during an assignment, the shearers and other casual workers return to the outspan by sundown, is some time spent eating and socialising around the cooking fires.

Usually shearing in teams of six to ten men from the same outspan, the core of which comprises kin, the shearers might be working on a particular farm from one to several weeks. Both the size of the team and the duration of the assignment depend on the size of the flock the farmer wants shorn.

Figure 4.3 *The twins Outjie and Rokkies with their father Koot Arnoster and uncle at the cooking fire.*

The shearers are paid from R1.50c to R2.50 (USD$1 = ± R6.60 GBP£1 = ± R11.80) per sheep shorn, the amount depending on the convention in the district, but more particularly on the farmer, and is not negotiable. The team also receives one sheep to slaughter for every 1000 shorn. For the rest shearers have to provide their own food as well as sheep-shears.

On a good day when the sheep are readily available in the shearing pen and there are no unexpected interruptions like unseasonal rain, the shearers each manage to shear on average 25 to 30 sheep per day, thus theoretically earning some R180 to R375 per week. Even with the possible additional income of some of the women and even children who may be employed on a temporary basis in the shearing shed or in and around the farmhouse (at anything from R2 to R10 per day), a shearer's family, after deductions for the shears and food and other purchases, often walks away with a net payment of only R50 to R100. The Karretjie People are hardly assured of shearing assignments for half of the months of the year, which puts the monthly average income for a *karretjie* unit at never more than around R300. This translates to an adult equivalent of less than R100 per month which is put into perspective by the figure of R178 per month which the Living Standards Development Survey identified some years ago as the adult equivalent cut-off expenditure for the *poorest of all* in South Africa (De Jongh, 2002; May et al., 1995: 7).

The Karretjie People are in every sense of the word poor and poverty is of course a matter of sufficiency, access and security (May et al., 1995: 5), where sufficiency is having, or not having enough food, income and essential services, as well as non material needs such as safety and opportunities. Access entails actually being able or unable to acquire sufficient food, income and services, and security is having or not having secure and sustainable access to essential commodities and services. Lack of security accentuates the vulnerability of the poor. In considering poverty in this context it is accepted that it entails much more than simply a lack of money and also a lack of secure and sustainable access to facilities, services and resources; it is, more importantly, a lack of opportunities to exercise choices. The Karretjie People and their underclass status as rural foragers are thus a good example of the consequences of denial of the most basic of resources, land, or space to exercise choices, for self-help, for devising strategies towards this end – beyond the domain controlled by capital or different levels of government (De Jongh, 2002). Lack of land or space is regarded as a basic resource not only in the sense of constraining agricultural production but also, and more importantly, as an environment where a person has control over the nature and level of her or his investment in order to live.

Ingenious as the adaptive strategies of the Karretjie People may be, their initiatives can only be properly interpreted as responses to a given set of circumstances and as actions taking place within parameters over which they have no control. The kind of space as resource that other South Africans have is what they are lacking, because historical events dispossessed them of their land but also because they were eventually classified 'coloured', i.e. something between the whites and the blacks and not indigenous to South Africa. Those individuals who are in possession of identity documents were, according to their own indignant insistence, incorrectly classified as coloured. Although the oral tradition of the Karretjie People is relatively 'shallow' and, with the exception of a few individuals, there is only a vague awareness of being descendants of the earliest inhabitants of the region, they clearly distinguish themselves from other people in the area (De Jongh, 2002).

No political party or any other organisation, whether government or non government, has effectively taken up the cause of the Karretjie People. Squatters on the fringes of urban centres, those who have suffered because of forced removals, communities with historical land claims and the dispossessed, disadvantaged and disempowered in general feature prominently on the agendas of various organisations and different levels of government, but almost universally to the exclusion of the Karretjie People. Census-takers have been generally oblivious of them, yet they are lumped into the category 'coloured' and are hence assumed, in the wider South African context, to be 'not so poor'. They have no land at all, are still almost totally illiterate, generate some of the lowest household incomes in the land and have hardly been able to avail themselves of the promise of access to social, medical and educational services, nor the mechanisms for general empowerment (De Jongh, 2002).

As not even census-takers conceive of enumerating a floating population like the Karretjie People, their likelihood of coming within the purview of policy-makers is slim indeed. The government has already demonstrated its commitment to education through the new constitution by recognising basic education as a fundamental human right. It has furthermore recognised the 'inheritance of inequality' of the previous South African dispensation. Thus it is acknowledged that the distribution of resources for education provision must address the fact that almost half of South African families live in poverty, mainly in rural areas. In so doing the new structure of the school system must ensure an equitable, efficient qualitatively sound and financially sustainable system for all its learners (Education White Paper – 2, 1996: 6). The instruments the government hence intend to employ are designed for, and directed at schools and learners as part of the existing, and known, structure. These instruments are not, however, calibrated to discern potential learners who have never been in the ambit of a school system conceived in a sedentist paradigm. Potential Karretjie 'learners', and this initially included all the children and all their parents, do in their wanderings encounter the proximity of schools. But a day or two near a town or a week or two on or near a farm which happens to have a farm school, hardly comprises access to schooling.

Official policy guidelines now make provision for new or reformed principles of organisation, governance, capacity building, financing and implementation in or of education – but in every instance exclusively directed at the formal school system. And even where initiatives are directed at actual schools, the premises are sometimes uninformed or preconceived. Farm schools, for example, are now regarded as belonging to one of only two categories of schools, i.e. public schools. This category also includes community schools, state schools and state-aided schools (including church schools, mine schools and others) and comprise over 98 percent of the country's primary and secondary schools and 99 percent of school enrolments. The other category, independent schools, comprise all current private and independent schools and account for not quite two percent of primary and secondary schools, and about 1.2 percent of enrolments (Education White Paper – 2, 1996: 8). The rationale for the public schools category is to ensure that the new organisation breaks with the past and lays a foundation on which a democratically-governed and equitable system of high quality can be built and while the funding will be public, and the property owned by the state, it will represent a partnership between provincial education departments and local communities.

Much maligned for many years, farm schools are singled out for special attention. The apartheid policies of an earlier minister of education, and later prime minister, H. F. Verwoerd, were partly instrumental in establishing farm schools for blacks. A more recent minister of education is on record as saying that '(t)he negative effects of apartheid education found its worst expression in the farm schools attended by African learners' (Asmal, 2000: 3). There are some 4,600 farm schools in South Africa with enrolments of around 600,000 learners. This is more or less 17 percent of all schools, which implies that one in every five schools in the country is a farm school. It is true that many of the children attending these schools walk long distances to be there and, again in the words of the minister,

> ... when these children arrive at school it is likely that they will enter a building that is in poor repair. They will probably not have access to clean water to quench their thirst. They will probably find it hard to concentrate on account of poor nutrition. They will have little protection from the weather. They will not be tired from carrying books because they do not have any. The teacher will be struggling to teach children of different grades in one class and without proper learning materials. (Asmal, 2000: 4)

It is also true, however, on the one hand, that children from the Karretjie context (and their parents) never even had, and often still do not have, access to such imperfect schools. On the other hand, the farm schools in the Karoo district we have been working in do not accord with the picture painted above. Many of the farm schools in these areas are not only situated on land made available by farmers but have buildings constructed and learning materials available – either due to funds initially advanced by the farmer or procured from provincial authorities through the intercession of the landowner or her/his spouse and/or by means of various and continuous fund-raising projects. In most cases the schools are staffed by dedicated and experienced teachers; and many of the children from farms in the area and from further afield are transported to the school, accommodated, and provided with regular wholesome meals. The 'Verwoerdian ideal' was said to have been 'a school on every farm' and the rationale 'to stabilise the labour force on farms; maintain the presence of women and children on farms as part of the labour force; and prevent migration from farms to the cities and towns'. But 'the current system with high drop out rates, the critically limited provision at secondary level and the lack of resources to implement an appropriate curriculum ... has outlived its usefulness even for those parties who had benefited from it in the past' (Education White Paper – 2, 1996: 35–36; Asmal, 2000: 3). But increasing demand for such schooling, steady growth in enrolment, a better pass-rate than many town and urban equivalents and national recognition and accolades for some of these schools' performance, put a lie to these allegations. Almost without exception the driving force behind such successful enterprises is a single individual (or just a few) who is vocation driven. The schools are situated on private land but are assisted by subsidies and salaries from official sources – but these are mostly inadequate. The role of farm schools and their teachers in the realm of the Karretjie People will be pursued later in this chapter.

Learning as Wanderers

Informal learning remains one of the main functions of the *karretjie* domestic unit. Older children not only play an active role with regard to sibling care, they are also a valuable source of domestic labour. Girls are more involved in activities surrounding the immediate *karretjie* unit with chores such as sweeping, washing clothes, preparing food and feeding pets and chickens. Boys look after the donkeys, fetch water and firewood and sometimes assist with chores such as washing clothing.

Berland (1982: 123–24) has found among the peripatetic Qalandar of Pakistan that 'from a very early age the child recognizes that the tasks he is assigned represent an important contribution to his own and his family's survival'. This principle applies equally to the Karretjie children. Depending on the number of members of a particular *karretjie* unit, very young children often get involved in domestic responsibilities. When the shearers are away on a shearing assignment, the mothers of the children would frequently 'borrow' children, especially boys, from other units to assist with collecting firewood and water in particular (Steyn, 2001).

From an early age boys accompany their fathers to the shearing shed. When they are skilled enough, boys start shearing independently and as a result, often form an independent *karretjie* unit. During her study among a group of Gypsies, Okely (1983: 162) observed that 'the learning context for travelling children is most often on the basis of one adult per child; a parent or relative. Learning is by direct example and practice in circumstances similar to those they will experience as adults'. Many boys start shearing when they are still in their teens. Often they are trained in shearing by accompanying and assisting their fathers during a shearing assignment. Children younger than 14 years are not recruited into activities such as shearing because the type of labour requires a certain amount of strength and can be done most efficiently by adults or older and stronger boys.

Another activity in which children are involved is harvesting of crops on neighbouring farms where their fathers usually shear. This kind of labour involvement is often condemned by the wider society as exploitation, but the reality is that the children's earnings make a very valuable contribution to the family income. The type of labour they perform, such as sweeping the shearing shed and picking and cleaning onions, does not necessarily imply keeping them out of school, because for many of these children school attendance is not an option at all.

Begging is another economic activity in which young children are involved, thereby contributing to the *karretjie* unit's economic resources. This activity mostly occurs at the outspans close to town where especially motorists passing through give the children money or food. Nowadays children who were previously from outspans far from town areas, but moved with their families to the informal settlements adjacent to towns, often begging to supplement the resources of the unit – are in fact 'deployed' by a parent or older sibling to do so (Steyn, 2001).

The following example is an excerpt stemming from longitudinal research of the lives of Karretjie children. These demonstrate something about their context and the challenges which they face, such as an unsettled existence, poverty, violence, discrimination, exclusion and separation from their parents. Their case differs considerably from the other children who were part of the study. Of our sample they are the only ones who advanced to a school in a rural town, previously designated for white children only, and will probably be the only ones to advance to the secondary level of formal education.

> Simon and Marie are twins. Their family and friends call them by their *klein naampies* (nicknames), Outjie ('little fellow') and Rokkies ('little dress'). They were born in 1988 on the farm Brandewynsfontein in the district of Colesberg in the Northern Cape Province. They have two older brothers, Pienkies and Toek-Toek. Their father, Koot Arnoster and mother Katryn Jacobs were never legally married or *ge-êg* as the Karretjie People refer to a 'proper' marriage, and for this reason the children take the last name of the mother. For most of their lives they lived semi-permanently at the outspan next to the Seacow River Bridge or on different farms. In 1991 Koot accidentally killed Katryn at the outspan during one of their regular weekend drinking bouts. They were arguing when he took his

shears and stabbed her in the groin, damaging an artery and she died as a result of arterial haemorrhaging. Their four children were present at the time of their mother's death and witnessed how their father was taken away to town in a police vehicle. While Koot was in prison awaiting trial in the nearby town of Hanover, Outjie and Rokkies along with their brothers stayed behind at the outspan with their elderly and partly disabled grandmother, Mieta Ackerman (Koot's mother) in her *karretjie* unit, which she shared with a daughter in law and her two children. Taking into consideration the circumstances of the Arnoster family, particularly the parentless children, the court decided on only a suspended sentence for Koot. He returned to the outspan and committed himself to responsibility for his four children. Two years later he 'married' Flora Swarts, a fellow resident at the outspan whose husband had previously died of tuberculosis. The children were very fond of her and while she was taking good care of them, Koot could continue his activities as shearer and spokesman for the shearing team. After visiting (and drinking) at a nearby farm one Saturday a year or so later, Koot and Flora, in their drunken state, started arguing while on their way back to the outspan. He hit her several times with his walking stick until she fell down. He then also sat down and after a while fell asleep next to her. The next morning when he woke up he realised for the first time that Flora had been dead for several hours. Two days later a farm labourer found Flora's body and soon afterwards the police arrived at the outspan to take Koot to the local prison. While he was awaiting trial his children once again were left in the care of their grandmother, travelling with her unit during shearing assignments. Koot was sentenced to six years imprisonment of which two years were suspended. Outjie and Rokkies' grandmother decided that in their interest they together with their brother Toek-Toek and the other school aged children at the outspan, should attend school. A fee of R7 per child per term was paid by the grandmother from her old-age pension of R380 monthly. A neighbouring farmer's daughter resides in town but is a teacher at one of the farm schools in the district and he volunteered to take the children to town on Monday mornings from where his daughter would take them to school on the eastern side of the district. The twins remained at this primary school for two years, without successfully completing the first grade, after which their grandmother withdrew them because of their extreme unhappiness. Toek-Toek quitted after one year due to a mental disability stemming from a fall off a donkey and returned to the outspan to assist his grandmother with her daily chores. For almost a year Outjie and Rokkies remained at the outspan and travelled with their grandmother's cart. The following year Koot sent a message from jail to his mother via his eldest son Pienkies that the twins should go back to school but this time to a primary school in the predominantly 'coloured' neighbourhood of town. They were to stay with a relative of their mother in the nearby informal settlement. They visited their grandmother and brothers during weekends and would tell of their experiences at school and in the informal settlement, often in negative terms. Towards the end of the same year the twins were put semi permanently in the foster care of a social worker in Lowryville (Extension 4) a new 'coloured' residential area next to the N1 national road, who lived in a two-bedroom house and received R240 per month for each child in her care. For the first time the twins were now living in a 'proper' house and it was also the first time that they had access to conventional beds and other facilities. In this small neighbourhood they soon befriended other children and seldom went back to the outspan to see their grandmother and brothers. The social worker used to take them once a week to see their father in prison, situated within walking distance from where they lived. However, their grandmother died the next year and the children's visits to their other relatives at the outspan became even more infrequent. Their father was released from prison towards the end of that year and moved back into his shack in the informal settlement adjacent to town. The twins remained in the care of the social worker but did see their father regularly. They are both currently enrolled at the previously exclusively white Colesberg primary school (having 'graduated' from the 'coloured' primary school) and by all accounts are doing well, both having advanced by several grades.

In a sense the twins are symptomatic of a new generation now emerging where boys no longer necessarily acquire the skill of shearing from their fathers, or girls do not follow in their mothers' footsteps; where in other cases increased poverty and unemployment lead to children leaving school to work or to help in the household while their parents work; where formal education is again a lower priority for many children and it becomes increasingly unlikely that they will return to school, and where an additional set of detrimental circumstances inevitably promotes a downward spiral of poverty and social problems (Steyn, 1995, 2001).

Childhood and Education: Wandering Learners

As mentioned earlier, the educational playing field in South Africa is not a level one, mainly because of a historical system of inequity and exclusion of certain communities from mainstream services. Education for previously disadvantaged groups, including the Karretjie People, should therefore be, and is, one of national government's main priorities. The Karretjie case, however, requires particular awareness and sensitivity. For most of the Karretjie children their childhood years entail times of great flux and fragmentation, a ceaseless process of shifting localities and changing relationships with others and where factors such as poverty, domestic disruption and personal uncertainty are the reality of their lives. Although they gain educational skills within their families and community, i.e. the *karretjie* domestic unit is the primary entity within which they acquire knowledge peculiar to their lifestyle and environment, they do not have the same access to formal schooling as children in other contexts.

In 1998 the Development Bank of Southern Africa stated that

> an education expands the range of options which a person may choose, thus creating opportunities for a fulfilling life. Education and training satisfy the basic need for knowledge and skills. Education also provides a means of meeting basic needs provided that adequate employment opportunities exist, and helps sustain and accelerate overall development. (Development Bank of Southern Africa, 1998: 45)

In practice, however, certain barriers prevent these children from accessing their basic right to education and its associated benefits. A peripatetic lifestyle has become increasingly more hazardous for some of these communities. Poverty-induced surrendering of cart and donkeys, for example, and the resultant loss of mobility and the concomitant increase in underemployment result in them being pushed to the fringes of towns and ultimately force them to become part of the squatter problem in South Africa.

Although most of the parents are illiterate and unemployed for large parts of the annual cycle, they acknowledge the importance of their children acquiring the basic skills of reading and writing. As people who have spent their childhood years and most of their adult lives subject to segregated governance, parents view their children as a new generation who should have, at least theoretically, better future prospects. Legislative and educational changes in the decade since the democratic election in 1994 have, however, had an insignificant impact on the children's lives because the Karretjie People lack the necessary mechanisms and resources to secure their educational rights. The reason is twofold: firstly, the farm school educational system and secondly, an itinerant lifestyle and its associated challenges.

Many of the children were only introduced to formal education, provided mainly by farm schools in rural areas, in the early 1990s. Furthermore, most have only brief encounters with schooling and with a few exceptions, never learn the skills of reading and writing. Although all South African schools have been theoretically accessible to every child since the advent of democracy, the Karretjie children still have little opportunity to attend schools other than secluded farm schools on a sporadic basis.

The education of non-white children in rural areas became the responsibility of the state after the Bantu Education Act was introduced in 1953 (Gaganakis and Crewe, 1987: 1). Previously, black children were mostly educated by either missionaries or under the auspices of farmers. The apartheid government of the time encouraged farm school education by providing subsidies and equipment to farmers to continue their educational endeavours. Other than this, farmers were prepared to contribute in this way because they wanted at least to have a semi-literate labour force (De V Graaff et al., 1990; Gaganakis and Crewe, 1987; Waldman, 1993).

Two of the major problems associated with the farm school system are that they are situated on private land and the farmer manages the school (so he, as a private individual, decides whether to open a school on his property, or to close it down). Furthermore, although the Department of Education and Training (DET) stipulated in its act of 1979 that '... any person who wishes to provide education for a black person, except at a State or community school, shall apply for registration of a school' (Gaganakis and Crewe, 1987: 4), the matter of school fees was determined by the farmer as school manager.

Since 1994, with a new dispensation in the country, the Department of Education has done little in terms of implementing new incentives as regards farm schools. These schools are still under the control of the farm owner, they provide schooling from grade 1 up to grade 7, and secondary education is mostly not provided.

As mentioned earlier, some Karretjie children started, for the first time, to attend some of these schools in the 1990s. The initiative primarily came from farmers or their wives or teachers who run these schools and fetch the children at their own cost from their semi-permanent settings, albeit on outspans or other farms. They provide board and lodging for the children and return them to their 'homes' on weekends or school vacations. At the time of doing this fieldwork the state contributed R98 per term (four months of the year) per learner to the schools where most of our data had been gathered (Steyn, 2001). It was clearly in the interest of the farmers and teachers to bolster the numbers of children attending their schools.

Although fees in schools, other than private schools, do not legally have to be paid, the level and effects of poverty these people have to endure still make formal education a difficult goal to fulfil. Many parents and children also realise that even with school education, the probability of procuring employment with a steady income is remote, especially given the high unemployment rate in the country generally. They are quite aware of the fact, having grown up in an environment with few employment opportunities, that even with an education, their life chances might not be improved.

The schools which do provide education for the children are often confronted with a shortage of space and lack of human resources, frequently resulting in combined class teaching. This severely affects the quality of teaching mainly because the individual needs of children are not monitored. Coming from functionally illiterate contexts, the children often require specialised attention in bridging the gap from home environment to school setting. Teachers also find themselves in difficult circumstances: in addition to the lack of space in classrooms and inadequate equipment to perform their task, they often do not have the background or training for dealing with children who are even more deprived than the farm children they already teach. Teachers therefore have to be innovative and have to make certain adaptations in order to satisfy the children's needs and to ensure that they persevere in their work. In most cases Karretjie children have to repeat their grades and their eventual success primarily depends on the commitment of teachers who provide them with personal and special attention and remedial teaching.

All schools in the country, whether in urban or rural areas, are now supposed to follow the same curriculum (Gaganakis and Crewe, 1987: 19). Given that most Karretjie People function in a particular rural context throughout their lives, the kind of education the children receive is mostly not designed with *their* immediate environment, needs or interests in mind. Although 'Education For All' is a relatively recent development for many groups in the country, the educational framework that applies to the

Karretjie children in particular, lacks in flexibility mainly because it was not planned to take cognisance of the context and conditions they find themselves in.

Even though relatively small numbers of Karretjie children initially started to attend school, many of them then dropped out, having mostly completed only two grades, and so leaving school before they attained permanent literacy and numeracy levels. Often children have no option but to leave school due to seasonal parental labour, increased poverty, the fact that children's earnings are needed to supplement family incomes and the discriminatory effects of a continuation of prejudices in many subtle and unsubtle ways against them. They also have virtually no access to educational support mechanisms and structures such as libraries and learning centres (and at home) when they leave school and therefore their rudimentary skills in reading and writing deteriorate rapidly.

An important reason for the high drop out rates is thus the perpetuation of discrimination against, and powerlessness of, the children and their parents. Within the school setting, the children's interactions with other children, i.e. those of farm labourers, often result in conflict. Children also find themselves in a position of defending their parents and their particular lifestyle on a regular basis. Even though the children of farm labourers who attend farm schools come from impoverished backgrounds with low levels of literacy, the gap between them and Karretjie children is still of much concern, especially to teachers. Abuse is often verbal and by way of physical harassment, and in more subtle ways in the form of low and negative expectations about the children's abilities to learn. The children, often very painfully, are aware that they are regarded as different and inferior in some or other way.

The itinerant way of life of many of these communities poses an immense challenge for the national educational system. Although schooling is legally compulsory until Grade 9 (*The Teacher*, 6 January 2000), it seems impossible to reconcile a shifting lifestyle and the consequences of rural poverty with an inflexible schooling system. Many families nowadays opt for a more sedentary lifestyle for various reasons, but even this lifestyle change offers little incentive for children to attend school. The reality is that, due to unemployment and the persistent financial constraints in a domestic unit, children are often left no option but to leave school and contribute to the income of their parents' unit.

Educating Itinerants

With a view to progressive empowerment and upliftment, we were instrumental in a comprehensive education programme being initiated in one of the Karoo districts a few years ago in an endeavour to facilitate a sustainable process for the provision of holistic education and development for the

Karretjie People. By bringing basic skills to, and developing a positive value system within this community, a significant contribution was envisaged to enable particularly the adults to compete socio-economically in a more equitable manner and to improve their quality of life. The programme included a literacy curriculum, practical and skills training as well as guidelines and procedures for health care, childcare, parental responsibility and hygiene. Portable educational facilities were taken to the Karretjie People at the various outspans, but given the mobility and fluidity patterns of individuals and *karretjie* units, especially the absence of the adult males as shearers, it soon became clear that careful planning and constant innovation and adaptation of the instructional process was essential.

The project was implemented in two stages, a stage of *communication, orientation and sensitisation* and a stage of *intensive instruction and tuition.* Given the fact that introduction and implementation of the programme had to be gradual, systematic and coordinated in order to be meaningful and also lasting and not disruptive, it was envisaged that the first stage should run for at least three months and the second stage for twelve to fifteen months. This

Figure 4.4 'Portable instruction' at the outspan.

latter stage was furthermore designed to set in motion a self-sustaining process.

The stage of *communication, orientation and sensitisation* was directed at the Karretjie community at large but also at farmers and key individuals and officials from the ranks of organised agriculture, the local government, political groupings, the clergy and health care. This stage served to explain the project's nature and aims and to gain the support and co-operation of all pivotal individuals and organisations. The need and strategy for introducing basic educational and health care values was explained, discussed and negotiated with all involved. This stage further served as a planning, orientation and training period for the teachers and facilitators to be employed in the project. The community facilitators had been strategically identified from their ranks and likewise had to undergo training.

The stage of *intensive instruction and tuition* embraced exclusively the Karretjie community and was designed to accommodate both adults and children. The programme for the adults (mainly females because of the frequent absence of the males who spend long hours in the shearing shed or doing other farm work), as was mentioned earlier, was designed to provide basic literacy and numeracy as well as fundamental, sustainable and

Figure 4.5 The first tentative steps to writing and literacy.

transferable guidelines and procedures for child care, parental responsibility, family planning, health care, dietetics and hygiene. The children from ages seven to sixteen received a similarly holistic educational orientation but with more specific emphasis on basic literacy and skills.

Given the itinerancy of the community, the initiatives and processes of the outreach programme had a dual focus. On the one hand, activities were concentrated at those outspans frequented on a regular basis by the largest number of Karretjie families. On the other hand, the more suitable facilities of a centrally located farm school were used in order to accommodate larger and combined groups for the purpose of discussions, interaction and tuition. In the case of the outspans, collapsible and portable basic equipment, in addition to the usual teaching aids, were taken to the people and in the case of the farm school, the participants were ferried to the central facility.

As the programme has now run its course a formal evaluation was done, and a number of practical and ethical issues emerged, many of which should serve as guidelines for future endeavours. Of equal importance, the circumstances of the Karretjie People have been subjected to continual change – particularly insofar as the variables and external factors which impinge upon them.

Conclusion: Practical and Ethical Issues

Clearly, a development initiative such as that outlined here implies a massive ethical responsibility. Education of whatever kind would, for example, result in an irreversible, even drastic, change in lifestyle for the Karretjie People. Adults, for instance, are generally positively inclined to education for their children, but already the advent of such tuition for some of the children had resulted in friction between the newly-created 'different worlds' of the older and younger generation.

Cognisance must, of course, be taken of the socio-political and socio-economic environment in which such endeavours are undertaken. For one, unemployment in the district concerned, and the country at large, is such that the acquisition of additional skills will result in expectations which, if unfulfilled, can only lead to yet more disappointment and frustration. The conditioned mindset of the wider community, particularly potential employers, is furthermore such that they would find it difficult to contemplate accommodating the 'new' Karretjie People in 'their' world. In fact, some members of the farming community perceive such initiatives as inconceivable because 'those Bushmen are uneducable', or if you do give them some education you will 'spoil' them, with the net result that farmers will 'lose' their shearers. An itinerant community such as the Karretjie People occupies a singularly sensitive and vulnerable socio-economic niche and by virtue of its position of almost complete dependency runs the risk of losing what little they have.

More practical considerations were also forthcoming. The movement of the *karretjie* units are not always predictable and a schedule composing regular tuition sessions is ill-suited to their pattern of activities. The suitability, also in practical terms, of the instructional strategy and content is unpredictable and uncertain as there is no appropriate precedent. Facilitators and teachers had to improvise on a weekly basis and although much benefit was gained from their individual and collective experiences and insights, design and application of an appropriate and effective strategy is still very much a nebulous affair.

The feasibility of 'taking the Karretjie People to the facilities' instead of the facilities to the outspans is informed by a number of factors. Mainly for logistical reasons, the facilitators had been providing teaching and instruction at the outspans, but it is impossible to provide infrastructure of the same standard 'on the run' as it were, as is possible at a fixed location. Given the fluidity of the *karretjie* unit, and especially the fact of the regular absence of the adult males as shearers, the further absence and commuting of adults for tuition and instructional purposes would need to be carefully planned and coordinated. Even if the *karretjie* moves as a unit to the educational facility the regular shearing cycle has to be kept in mind, particularly as outspans are selected for strategic reasons in order to take maximum advantage of shearing opportunities. In all cases supervision and care of the small children, in the absence of some of the adults, remains a priority.

To comprehend policy analysis and implementation, we have found it helpful first to consider how decisions are made in a particular context. Many factors or variables play a role in decision-making – the socio-cultural system involved, the values, the information available, perceptions of such information, political (and other) agendas and the power relations and influence between individuals and groups and levels of authority. We furthermore understand policy to entail intentions which are associated with deliberate action in all spheres of human activity. For any action there is always some preceding idea or conception of the eventual result of such an action – irrespective of whether it affects only an individual or many people. These preceding ideas, conceptions or notions are what policy is all about i.e. intentional human behaviour. Such predetermined notions or 'plans' may be formal or informal, specific or general, appropriate or inappropriate, but they still represent human intention (Chambers, 1989).

In the case under consideration here we are more concerned with formal policy stemming from the public (government, administration) sector because whole communities are affected or not affected, and programmes or activities deliberately designed to bring about change are at issue. Given different and often conflicting intentions of individuals, stakeholders and other interest groups, the policy domain is thus a contested one. The outcome of such interactions is the reality of socio-cultural contexts that people find themselves in. The effects of globalisation have complicated these interactions; communication and transportation have become more rapid, efficient and immediate. People are no longer sheltered in a community context, many more variables play into their lives. Generally people have become more aware that bureaucratic and other decisions can drastically affect their lives and their destiny – except the Karretjie People. Apart from being 'discovered' for the first time by every political party in the run-up to South Africa's first democratic election in 1994 (and then in subsequent elections), they have been unaware, and have certainly not experienced the benefits, of any decisions or policies designed to address their particular circumstances. They have never been sheltered in community context and are now even more vulnerable than before. Exploited or ignored at the local level, the variables, interactions, intentions and even contestations at the higher levels have washed over or past them as if they do not even exist.

For too long we anthropologists, and many other social scientists, have been preoccupied, even obsessed with a fixed site or location for our fieldwork endeavours. Even when anthropologists followed their informants into the cities, they looked for, and found, their 'village' in the urban context. Only with the advent of our interest in 'travelling cultures' did we undergo a mind and paradigm shift which enabled us to be sensitive to the distinctive context, perspectives, values and needs of shifting and multi-sited communities – this can quite simply be reduced to antithetical theoretical perspectives and paradigms: sedentist, centrist, localised, situated vis-à-vis itinerant, 'decentred', multi-sited, travelling culture. This clearly has methodological and theoretical implications and it is incumbent upon us to translate these for decision-makers and bureaucrats at all levels of government.

The Karretjie example suggests that only through case- and context-specific data which stem from participatory research, can the required sensitivity and understanding of problems of rural poverty and educational needs be developed. Sound macro policies can only be designed by development organisations and different sectors and levels of government if such recent and 'dense data' of not only the different 'geographies of poverty' but also of pockets of 'invisible educationless people' such as have been depicted here, are utilised in order to ensure that those who initiate programmes are aware of not only the extent and nature of the problem, but also who the people really are, and exactly where and how they live.

References

Asmal, K. (2000) 'Address by the Minister of Education, Professor Kader Asmal, MP, to the National Conference on Farm Schools', Saturday 13 May 2000. http://education.pwv.gov.za/Media_Statements/Speeches00/May00/Farm_scho ols.htm

Berland, J. (1982) *No Five Fingers are Alike: Cognitive Amplifiers in Social Context*. Cambridge: Harvard University Press.

Chambers, E. (1989) *Applied Anthropology. A Practical Guide*. Englewood Cliffs: Prentice Hall.

Chambers, R., R. Longhurst and A. Pacey (1981) *Seasonal Dimensions to Rural Poverty*. London: Frances Pinter (Publishers) Ltd.

De Jongh, M. (1997) 'Conventional Strangers: Itinerant Agency, Asymmetry and "Karoo Culture"'. *African Anthropology* 4 (2) pp. 89–109.

—— (2002) 'No Fixed Abode: the Poorest of the Poor and Elusive Identities in Rural South Africa'. *Journal of Southern African Studies* 28 (2) pp. 441–60.

—— (2004) 'Strangers in Their Own Land: Social Resources and Domestic Fluidity of the Peripatetic Karretjie People of the South African Karoo'. In: J.C. Berland and A. Rao (eds) *Customary Strangers. New Perspectives on Peripatetic Peoples in the Middle East, Africa, and Asia*. Praeger: West Port, pp. 155–77.

—— and R. Steyn (1998) 'Karretjie People'. In T.L. Gall (ed.) *Worldmark Encyclopedia of Culture and Daily Life*, vol. 1 – Africa. Cleveland: Eastword Publications Development.

De V Graaff, J. et al. (1990) *Farm Schools in the Western Cape: a Sociological Analysis*. Stellenbosch: University of Stellenbosch.

Development Bank of Southern Africa: Development Information Business Unit (1998) *Northern Cape: Development Profile 1998*. Paper 131. Johannesburg: Development Bank of Southern Africa.

Education White Paper – 2 (1996) 'The Organization, Governance and Future Funding of Schools' (Notice 130 of 1996). Pretoria: Department of Education.

Gaganakis, M. and M. Crewe (1987) *Farm Schools in South Africa. An Introductory Review*. Johannesburg: South African Institute of Race Relations.

May, J., M. Carter and D. Posel (1995) *The Composition and Persistence of Poverty in Rural South Africa. An Entitlements Approach to Poverty*. Johannesburg: The Land and Agriculture Policy Centre.

Okely, J. (1983) *The Traveller-Gypsies*. Cambridge: Cambridge University Press.

Steyn, R. (1995) 'Child-Rearing and Child-Care in a South African Nomadic Community'. *African Anthropology*, 1995, 11(2). pp. 82–89.

—— (2001) 'Some Notes on Childhood in a South African Peripatetic Community'. *Nomadic Peoples*, 2001, 5(1). pp. 28–36.

The Teacher, 6 January 2000, Johannesburg, South Africa.

Waldman, L. (1993) 'Here You Will Remain: Adolescent Experience on Farms in the Western Cape'. M.A. Dissertation, Cape Town, University of Cape Town.

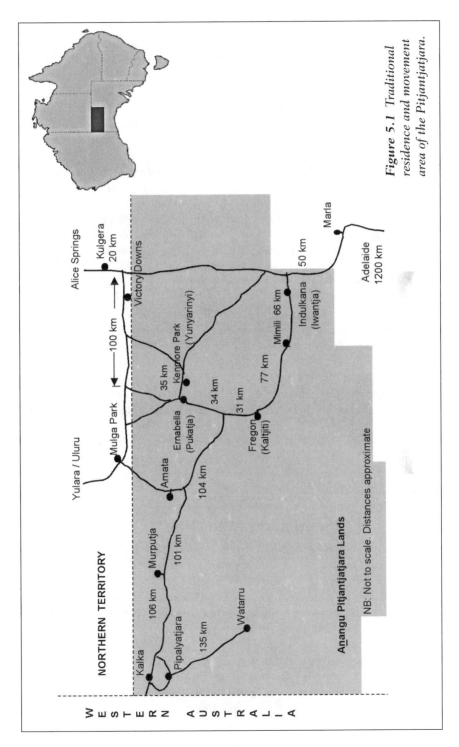

Figure 5.1 Traditional residence and movement area of the Pitjantjatjara.

The Anangu enshrine their understanding of the world and their place in it in a complex of stories referred to as *Tjukurpa*, glossed in English as The Dreaming (Edwards, 2004: 16–32). According to the Dreaming stories, ancestor spirit beings lay dormant within a pre-existing formless substance. In this creative epoch, the spirit beings emerged from within the earth, took the identities and shapes of the various faunal and floral species of the region, and moved across the surface of the land, performing the activities appropriate for the species. These beings shared human identity as well as that of the particular species, for example as kangaroo-man, emu-man, bowerbird-woman, and fig-man. Each clan group traces its descent from one of these species. The activities of these beings in hunting, making implements, fighting, digging, vomiting, and travelling, formed the features of the environment. For example, small water holes in a flat rock were made by three of the species digging for water, a winding watercourse was made by a water serpent, a leaning tree was a man in the act of spearing and clusters of small stones are the leftovers of bush tomatoes collected by women.

As well as providing an explanation of the creation of all aspects of the environment, the stories of the *Tjukurpa* also provide a pattern for life. As the Ancestor Spirit Beings are recorded in the oral stories as hunting and gathering foods, making implements, punishing offenders, fulfilling kinship obligations, performing ceremonies, painting on rock walls, and marrying within specified section groups, so people in each generation are to follow these examples in their daily lives. Not that the activities of the ancestors were perfect: the mythology included both good and bad elements of life. People thus reflect on the total condition of life and make decisions on the basis of this reflection. According to Stanner (1984: 145), this 'religious belief expressed a philosophy of assent to life's terms'. This emphasis on the centrality of The Dreaming and the conservation and transmission of cultural tradition largely determined the role and content of traditional Aboriginal education.

Traditional Pitjantjatjara Education

There were no formal educational structures, specialist teachers or schools in traditional Pitjantjatjara society. There were no separate domains identified as educational, religious or economic. All aspects of life were part of an inter-related and unified whole, centred on The Dreaming. Pitjantjatjara children learned the skills, knowledge and values to equip them for participation in all aspects of this total life through observation, imitation and participation in everyday activities. Divisions based on sex and age are important in Aboriginal societies as they determine rights, responsibilities and restrictions in regard to knowledge. For example, knowledge of some stories and ceremonies is restricted to older males and of others to older females. Rights to some foods are restricted to certain categories. As children grow, they are increasingly prepared for entry into their respective male or female domains of life. A Pitjantjatjara woman, born in the late 1920s, recorded her memories of socialisation in traditional settings:

> I lived as a child at Angatja. My father, mother, grandmother, older brothers, aunties and uncles taught me there and I learned from them. I learned from my mother about collecting the plant foods. She collected the foods and prepared them and I learned from watching her. (Ilyatjari, 1988: 6)

The enculturation of Pitjantjatjara children took place within small local clan-based groups which hunted, gathered and utilised the resources within their areas. Larger assemblies gathered for ritual and social purposes when sufficient water and food were available. Children were taught the location of water supplies and plant foods, such as native millet, bush tomatoes and native peaches, and to identify the tracks left by the various animals such as kangaroos, emus, bush turkeys and reptiles. Boys observed the hunting techniques employed by their fathers and other male relatives and used miniature spears and throwing sticks in play. Girls observed the women of the group digging for roots, witchetty grubs and honey ants, collecting fruits and gathering and winnowing seeds. They imitated the women, using small digging sticks, wooden dishes and grindstones. As the children grew they hunted some of the smaller animals, reptiles, and birds and gathered vegetable foods. Learning in the natural environment also included instruction about what should be avoided:

> We learned too about the things that were dangerous. We were told to avoid snakes and to be afraid of them and which ants would bite us ... And we had to learn that there were some things that we could not say. If we said them our mothers hit us. They told us that some places were sacred and we must avoid them. (Ilyatjari, 1988: 7)

At well as learning the knowledge and skills appropriate to the physical world, Pitjantjatjara children are taught about the relationships which determine their rights and obligations in daily life. Under their classificatory system of kinship each person identifies a specific relationship with all other members of the society. An individual has many fathers, mothers, brothers, sisters, aunts, uncles and grandparents. Most everyday behaviours are determined by these relationships, for example, sharing of foods, inflicting punishments, passing on knowledge, roles in ceremonies and selection of marriage partners (Edwards, 2004: 57–61). Children are constantly told of their relationships to others and reminded of the behaviours expected of them. Older girls and women tell stories incorporating this knowledge to younger girls. In story telling games, *milpatjunanyi*, marks traced in the sand symbolise the stories. Oral transmission of knowledge through story and song is reinforced by artistic symbolism and ritual.

During early years this education is informal and children have a great deal of freedom. They are made aware that the land is imbued with the presence of spirit beings, and taught to walk with care and respect so that they do not offend these spirits and risk dangerous consequences. Following puberty they are subject to strict discipline, as youths are segregated for intensive teaching leading to initiation into manhood. Girls learn the women's parts of the stories and their parts in ritual to prepare them for their roles as wives, mothers and keepers of the women's knowledge. This learning continues throughout adulthood as men and women pass through stages of advancement in ritual, knowledge and authority.

Thus in most respects, education in traditional Pitjantjatjara societies contrasts markedly with Western systems of education. There was no written language. Learning took place in natural settings, and was closely related to the physical environment. It occurred within everyday social contexts. There was no formalised teaching profession. All members of the group participated in teaching. There was an emphasis on imitation and participation. The children learned by doing it, not by learning how to do it. There was no training of specialists, apart from the recognition that a few people had special powers to heal or perform sorcery. There was a stress on conformity with little encouragement to experiment or question. In contrast to Western societies where discipline in early years gives way to greater freedom at adolescence, the freedom of early Pitjantjatjara life was replaced by strict discipline following puberty.

Early Contact History

Aboriginal groups living in areas of initial colonial settlement, for example in the Sydney region first settled in 1788, suffered severely from this overwhelming contact through dispossession of land, massacres and exposure to illnesses to which they had little or no resistance.

Isolation in the interior of Australia provided some security for the Pitjantjatjara people. The Pitjantjatjara heartlands are 1500 km from Adelaide, the capital and administrative centre of the State of South Australia. The first European explorers entered their territory in 1873. Contacts in the following decades were spasmodic as explorers, surveyors and prospectors passed through the region. Further protection was provided by the proclamation of a large Aboriginal reserve in 1921. Some Pitjantjatjara people moved east to work on cattle stations. Droughts during the 1920s and 1930s encouraged this movement as did the attraction of new foods, such as flour and sugar, tools, clothing, blankets and other goods introduced by the settlers.

While the Aborigines obtained food and goods in return for work in the cattle industry, where their abilities at tracking and adaptation to horsemanship, made them valuable employees, there were increasing reports of occasional conflict, abuses of labour and sexual exploitation of women (Edwards, 1992: 6–7). These reports led to the opening of the first settlement established to provide a place where Pitjantjatjara people could settle and receive educational, employment, health and other services to prepare them for participation in the wider Australian society. The gradual change for the Pitjantjatjara people from the hunter-gatherer lifestyle in small local groups to relatively permanent residence in established communities was motivated by their desire to have access to the new foods and other resources and subsequently, a developing dependency on the health, store, employment, educational and social security services which were made available on these settlements.

Ernabella Mission and the First Pitjantjatjara School

Ernabella Mission was established on a 500 square mile pastoral lease by the Presbyterian Church of Australia in 1937. This was increased later to 2000 square miles. A lay Moderator of the Presbyterian Church, Dr Charles Duguid, visited the region and expressed concern about the indiscriminate contacts with Europeans. He advocated the establishment of the mission as a buffer settlement where the people would receive health services, training and employment in a context of mutual respect. Duguid laid down the following principles for the mission:

> There was to be no compulsion nor imposition of our way of life on the Aborigines, nor deliberate interference with tribal custom ... only people trained in some particular skill should be on the mission staff, and ... they must learn the tribal language. (Duguid, 1972: 115)

Figure 5.2 *The first Ernabella School building and Pitjantjatjara students, 1941.*

Sheep had been grazed on the pastoral lease and the sheep industry was developed to provide training and employment for Pitjantjatjara people as shepherds, shearers, fencers and well-sinkers.

As families began to settle, a mission school with one teacher was opened at Ernabella on 1 March 1940. The early classes were held in the open in the mornings only, with children encouraged to engage in traditional games and food gathering in the afternoons. The children lived in camp conditions with their families and continued to hear traditional stories and to observe ceremonies. School attendance was spasmodic as families moved back to their homelands. The school and other activities at Ernabella usually closed during the summer and late winter for holiday periods and the residents were encouraged to visit their clan territories. These periods were used for initiations and other traditional ceremonial purposes.

The Ernabella Mission School was notable as the only Aboriginal school where a policy of vernacular education was followed consistently for several decades. In line with the mission's policy, the instruction in early years was in Pitjantjatjara (Edwards, 1969: 278–82). A phonetic orthography was introduced and a syllabic method of teaching literacy enabled the children to learn to read and write Pitjantjatjara within a short time. According to a 1942 report after 'an equivalent of 12 months' tuition at the school (a very interrupted 12 months) some of these children are writing their own language as fluently, neatly and correctly as white children in Grade VII at our schools' (Trudinger, 1942). In 1944, English was being taught in the school as a secondary language (*Ernabella News Letter*, October 1944: 8). Up to 200 children had attended the school at some time during the first five years. Despite irregular attendance as families moved in and out of the mission, 80 children had some degree of literacy (*Ernabella News Letter*, October 1945: 2–4).

Figure 5.3 *First day of the Ernabella School held in the creek bed, 1940.*

In the early years the curriculum focused on Scripture, writing and spelling, composition, reading, number, manual work, English, music and drawing (*Ernabella News Letter*, October 1945: 4). The children were trained in four-part singing and hymns were translated into Pitjantjatjara. This early training in the school laid the foundations for the Ernabella Choir which in later decades travelled to Alice Springs, Adelaide, Melbourne, Sydney and Fiji. Traditional songs were also performed on these tours. Development of traditional symbolic forms in the school classes led to the development in 1948 at Ernabella of the longest continuing Aboriginal handcraft industry in Australia.

Until 1959 only one trained teacher was employed although the school attendance reached 80 children at peak times. The emphasis on vernacular education enabled the employment of Pitjantjatjara assistants who did much of the teaching in the earlier years (*Ernabella News Letter*, March 1952: 3). The white teacher concentrated on preparation of materials and teaching the older children. While Pitjantjatjara remained the language of instruction in earlier years, the use of English increased as the Pitjantjatjara people were increasingly exposed to wider Australian society. According to the 1957 School Report, 'More stress has again been placed on English, and the progress made is a little more encouraging both in reading and conversation'.

A second school for Pitjantjatjara children in South Australia was opened in 1961 at Fregon, 60 kilometres south-west of Ernabella. Fregon was established as an out-station of Ernabella to decentralise, and provide more opportunities for employment through the development of a cattle industry. Through the 1960s the schools at Ernabella and Fregon continued under mission administration with two teachers employed at Ernabella and one at Fregon. Pitjantjatjara assistants continued to fulfil important roles, especially in relation to the Pitjantjatjara language literacy programmes. While the vernacular policy was maintained, the use of English in the schools increased (Edwards, 1969: 281). Attendance levels at the mission schools were high.

During this era, the Australian federal and state governments followed a policy of assimilation in Aboriginal affairs. The earlier policy of protectionism was replaced by one of assimilation in 1951 and this was reaffirmed at a conference of Commonwealth and State Ministers in 1961 (*One People*, 1961: 9–10). While the South Australian government gave limited financial support to the Ernabella and Fregon schools, government officials opposed the use of Pitjantjatjara in the schools, seeing it as hindrance to the process of assimilation. In 1961 the South Australian government established a government Aboriginal settlement, Musgrave Park (later known as Amata), to the west of Ernabella. Some Ernabella families moved to the new settlement. The Department of Education commenced a school at Amata in 1968.

Government Schools

A Labor Party government assumed office in South Australia in 1965. The Minister for Aboriginal Affairs, and later Premier, Donald Dunstan, supported the bilingual policy practised at Ernabella and decreed that government Aboriginal schools in remote areas should be bilingual. In 1968 a section of twelve square miles was excised from Granite Downs pastoral lease to establish another government Aboriginal settlement, Indulkana, for people who had lived on nearby cattle stations. The Education Department opened a school there in 1971. The Presbyterian Church handed over the schools at Ernabella and Fregon to the Department in 1971. While the mission schools were poorly resourced and had low staffing levels, they were also characterised by the commitment of teachers who remained for long periods of service; steady development in the learning of both Pitjantjatjara and English literacy; high levels of attendance; and good relationships between schools and communities.

In the early 1970s, Aboriginal affairs policies changed from assimilation to self-management. The Church transferred administration of Ernabella and Fregon to local incorporated communities from 1 January 1974. This process was followed later by the South Australian government at Amata and Indulkana. During the 1970s two cattle stations, Everard Park (Mimili) and Kenmore Park (Inyarinyi), were purchased by the Commonwealth government and the leases transferred to the Aboriginal communities. Schools were established on these communities. With the political changes in Aboriginal affairs, the availability of more funding and a growing independence amongst the Pitjantjatjara people as they had access to social security benefits and ownership of motor vehicles, some families returned to their traditional lands to the west of the established communities and created homeland communities. Pipalyatjara community was settled 200 km west of Amata in 1975. The Education Department opened a school there in 1976 (Edwards, 1992: 16–17).

Although the Department of Education espoused a policy of bilingual education during this period, the principles of the assimilation policies continued to influence school practices. The provision of support infrastructure for bilingual education was spasmodic. The implementation of the policy depended on the understanding, interest and commitment of principals and other staff to such a policy. One observer noted:

> An assumption of schooling in this era was that Pitjantjatjara culture and society would soon give way to the 'superior' European ways and that Anangu must find an economic role outside the settlements. (Folds, 1987: 9)

In the early years of Ernabella there were approximately 500 Aborigines in contact with the mission. The population of the region grew through natural increase, the return to the area of people who had moved to cattle stations and towns further east and south and an influx of other Aboriginal people, to approximately 2,000 by 1990 and 2,800 by 2000. There was a concomitant increase in non-Aboriginal staff to service the health, educational, administrative, store, mechanical and building needs in the region. The Pitjantjatjara/Yankunytjatjara people are now living across their traditional lands in several larger communities and smaller homelands. While there is still some utilisation of traditional foods, there is a greater dependency on introduced foods, motor vehicles and social security benefits.

Despite political development with the establishment of a Pitjantjatjara Council in 1976 and the granting of freehold tenure in 1981 to the Anangu Pitjantjatjara Incorporated of 102,360 square kilometres of land, there has been an increase in social problems with substance abuse, including alcohol consumption by adults and petrol sniffing by children and youths. The latter has seriously affected school attendance by older boys. Traditional rituals are not accompanied by the same depth of instruction and discipline, and there has been a breakdown in social control. A research report in 1977 concluded that the Anangu people saw the increase in school absenteeism and petrol sniffing as 'the result of the destructive impact white school education and contact with white materialist values generally has on the respect of the young for Aboriginal law' (Coombs, 1977: 24). School attendance figures issued in South Australia in 1999 indicated that Aboriginal schools had the highest levels of absenteeism in the State, with attendance levels at Anangu schools varying between 41.7 percent and 52.2 percent (*The Advertiser*, 16/6/99). According to the Department of Education and Children's Services report, the average attendance at all Anangu schools in 2003 was 72.5 percent, compared with a figure of 91.4 percent for all schools in South Australia.

Whereas many of the people had been employed in earlier years in cattle and sheep industries, handcrafts, building and community projects, much of this employment no longer exists and non-Pitjantjatjara people are employed in many areas of administration and services where professional skills are required. While some Anangu people are still employed in clinics, schools and craft rooms, many are unemployed or working in community projects which do not provide motivation for children to apply themselves to schooling. Several initiatives have been implemented by the Department of Education and other bodies in attempting to meet this challenge.

Wiltja Programme

A teacher of senior girls in the Ernabella school in the late 1970s was concerned that girls aged in their upper teen years were attending a primary school, with no provision for secondary education. Her concerns and recommendations to the Department of Education led to the establishment of the Wiltja Programme in 1980. Wiltja Hostel, established in Adelaide in 1957 by the Aborigines Advancement League Incorporated for Aboriginal children from rural areas (Barnes, 2000: 94), was made available for groups of eight Anangu children to attend a special programme in a suburban high school in Adelaide. Initially the students visited for periods of four weeks. They then returned to their home schools. There was an emphasis on learning social skills, handling money, using public transport and English language acquisition.

The programme expanded with children staying longer and the emphasis on academic progress rising. Increasing demand for access to the programme from Pitjantjatjara communities led to the expansion to other hostels and the movement of the programme to Woodville High School. Students stayed in Adelaide for the whole year. By 1995 the vision of the Wiltja programme was to 'develop the skills, talents, abilities and confidence of Anangu students in the mainstream education and cultural process to enable them to gain greater self management of their communities as adults within these communities' (*Desert Schools*, 1996: 373). In 1998, with enrolments in the programme at over 60, the accommodation was centralised in a larger hostel. This programme is an example of the provision of boarding facilities (Krätli and Dyer, this volume).

Anangu Teacher Education Programme (AnTEP)

From the early years of the Ernabella Mission school, Pitjantjatjara assistants played an important role, especially in the teaching of Pitjantjatjara literacy and maintaining a link between school and community. This continued with the employment of Aboriginal teaching assistants in the government schools as they were established in the region. However, as the staffing levels of trained teachers increased, teacher aides expressed frustration at the fact that they lacked professional training and recognition. Two Pitjantjatjara teaching assistants enrolled at Batchelor College near Darwin in the Northern Territory but the requirement to reside at Batchelor, approximately 1,800 km from their home communities, proved impractical as they felt isolated and homesick (Gale, 1996: 20).

Figure 5.4 Music lesson, Wiltja secondary education programme, Adelaide, 1982.

In a 1976 report, Dr H.H. Penny recommended that 'systematic training in a Pitjantjatjara settlement replace the present form of "on the job" training' (Penny, 1976: 5). The Aboriginal Studies and Teacher Education Centre at the South Australian College of Advanced Education (absorbed into the University of South Australia when it was established in 1991) was asked to investigate the need for a special course to provide training and an appropriate qualification. A coordinator was appointed to survey needs. From the beginning it was agreed:

> non-Aboriginal definitions of 'appropriate' education imposed upon Aboriginal people in the past have had a notable lack of success in raising academic performance, and have often seriously conflicted with the social, cultural and religious fabric of Aboriginal life. (French-Kennedy, 1982)

Consultation with Anangu communities and the preparation of a course accreditation document continued over a period of four years. The communities confirmed that they wanted Anangu people to teach in their own schools, these teachers to be trained in their own communities and that the course should lead to a genuine qualification so that the graduates would be recognised as 'real' teachers. Two awards, an Associate Diploma of Education (Anangu Education) and a Diploma of Teaching (Anangu Education) were accredited. They qualify graduates to be registered as teachers in Anangu schools only. In 1984, the first group of ten students commenced study at Ernabella where a lecturer was based to provide day-to-day teaching. Students visited Adelaide for specialised workshops. In 1988 the programme was extended with part-time staff and students based in other Pitjantjatjara communities.

The AnTEP programme is based on a bicultural approach with a negotiated curriculum and competency-based student progression. Most of the students have been women and the programme recognises that they have other commitments related to child-rearing, traditional cultural activities and other family and community obligations. A basic assumption of the programme is 'that the expressed desire of Anangu to maintain the integrity of their culture within the wider context of Australian society must be acknowledged and supported' (ASTEC, 1983: 13). As some students found that other obligations made it difficult to complete the Associate Diploma and Diploma levels, a Stage 1 Certificate was introduced for those who completed the equivalent to one year of full-time study (Gale, 1996: 18).

By the end of 2004, 37 students had graduated from the programme with a Diploma of Education (Anangu Education), and 18 with what is now a Bachelor of Teaching (Anangu Education). Of the 18 graduates in the Bachelor award, 9 are currently teaching in Anangu schools.

While AnTEP graduates are employed in Anangu schools, some have continued to experience frustration as teachers trained in traditional

Western teacher training institutions often find it hard to adjust to the particular needs of Anangu schools and to accept the different roles of Anangu teachers. These problems have been exacerbated by changes in language policy. An English-only policy introduced into Anangu schools in 1992 was in conflict with the philosophy of the AnTEP programme and undermined one of the strengths which the Anangu teachers brought to the educational programme of the schools. 'The greatest skill AnTEP students develop – Pitjantjatjara literacy – is not utilised because English is the prevailing language of instruction' (Macgill, 1999: 123). The influence of these Anangu teachers has been a major factor in the revision of this policy in recent years. This now allows local community schools to once again incorporate the teaching of Pitjantjatjara literacy in the school curriculum.

Pitjantjatjara/Yankunytjatjara Education Committee (PYEC)

During the 1970s and early 1980s the government schools on Anangu communities were administered by the Department of Education, Training and Employment (DETE) from distant Adelaide. A costly infrastructure of well-equipped school buildings and teacher housing was constructed on communities and a high teacher: student ratio was maintained in the schools. In 1988 there were 24 Department of Education non-Anangu employees at Ernabella alone. In 1987 an Anangu Schools Resource Centre was established at Ernabella to produce materials for the bilingual programme: teacher-linguists were employed and computers and desktop publishing facilities were provided (Macgill, 1999: 121).

As Pitjantjatjara and Yankunytjatjara people had gained more political power through their Community Councils and the Pitjantjatjara Council, some questioned the continuing control of education on their lands by the Department of Education based in Adelaide. In response to this, in 1987 operational and policy control of education was transferred to Anangu people through the Anangu Pitjantjatjara (AP), the land-holding body, established under the Pitjantjatjara Land Rights Acts (1981). A sub-committee, the Pitjantjatjara/Yankunytjatjara Education Committee (PYEC) was established. This committee consists of representatives from each community and Anangu schools. They are to make or approve all decisions relating to education in Anangu schools. The schools' representatives include the Anangu Coordinator from each school, a person who works alongside the school principal. PYEC has a full-time director selected by Anangu and an elected chairperson.

A small agency of the Department for Education, Training and Employment (DETE), Anangu Education Services (AES), was established to support PYEC. Staff of AES, in consultation with Anangu people have prepared a curriculum document, Skills for Self Determination, to guide and assist PYEC and school staff in implementing strategies which will enable Anangu students to develop skills necessary to successfully manage their communities in the future (AES, 1996). The PYEC determined the following priorities:

1. We want to control our own education.
2. We want to have equal opportunity for education.
3. We want more Anangu teachers in our schools.
4. We want the best teachers in our schools.
5. We want all students to do well in education.
6. We want to have education which respects our ways.

As younger Anangu people interacted with non-Anangu professionals such as lawyers, anthropologists, accountants and doctors through their political organisations, some expressed concern that none of their young people had reached educational standards which enabled them to enter training for these professions. They blamed the bilingual approach for the low standards of English literacy and for thus limiting educational opportunities for Anangu young people. Macgill (1999: 122) suggests that there was coercion from some teachers who had been opposed to the use of indigenous languages in the schools. Arguments and statistics which purported to show that the falling literacy rates were the result of the bilingual policy were put to a newly elected PYEC, which decided to introduce a policy of English language only in Anangu schools in 1992.

This policy was based on a method known as Two-Way Schooling, which recognised the existence of two domains and assumed that learning would be more effective if the teaching of Anangu and non-Anangu ways takes place in different areas (Hughes, 1990). The policy was controversial as some older Anangu expressed concern that an English-only policy in the schools weakened their culture. In 1992 Aboriginal Education Workers and Anangu teachers were instructed that they were expected to use English whenever possible, while non-Anangu teachers were to use English only. Some non-Anangu teachers have expressed concern that this has restricted their interaction with students and their families. Soon after the implementation of the policy, the Director of the PYEC wrote to AnTEP students to let them know that 'when you graduate as teachers from AnTEP, we want you only to speak in English to your students'. This directive was given despite the fact that the local dialects remain as the first languages in daily use in the communities. The policy is in contradiction to the basic philosophy of the AnTEP programme and has led to continuous frustration and conflict between PYEC and Anangu teachers, although the appointment of an AnTEP graduate as Director of PYEC since 2000 has enabled resolution of some of the frustration and conflict. As noted earlier, the language policy has been revised since 2002. According to a former Lecturer in the AnTEP programme who has researched the professional development of Anangu teachers:

> There are now nine Anangu teachers working in schools and from this critical mass has emerged a strong body of teachers who are interested and competent in taking a more active role in determining the business of education in their schools and across the Anangu Pitjantjatjara Lands. (Atkinson, 2000: 33)

Conclusion

At the beginning of the twentieth century the Pitjantjatjara/Yankunytjatjara people lived in comparative isolation with little disruption to their traditional life which had been developed and maintained over many millennia. Children were enculturated into the hunting and gathering mode of existence through traditional methods of learning. Over the course of the century, these societies have faced severe challenges to their traditional structures. During the middle decades of the century they retained much of their traditional knowledge and practices while accommodating to opportunities to engage in employment on cattle stations and in schooling, training and employment in the buffer situation of Ernabella Mission where their culture and language were respected.

The closing decades of the last century saw a sharp increase in population, changes in local demography, with the influx of other Aboriginal people to the region, the emergence of welfare dependency, the development of political and bureaucratic structures, and a significant increase of the non-Aboriginal population in the region to service educational, health, administrative, policing, store, power and other needs. People who moved almost constantly across their country on foot now reside in communities to access these services, and movement between communities is by motor vehicle. Traditional values endure at the same time as people seek to engage in the modern economic and political structures: this gives rise to considerable tension. They are caught between a desire to maintain their identity with their language and culture, and an ambition to involve themselves more fully in mainstream Australian society, an ambition made difficult because of both physical and cultural distance. As an earlier writer observed, the Pitjantjatjara people are a people 'in between' two vastly different worlds (Hilliard, 1968). All those involved in Anangu education find themselves struggling with the paradoxes, pressures and frustration inherent in this situation.

The Anangu people are not alone as indigenous people in Australia in this struggle. A 1999 review of indigenous education in the Northern Territory established that while there is 'a widespread desire amongst indigenous people for improvements in the education of their children,' there is 'unequivocal evidence of deteriorating outcomes from an already unacceptably low base, linked to a range of issues, led primarily by poor attendance which has become an educational crisis' (Collins, 1999: 1). At that same time, the Northern Territory government withdrew funding for bilingual programmes in indigenous schools. The report noted that the failure of the bilingual programme was not due to its underlying philosophy but to incompetent pedagogy and unsound teaching practice. It recommended that 'the NT should be leading Australia in policy development and pedagogy for the use of original Australian languages in education' (Collins, 1999: 127).

A community worker, encouraged by Yolngu people of north-east Arnhem Land in the Northern Territory, has focused attention on social problems arising from a lack of good communication and the need for education to be based on sensitivity to local values and concepts rather than to be shaped totally by the dominant culture.

> For Yolngu to learn, however, they need special education to first fill in the 'missing links' or 'gaps' in their 'conceptual universe' regarding the contemporary world. Only when their conceptual universe is adjusted and well-developed in relation to this 'new world' knowledge will they be ready for more 'normal' skill-based education programmes. (Trudgen, 2000: 234)

Noel Pearson, an Aboriginal historian, lawyer and community leader in north Queensland, has drawn attention to the crisis in his communities, where despite government funding of health and education programmes there is a decrease in life expectancy, increase in illiteracy and 'our society is in a terrible state of dysfunction' (Pearson, 2000: 1). He blames the overwhelming imposition of the welfare state for this state of affairs: motivation for education has been undermined by dependency.

These experiences in other regions of Australia reinforce the picture of contemporary Anangu life and the problems which face educators in Anangu schools. Some of the factors acting against achievement of educational aims are beyond the control of schools and educational authorities. They involve major social issues which require comprehensive analysis and attention on the part of government departments, Aboriginal organisations and local communities. This experience reinforces Krätli and Dyer's argument (this volume) that the 'lack of relevance of the standard curriculum appears to be an inadequate explanation for low enrolment and high drop out rates.'

Although the general picture of Anangu education is rather negative, there are a few signs of hope, such as the commitment of AnTEP trained Anangu teachers to make a difference in the schools, the progress made by some students in the Wiltja programme, through which by the end of 2003, 19 students had completed the Year 12 South Australian Certificate of Education (SACE), and the success of two students from Indulkana Anangu School in completing Year 12 while studying in their local school, with assistance from the Open Access College (*The Advertiser*, 30/11/00).

Further positive developments in Anangu education will depend partly on effectively tackling the wider social issues, so that the prospect of future employment will motivate improved school attendance. Within the Anangu education sector, further attention needs to be given to resolving issues relating to the importance of language in learning, so that the Pitjantjatjara and Yankunytjatjara dialects can again receive fuller recognition within the schooling system, thus enabling students to master concepts confidently in their own language and then progress to understanding concepts in the second language of English.

References

AES (1996) *Skills for Self Determination,* Anangu Education Services, Department of Education, Training and Employment, Adelaide.

ASTEC (1983) 'Submission for Re-accreditation of the Associate Diploma in Education (Anangu) and the Diploma of Teaching (Anangu Education)' Vol. 1, Sept 1983. Adelaide: South Australian College of Advanced Education.

Atkinson, K. (2000) Holding the Knowledge: Partnerships for Professional Development on the Anangu Pitjantjatjara Lands, Unpublished M.Ed. Thesis, University of South Australia.

Barnes, N. (2000) *Munyi's Daughter: a Spirited Brumby.* Adelaide: Seaview Press.

Collins, B. (1999) *Learning Lessons: an Independent Review of Indigenous Education in the Northern Territory.* Darwin: Northern Territory Department of Education.

Coombs, H.G. (1977) *The Pitjantjatjara Aborigines: a Strategy for Survival.* Centre for Resource and Environmental Studies Working Paper. Canberra: Australian National University.

Desert Schools, Volume 2, Research Report (1996) Adelaide: The Department of Employment, Education, Training and Youth Affairs.

Duguid, C. (1972) *Doctor and the Aborigines.* Adelaide: Rigby.

Edwards, W.H. (1969) 'Experience in the Use of the Vernacular as an Introductory Medium of Instruction'. In S.S. Dunn and C.M. Tatz, (eds) *Aborigines and Education.* Melbourne: Sun Books.

—— (1992) 'Patterns of Aboriginal Residence in the North-west of South Australia'. *Journal of the Anthropological Society of South Australia* 30 (1&2): 2–32.

—— (2004). *An Introduction to Aboriginal Societies,* 2nd edn. Wentworth Falls (NSW): Social Science Press.

Elkin, A.P. (1956) *The Australian Aborigines: How to Understand Them.* Sydney: Angus and Robertson.

Ernabella News Letter (October 1944) Melbourne: Board of Missions of the Presbyterian Church of Australia.

Ernabella News Letter (October 1945) Melbourne: Board of Missions of the Presbyterian Church of Australia.

Ernabella News Letter. (March 1952) Melbourne: Board of Missions of the Presbyterian Church of Australia.

Folds, R. (1987) *Whitefella School: Education and Aboriginal Resistance.* Sydney: Allen and Unwin.

French-Kennedy, T. (1982) *Anangu Teacher Education – a Survey of Community Needs*. Underdale: South Australian College of Advanced Education.

Gale, M-A. (1996). 'AnTEP Comes of Age'. *The Australian Journal of Indigenous Education* 24 (1): 17–25.

Hilliard, W. (1968) *The People in Between: the Pitjantjatjara People of Ernabella*. London: Hodder and Stoughton.

Hughes, P. (1990) *Two-way Schooling, Discussion Paper*. Adelaide: Aboriginal Education Curriculum Unit.

Ilyatjari, N. (1988) 'Traditional Aboriginal Education'. In Hyams, B. et al. (eds) *Learning and Other Things: Sources for a Social History of Education in South Australia*. Adelaide: South Australian Government Press.

Macgill, B. (1999). 'Ernabella Mission School: a Critique'. *Journal of the Anthropological Society of South Australia,* 32 (December): 110–38.

One People (1961) Canberra: Department of Territories.

Pearson, N. (2000) 'The Light on the Hill'. Ben Chifley Memorial Lecture, Bathurst Panthers Leagues Club, Saturday, 12 August 2000.

Penny, H.H. (1976) *The Training of Pitjantjatjara Aborigines for Greater Teaching Responsibilities in South Australian Tribal Aboriginal Schools: Report and Recommendation to the Education Department of South Australia*. Adelaide: Education Department of South Australia.

Stanner, W. (1984) 'Religion, Totemism and Symbolism'. In: Charlesworth, M. et al. (eds) *Religion in Aboriginal Australia*. Brisbane: University of Queensland Press.

The Advertiser, Adelaide, 16.6.1999.

The Advertiser, Adelaide, 30.11.2000.

Trudgen, R. (2000) *Why Warriors Lie Down and Die: Towards an Understanding of Why Aboriginal People of Arnhem Land Face the Greatest Crisis in Health and Education Since European Contact*. Darwin: Aboriginal Resource and Development Services Inc.

Trudinger, R.M. (1942) 'An Educational Experiment'. *The Messenger*, Presbyterian Church of Victoria, 17 July 1942.

CHAPTER 6

CULTURAL ROOTS OF POVERTY?
EDUCATION AND PASTORAL LIVELIHOOD IN
TURKANA AND KARAMOJA

Saverio Krätli

Introduction

*T*urkana, northern Kenya, food relief distribution centre of Lokiriama, dry season, early afternoon. The sun is holding in the rare shaded spots the handful of officers attached to the centre. In the open, a small group of women have just arrived after a two-day march across the hills, from a locality called Loteere ('the border'), where their families are camping with the livestock. The women are taking two young children to the dispensary, as they come out again, they hold in their hands four small pockets of paper, each one containing a few pills with the name and use of the drug written on the outside by the health officer: there are pills for malaria, 'chest problems', cold and stomachache. A card of instructions, scribbled quickly and hardly readable, accompanies the drugs but it does not refer to them. The officer at the dispensary has picked up the wrong card. However, it doesn't matter: none of the women can read, nor can anybody else at their camp. 'We just take one or two tablets – they tell us – and usually we get better'.

Beyond its apparent triviality, this episode raises some important issues. What makes a relatively well educated health officer think that it is alright to give different drugs, only identifiable by written names and accompanied by written instructions, to people who cannot read? Turkana pastoral people, who spend most of their life outdoors in remote areas, can make sophisticated distinctions when it comes to medicinal plants. Is there a link between the opacity of the process through which drugs are administered and the surprising failure of otherwise therapeutically sophisticated users to differentiate within the category of 'drugs'? More generally, in which way do mainstream cultural attitudes towards pastoralism interlock with service provision to pastoral people? How do they affect the potential of service provision for knowledge exchange, social integration and poverty reduction?

This chapter looks at the relationship between culture and poverty, focusing on the role of education in cultural reproduction and as a vehicle for the myths and negative clichés that constitute the public image of mobile pastoralism. The review of the literature on education provision to pastoralists (Krätli, 2001a; Krätli with Dyer, this volume) concluded that it is time to look at education with a broader vision and reconceptualise it as a discourse. This chapter is an attempt to apply such a perspective. The popular view that attributes the poverty of pastoral people to their 'traditional' culture and their lack of modern education is questioned. In as much as the increasing insecurity of pastoral livelihood has cultural roots (besides and not instead of, the political and economic ones), these roots are more fruitfully studied by turning our attention to mainstream culture (within each respective country) rather than just focusing on pastoral people. Similarly, the link between pastoral poverty and education concerns (via development policies and practices) the nature of the education undergone by pastoralists' fellow citizens (with their consequent 'knowledge' of pastoralism), at least as much as it concerns the knowledge gap about the 'outside world' amongst the pastoralists themselves.

The chapter is based on data collected in Turkana (Kenya) and Karamoja (Uganda) between January and May 2001, during a study funded under the World Bank's Learning and Research Program on Culture and Poverty (LRPCP). The Program's objective was to learn about how attention to aspects of culture can help reduce poverty and improve the well-being of the poor. Defining culture is controversial ground, but broadly speaking, current debate is stretched across two perspectives. At one extreme, 'culture' is used to mean a stable and pervasive set of characteristics, shared within social groups and varying across them. This idea of culture as a 'thing', largely dismissed within anthropology since the 1980s (Clifford, 1986) is resilient within the mainstream domain of development (e.g. the final report on the UN decade for culture and development, UNESCO, 1995). At the other extreme, 'cultures' are understood as dynamic processes of negotiation of meaning rather than stable and coherent systems. Scholars from this perspective underline that the objectification of culture masks the political dimension of any definition of 'culture'. They show how such definitions are constantly used in political strategies as a resource for establishing or challenging processes of domination and marginalisation, for example by setting the terms of the relations between marginalised groups and mainstream society (Street, 1993; Wright, 1998). LRPCP defined 'culture' as: 'the particular shared values, beliefs, knowledge, skills and practices that underpin behaviour by members of a social group at a particular point in time (with potentially good and bad effects on processes of poverty reduction)'.

The analytical strategy followed in this chapter is to hold onto this definition as an operative tool but, in light of the recent reflections in anthropology, acknowledge its political dimension. As a result, the popular and institutional descriptions of the 'pastoral culture' in Kenya and Uganda are here treated as, themselves, an expression of culture, 'shared values, beliefs, knowledge, skills and practices' particular to the social group who defines, rather than to the group who is defined. The aim of this approach is not to rectify a 'false' representation offering a 'true' one, but rather to shed some light on the *consequences* of pastoralists' public image (with regard to development). Following the definition of culture adopted by LRPCP, I ask how such a culture 'underpin[s] behaviour by members of [both the defining and the defined] social group[s] at a particular point in time (with potentially good and bad effects on processes of poverty reduction)'.

'Pastoralism' is far from a straightforward concept. Over the years, definition has proved a difficult and controversial issue (Bonte and Galaty, 1991; Chang and Koster, 1994). In as much as attempts to define pastoral societies have centred on some 'essential feature' (nomadism, subsistence economy depending on livestock, egalitarian social organisation, etc.) the same theoretical problems are also met in defining 'culture'. Today's social reality in pastoral areas presents huge variations across many intertwining levels. Research on 'pastoralists' can look, for example, at people who have few animals, if any, and live in slums on the outskirts of a town; or at people who control substantial capitals in livestock, labour and social networks (including powerful connections in town), but spend most of their time in the bush. Whilst mainstream representations of pastoral 'culture' overlook such distinctions, they always emphasise its 'traditional' character. This study sought a sample group that would enable comparison of the public image of pastoral 'culture' with people who, within the same representational framework, are considered very 'traditional' and conservative: in Turkana, groups living in the Loima Hills; in Karamoja, the Jie of Panjangara sub-county and the Matheniko-Karimojong.

The public (both popular and institutional) image of pastoralism was investigated across a wide range of sources, including textbooks, newspapers, development reports and policy documents, local administrators, health officers and education personnel.

The findings suggest that, in as much as the increasing insecurity of pastoral livelihood has cultural roots (besides and not instead of, the political and economic ones), those roots are more fruitfully searched in mainstream cultures (within each respective country) rather than in the cultures of pastoral people. Similarly, the link between education and poverty of pastoral people concerns (via development policies and practices) the nature of the education undergone by pastoralists' fellow citizens, and their consequent 'knowledge' of pastoralism, at least as much as it concerns the knowledge gap about the 'outside world' amongst the pastoralists themselves.

Pastoral Culture in Mainstream Culture

Seen from Kampala and Nairobi, Karamoja and Turkana are little more than words evoking a wild place of violence and lawlessness. The people I met every day, taxi drivers, shopkeepers, hotel staff, sometimes did not even know where exactly those places were. Those who did know were surprised to hear that I was heading there: why on earth? Wasn't I afraid to be killed? With all the nice places to visit in the country ... As I offered a more positive view, people who had been chirpy became quiet, perplexed, even suspicious. But what do people in town really know about pastoralists, and where does their knowledge come from?

A Social Studies textbook series for Primary 1–7 (widely used in Karamoja), in more than 500 pages of text, mentions Karimojong once, in a few lines on Maasai and Turkana. One chapter on grassland environments (Book 7) shows pictures of cattle herds in Great Britain and Australia, and describes the life of Twareg and Fulani. The basic needs of 'Ugandan people' are compared to those of Twareg on two opposed pages, one showing a drawing of a rural house made of bricks, with an iron sheet roof and glass in the windows; the other featuring the photograph of a group of Twareg having tea sitting on the ground in front of a tent. The text underlines that, while crops cannot be grown where the Twareg live, 'in Uganda we are able to grow most of the basic food we eat'. A four-page chapter on cattle-keeping in Uganda, in Book 4, describes the Ankole-Masaka ranching scheme, but makes no mention of Karamoja (National Curriculum Development Centre, 1995).

When the Karimojong actually receive some attention in the national curriculum, they are represented as the opposite of modernisation, always in a light that makes them appear like something from the past. In a geography textbook for the Higher School Certificate (National Curriculum Development Centre, 1989), the front cover could hardly be more emblematic. A picture of the Kariba dam in Zimbabwe catches the eye in the foreground while, covering the whole page, one can just make out in the background a faded aerial photo of a Karimojong homestead. The composition is clearly suggestive of a world of the past fading away under the 'bold impression' of modernisation. This book contains almost a whole page on nomadism and half a page on the pastoral system in Uganda. These are part of a 35 page chapter on agriculture that features, among the rest, two pages on the 'case study of Court Lodge Farm in the south-east of England'. In the few paragraphs about pastoral nomads, we learn that they are among 'the less developed societies'. They cause land degradation and social problems by burning the grass and keeping unreasonably large herds – a habit that forces them, 'in their search for new grazing ... to encroach on arable land causing conflict with the farmers'. The recommended solution to these problems is 'to get the nomads to settle ... if they did it, disputes over grazing would be avoided and the quality of the herds would be improved' (pp. 61, 41). In the short reference to the Karimojong, we are informed on page 73 that 'the growing of crops is left to the women, whilst the men lavish attention on their animals' and that 'Karimojong can live quite independently from crops as they drink the blood and milk of their cattle on a daily basis'.

Old clichés do not just inhabit out-of-date school textbooks. They also characterise the way pastoralists are represented in the media. Over the last few years, Karamoja has become increasingly popular with the media, but pastoralists are usually represented with uncritical generalisation. All violence in Karamoja is described as 'traditional' and all Karimojong appear to be 'warriors', depicted as threatening-looking armed men with picture captions like 'Karimojong vigilante cuddles his gun' or 'Karimojong warrior caresses his rifle' (*The Monitor*, 9 August 1999, 16 April 2000). Caricatured images of pastoral 'traditional culture' are used to provide, by contrast, the English-reading urban middle class and the rapidly swelling ranks of unemployed literate young people, with confidence about their own modernity and 'development'. Following an incident between a nurse and one of her patients at Matany hospital, an article entitled 'Karimojong harass nurses' (note the plural), in a national newspaper, read:

> Many things have been said about the Karimojong – raiding, cattle rustling, killing innocent people, highway thuggery [sic] – but one thing had been left out – the biting of nurses [...] the authorities were forced to close the hospital for three days in the hope that that would change Karimojong attitude towards hospital staff [...] Medical staff in Matany hospital are often unjustly criticized and sometimes tormented by Karimojong, because of the Karimojong's ignorance and inability to differentiate between good and bad. (*The Monitor*, 18 August 1999)

More recently, the creation of a Karamoja Data Centre seems to have fed on the old myths with incredible ease. Described as 'the Government's focal point for the coordination of all data and information generation activities in the Karamoja region', the project was put on line in June 2002, with assistance from the Italian Co-operation (KDC, 2004). Although pastoralism is by far the most important economic activity in the region, in order to find some information about it one has to follow a link to 'Agriculture', then scroll down, after the list of agricultural issues. In the overview of problems affecting agriculture we read: 'Conservative Culture of the Karimojong ... the Karimojong practise a ritual attachment to cattle, sometimes referred to as a "cattle complex"'. This colonial cliché (Herskovits, 1926) dismissed by serious scholarship at least since the 1980s is just repeated online in the years 2000 as if it was a cutting edge analytical tool. The section on 'Culture' is even more outrageous:

> ... the Karimojong believe that God has given all cattle to them. The implication of that is that God has not given any cattle to their neighboring tribes. Unfortunately, the Pokot in Kenya, living right on the Karamoja border of Uganda,

have the same conviction about their divine right to cattle. As a result, both tribes are continually trying to re-collect 'their' cattle. Violence occasionally results. It is no wonder that our guide calls Karamoja 'the Wild West'. (KDC, 2004)

Even in pastoral districts, negative images of pastoralism are a common place, repeated almost identically like a lesson learned by heart. Although a few government officers and education personnel offered alternative views, the majority of those interviewed 'played safe', sticking to the mainstream representation whether they believed it or not (indeed, some of the interviewees appeared quite happy to have such views challenged). When mainstream representation was seriously supported, the most common arguments used concerned pastoralists' low levels of living conditions, particularly with regard to health, education, and gender balance. Some of these arguments at the core of pastoralists' public image are described below.

Non-disaggregated district figures for low life expectancy and high infant and maternal mortality (usually based on data gathered in settlements and including a majority of non-pastoral population), are used as hard evidence of the inadequacy of 'pastoral culture'. Pastoralists' 'traditional practices', equated with backwardness, are pointed out as the main cause of disease. Pastoralists are depicted as ignorant and dirty as they, supposedly, neglect to send their children to school, don't wash regularly, and refrain from using latrines. A recent needs assessment states that 'most people in Karamoja hardly bathe throughout the dry season [whilst] the scarcity of water has apparently turned mud into a valuable item of beauty and toiletry'. Meanwhile, 'people do not have any disgust for human excreta and as a result freely dispose of it all over the place' (Okech, 2000: 11). Although according to the people interviewed during the assessment, the main cause of death was malaria, 'traditional attitudes' towards hygienic practices are said to have a 'major impact' on health. Even the editors of a Participatory Poverty Assessment carried out in Kotido cannot report on local hygiene practices without distancing themselves from them: 'women in Jie are said to take about seven days before bathing after delivery. This seems to be unhygienic but it is their culture' (UPPAP, 1999: 36).

Hygiene is seen as a measure of modernisation and a lot of basic health education is about becoming 'modern' as much as is about getting rid of bacteria. 'Modern' norms of personal hygiene are among the first things that children are taught at school and the topic is commonly loaded with moral value and status: good children wash their hands, only lesser children do not. A primary school Science textbook used in Moroto lists 'wash hands' and 'pray' amongst 'the important jobs we must do before and after eating' (National Curriculum Development Centre, n/d: 3). On the other hand, ignorance is officially represented as a 'dirt' in which 'diseases' like poverty and violence proliferate. Within such a framework, often schooling takes the role of a 'cleaning' process: from superstitions, from traditional beliefs, from one's past in the darkness of a primitive life. A teacher in a rural school in Moroto district described his work and the mission of education as 'fighting the community ... in their beliefs and behaviours'.

Finally, the popular discourse about pastoralists portrays women and children as subjugated creatures. Children are thought to be neglected by mothers who don't wash them enough and fathers who exploit their labour but do not refrain from risking their life for starvation or disease, instead of selling a few goats to buy food or drugs. Women are supposed to be forced by greedy fathers into early marriages with lusty old men, raped by the 'warriors', overloaded with work and enslaved by husbands who sleep and drink all day long and only care about cows. These images are presented in contrast with 'modern' and 'enlightened' attitudes about children's rights and gender issues, as prescribed by international development policies and mirrored by national governments. Without denying the reality or the gravity of specific cases of abuse in pastoral districts (not unlike everywhere else), the point made here is that there is a common narrative that 'explains' them by force of logic as 'pastoral traditional culture', a mere corollary to the supposedly primitive state of pastoral society, that requires no further analysis. Women's supposed subjugation also comes in handy to explain why their voice is largely missing from the findings: 'the traditional authority system in Karamoja ... keeps women in the background when it comes to speaking to outsiders' (Okech, 2000: 16).

On the same basis, pastoralism is often associated with supposedly underdeveloped living conditions following from its 'irrational mode of production'. This results in part from culturally limited livelihood analysis indicators as, for example, the emphasis on income, ill-fitted to represent an economic reality in which security is largely based on non-monetary and intangible assets. The number of permanent houses, corrugated tin-roofs or latrines, says little about living conditions in which shelters need to be mobile, while low population density, mobility and burning hot sun make the idea of a latrine, where all the excreta of the neighbourhood are collected in the same bug-infested smelly hole in the ground, something of an exotic perversion.

In this section, I have attempted to reconstruct the public image of pastoralism in mainstream society in Uganda and Kenya. To summarise, pastoralism is either represented through a deforming lens or removed altogether from the social, cultural and economic landscape of the country. Pastoralists are supposed to be backward and unproductive, locked into a way of life that belongs to the past, their 'culture' frozen in tradition and impermeable to innovation and development, ultimately separate from, and alien to, 'modern' society. In general, such a representation of pastoral culture is in continuity with the bi-polar opposition modern *vs* traditional, developed in many social theories of the last two centuries (Wolf, 1982). Pastoral 'culture' (often pastoral development too) is conceptualised around a variety of hierarchical and teleological pairs: nature *vs* civilisation; nomadic *vs* sedentary; traditional *vs* modern; ignorance *vs* education; irrational *vs* rational; dirty *vs* clean; women's subjugation *vs* gender sensitivity; group tyranny *vs* individual freedom; poverty *vs* prosperity; chaos *vs* order; barbarian violence *vs* Christian values; etc. In a way that recalls the implicit denial of the coequality of the 'observer' in typological time (Fabian, 1983), pastoral culture is depicted as a world apart and assigned to a different 'time', in which its whole and only destiny is to upgrade to the present of modern society. Given this framework, there is no conceptual ground on which pastoral and modern society can meet and communicate. The only legitimate relationship between pastoralists and mainstream society is 'change' – not, however, intended as creative adjustment to globalising forces but, in a narrower and limiting sense, as imitation or as a guided procedure through a pre-ordained sequence of steps.

These ideas are by no means particular to Kenya or Uganda. They have a long tradition, both within pastoral development discourse (Anderson, 1999) and, in various forms and degrees, within the academic work on pastoralism, where they were largely dismissed by scholars only during the late 1980s and 1990s (Bonte and Galaty, 1991; Fratkin et al., 1994). On the other hand, a wealth of research has been accumulated over the last two decades, revealing much more complex dimensions of pastoralism. While the myth of pastoralism as a mode of production preceding the development of agriculture has been clearly disproved (Khazanov, 1984; Sadr, 1991; Smith, 1992), the rationality and productive efficiency of extensive pastoral systems has been widely recognised (Dahl and Hjort, 1976; Scott, 1984; Johnston and Anderson, 1988; Galaty and Johnson, 1990; Muhereza and Ocan, 1994; Scoones, 1995a; Little and Leslie, 1999; Niamir-Fuller, 1999; UNDP-GDI, 2003). With particular reference to Uganda and Kenya, when the full range of costs and benefits are calculated (in Table 6.1 in Scoones, 1995b) the figures show that returns per hectare and per animal are higher in 'traditional' systems than in ranching. The popular association of pastoralism and women's low status has been questioned in favour of a more critical approach that recognises the complex dynamics of gender relations, among pastoralists as among other groups. Anthropological research points out that imbalance in gender relations and a supremacy of livestock production over other domains of pastoral livelihood (for example material culture), far from being 'traditional', has appeared as a result of decades of male-centred development policies (Hodgson, 2000). The straightforward association of pastoralism with poverty has also been problematised, questioning the adequacy of standard indicators. Turkana, for example, distinguish several dimensions of poverty and prosperity, focusing on three parameters: labour (a large family with a balanced proportion of boys and girls), livestock and social network, the latter being considered the most stable of all the assets (Broch-Due and Anderson, 1999).

Finally, several studies have questioned the association of 'traditional' pastoralism with poor health conditions or children's malnutrition. Comparative research has found that nutritional status and health conditions in pastoral areas are worse in settlements than among nomadic groups (Nathan and Fratkin, 1996; Campbell et al., 1999; Shell-Duncan and Obiero, 2000). Pastoralists' dietary practices, once considered to heighten the risk of malnutrition and infections in children, are now thought to produce the opposite results (Gray, 1998). High incidence of health problems amongst pastoralists are attributed to forced concentrations of people in settlements lacking adequate health care services (Sheik-Mohamed and Velema, 1999). Scholars have also pointed out that the infant mortality rate is not a reliable parameter with populations where accurate accounting of age is not routine (Wiley and Pike, 1998).

The data collected in Turkana and Karimojong camps during the fieldwork for the present study support these perspectives. The next section offers some examples with regard to gender, children, health and resistance to change (for a complete description see Krätli, 2001b).

In the Field

In both Turkana and Karamoja, I worked with a research assistant. The dry season's herd management involved an extremely busy schedule and dangerous grazing conditions: cattle herders were leaving the camp at about five in the morning, returning only after nine at night. They were taking their animals to graze in Uganda and back every day, under security precautions that made me think of a commando operation. Such a situation made it infeasible for the herders to take us with them without putting everybody's life at risk. Consequently, during the month we stayed in Loteere we spent quite a lot of time in camps or at water points, and most of it with women.

Women stopped by for a chat in small groups or alone. They asked us a lot of questions, curious about life in Nairobi and in Europe, trying to understand what kind of people we were, to travel so far away from friends and families. How could our children be fed in the meanwhile? Were we not worried about leaving our wives alone for so long? Did we take some special medication to inhibit sexual desire, or simply 'endure the suffering'? In the camp, they were in charge of almost everything, from shelter building to food storing, from water fetching to milking. By and large, far from subjugated, they appeared independent, assertive and confident.

Once, three young 'warriors' who were paying us a visit asked us to offer them some tea. We agreed but told them that they would have had to make it themselves. The two more senior men tried to make the youngest boil the water, but he politely resisted, arguing that as his girlfriend was in the camp, there was no way he could afford to been seen 'doing the work of a woman'.

His fellows turned then to us but we also refused, on the grounds that we should not be seen cooking for younger men. They called a girl of about fifteen who was passing by and asked her boldly to make a fire and boil some water for tea. Not at all impressed, she shortly told them that she had other things to do and walked away. After some minutes of further unfruitful negotiation with us and their young colleague, the two senior herders tried again, this time with a little girl of about eight. She stopped, looked at us with curiosity, then suggested that we could have boiled the water ourselves as we normally did. We made it clear that the tea was not for us but for the young men. Only after they had openly admitted that they did not want to be seen cooking in the camp, and asked the girl again politely, as a favour, did she finally agree.

Also with regard to children's living conditions, we saw nothing to confirm the popular narrative in town, but rather the contrary. In the camp, sick children were kept at home to rest, even when this meant that their mothers had to defend their decision with the other women in the face of the heavy labour requirements of the dry season. In all the families we visited, work never seemed to be a burden for the children, no more than going to school can be in a 'modern' context. Some like it more than others, some look forward to going and others fake illness in order to be kept at home for the day. During the fieldwork in a camp in Karamoja, a boy of about seven screamed at the top of his voice every time his older brother tried to force him to help with the flock. The scene, repeated day after day with increasing drama, usually ended with the grandfather intervening in favour of the child, telling the shepherd to stop making him cry. On the other hand, the shepherd complained that the child was only a problem when the old man was in the camp (as he always took his side) otherwise the child made no fuss. Another child in the camp, cousin of the reluctant boy and just slightly younger than him, often asked to go out with the flock but was told to wait for fear that, not knowing yet the whereabouts of the camp well enough, he could have got lost. The two boys were good friends. When in the camp, they spent most of their time around the old man doing little jobs or playing 'herding', using small stones as livestock. They ate with the old man in the evening and slept by the fire next to him.

We only witnessed one punishment, in Turkana, when a boy of about six lost a lamb in the bush. The child had a mild eye infection and the father asked him about it, then, without raising his voice, asked what happened to the lamb and whether it was his fault. As the boy admitted his responsibility, the father used a long twig to whip him, more symbolically than for real, once on the top of each shoulder and once on the top of the head, then he dismissed him. The child, mortified, shed some silent tears sitting away from the fire. Some ten minutes later the father called him again, asked him to bring some water, then sat on his heels and carefully washed the boy's face and his eyes, talking to him with a calm voice. In this case, we happened to watch an intelligent man under no special pressure, acting within a very united and rather happy family. Pastoralists themselves, interviewed on the topic, say that punishments should be good and reasonable but can sometimes be inappropriate or even cruel, depending on who deals with it. As in other societies – some pointed out with an admirably open mind – some parents do better than others.

As much as it could have been visible to non-specialists, the people in Loteere seemed strong and healthy. Every evening, as they finished their tasks, the children spent hours singing together or running around playing often until midnight (waking up again at five). Although we did not investigate health conditions, people assumed that we had drugs and came to ask for help when they had a health problem. In almost two months, coming into contact with about 400 people, we were asked to give medical help 15 times, mostly for headaches and eye infections. Because of the season and the distance from the water, out in the camps we saw no mosquitoes at all, although there were plenty by the permanent settlements.

In Loteere, when the wind blows you literally get covered in dust. Your hair, your eyes, your ears fill up with dust, and it is in your food and your water. People didn't seem to mind dust any more than the English mind rain. However, on average they seemed to wash themselves as often as they could. Women did not bathe in public but men did, and despite the dry season we saw men bathing at water points almost daily. Of course, when water is scarce, washing comes low on the list of priorities. As a general rule, at least in the dry season, one's cleanliness tends to be inversely proportional to the amount of clothes one wears, as it takes three times more water to wash a shirt than to have a bath. Fully dressed in 'modern' clothes, in a few days we were the filthiest people around the camp.

We also saw that people avoided defecating close to the camp. When very small children freed themselves within the area of the camp, whoever was in charge (even if this was another child) carefully collected the stool, together with the soil underneath, and disposed of both outside of the camp. A leaf was used, or two pieces of wood, or the underneath of a hide sandal, in order to avoid touching the faeces with the hands.

The Loima Hills are considered one of the last strongholds of Turkana 'traditions' but we found no trace of blind conservatism. In fact, people said that for decades they had been asking for better communications, more water security, a school, and a dispensary. They appeared curious and open to useful innovation.

On a rainy day, my assistant wore his raincoat bought in Nairobi for our trip, two sizes too small (he had forgotten to try it on) and with a pattern probably designed for a city girl. The way he looked could hardly have been more distant from the front-page image of Turkana warriorhood. Nevertheless, the garment immediately became very popular amongst the herders who had never seen one and were tantalized by the possibility of keeping dry under the rain. In the following days we had several orders: 'the next time you come, bring many of these and you will sell them all!' people told us.

Somebody asked for tarpaulin, and was ready to give a cow for it. A stock of second-hand lorry tarpaulins from a closed down World Food Programme operation had recently been sold in northern Uganda and one or two had ended up in herders' hands. The news had spread that they were good as a quick-to-set-up rainproof shelter, particularly handy during the frequent movements at the beginning of the wet season. Could we send one from Nairobi? Commercial outdoor equipment of any kind or quality is impossible to find in pastoral areas, despite their largely nomadic population. As pastoralists' needs are deduced from the modernisation paradigm, their priorities are supposed to be building latrines and tin-roofed brick-houses. Equally (or more) 'modern' opportunities to provide better protection from the weather while living outdoors are excluded in principle. When, back in Moroto, I mentioned the request for tarpaulin to an officer at the District, the man laughed and said that I should have persuaded 'my friend' (who turned out to be his cousin) to get iron sheets rather than tarpaulin, and build a 'proper' house.

Over the years, pastoralism has become an increasingly complex social reality and it is now more difficult than ever to separate pastoralists from the wider society. As pastoral social capital networks expand, they include increasing numbers of people from the 'outside world': educated people in town, soldiers and police, government officers, politicians from as far as Kampala and Nairobi, nuns and priests of various denominations, NGO staff and even expatriates. Moreover, if the pastoral homestead relies on educated members in times of crisis, family members in town rely on the rural family for cheap labour and capital. When the need for a lump sum suddenly arises in urban households (for continuing education, building a house, or buying a vehicle), the money is likely to come from the sale of livestock from the family herd. When, as is often the case, town people have their own livestock, the animals are looked after by the children of their relatives in the bush. Within the labour intensive African household routine (even in town), educated Turkana and Karimojong women can have a salaried job, and all their children can go to school, because dependent young rural relatives act as baby-sitters and do most of the housework. In a way, part of the pastoral family 'co-operative' now lives permanently in town, just as other sections live periodically in the kraal and the village. However, whilst the relationships between village and kraal are clear and well established, those between bush and town appear still imprecise and unstable. Although almost everybody lives somewhere in between the two supposedly separated worlds, 'in between' there is a grey zone, a cultural and conceptual void, a place that is not on the map.

'Culture' and Development

Negative images of pastoralism (and pastoralists) did not appear to be isolated prejudices but, rather, part of a broad representation pervading major dimensions of the mainstream culture, including key institutional contexts such as the education system. Issues associated with pastoral areas are interpreted through such a 'cultural' filter, from labour requirements to livestock management, from health to gender relations, from service provision to political representation, from economic performance to security. In this way, the mainstream representation of pastoralism plays a silent but pervasive role in informing policy-making and project implementation concerning pastoral people.

A recent needs assessment for a project of functional adult literacy in Karamoja, produced by the Ugandan government in collaboration with the World Food Programme (Okech, 2000), offers a good example of this process. As the assessment concerns Karamoja, the report begins with an introductory overview of the 'problems of pastoral people', repeating all the clichés of pastoralists' public image. On those bases, the report explains that at the root of food insecurity in the region is *traditional* gender inequality among *pastoral* people: 'men look after the cattle, leaving the women to do all the domestic work, including all crop cultivation and even construction of huts. Obviously, the women are too overburdened with work to produce enough food during the short single rainy season' (Okech, 2000: 9). However, further on the reader is informed that most of the data were collected among the settled farming communities in Labwor county (the most fertile county in Karamoja) and more than 60 percent of the respondents described themselves as 'non-pastoralist'. Puzzled by the high proportion of 'non-pastoral' respondents, the authors suggest that 'people of Karamoja are indeed becoming increasingly an agricultural people [...they] see a better future for themselves in agriculture: that is where they have plans to improve their lives. Information received from the WFP showed that a number of households, even in the cattle-keeping parts of the two districts, do not even own cattle' (Okech, 2000: 19). That the absence of livestock might represent an undesired situation rather than a choice for the better is not even considered. As the public image of pastoralism is conducive to an understanding of pastoral development as alternative to and away from a pastoral livelihood, decreasing numbers of livestock and increasing dependence on agriculture tend to be seen uncritically, always as a positive change. In fact, even in Labwor county the number of cattle owned by a family was considered, at the time of the assessment, to be the first indicator of livelihood security, with people lamenting having become increasingly vulnerable over the last 20 years, due to the loss of cattle which has forced them to depend exclusively on agriculture (UPPAP, 1999: 11, 16).

Figure 6.1 *Primary school classroom entirely built from corrugated tin sheets in Moroto district, Uganda. The sign above the entrance says: 'Welcome to P. 2'.*

The misinterpretation of data as in Okech (2000) is not unusual. Government administrators and education personnel in pastoral districts quote the increase in pastoralists' demand for primary education over the last decade as a straightforward indicator of development. However, interviews with Turkana and Karimojong parents from pastoral households suggested a rather different explanation. Although formal education strategies vary from family to family, the choice of sending children to school seems to be most commonly linked to an overall increase in vulnerability. Families without strong and balanced assets (labour and livestock), or without a large network of potential supporters (social capital), are at great risk of being ruined by unpredictable crisis such as human or animal diseases, raids or drought. It is these families, above all, that increasingly turn to education, as a last resort, in the hope of gaining access to resources outside the pastoral sector. Moreover, decades of 'sensitisation' and pro-schooling propaganda conspire to generate the feeling that by sending a child to school one is pleasing the government and other powerful networks. Pastoralists greatly value any membership in a powerful network. People have learned that priests, nuns and development workers can often be moved into sponsoring a 'poor' child throughout school. But that is not the only advantage. Sending a child to school opens an avenue to contact powerful outsiders on a common ground. Some kind of support is likely to come (in fact, perceived as almost due) establishing a bond between those outsiders and the family, that may last for years. Although modern education is typically offered to individuals as a one-way ticket for leaving pastoralism, pastoral households in Turkana and Karamoja seem to use it as a family chance to remain *within* the pastoral economy, by accessing external resources (money and social capital).

The emphasis on 'traditional culture' draws the attention away from a history of inappropriate policies and great imbalance in service provision to pastoralists, in comparison with other productive groups. Long-lasting programmes of 'food relief' in pastoral areas are seen as evidence that pastoralism is economically unviable, an idea that fits well within the public representation of pastoralism as a primitive stage of development with inherently irrational production strategies. However, to the extent to which food relief is an injection of external resources into the pastoral economy in order to keep it going during periods of difficulty, it is no different from what, in other contexts, would be called subsidy (cf. WTO, 2000). In 2000, the European Union was paying out an average subsidy of US$17,000 to every full-time farmer in the Union (*The Economist*, 3 March 2001). According to a recent forecast, government handouts to farmers within OECD in 2002 will exceed Africa's GDP (Economist Intelligence Unit, 2001: 97). Subsidies to modern farmers are considered an economic intervention: why are subsidies to pastoralists seen as a humanitarian affair?

Statistically, a high rate of child mortality in pastoral districts contributes towards exceptionally low life expectancy figures. The received wisdom on the problem blames lack of prevention and irrational 'cultural' practices due to women's lack of education. Such a view contributes to a policy-making culture that blindly promotes sedentarisation and urbanisation on ideological bases (thus no matter how unplanned and chaotic), using education itself (seen as a crucial step forward against child mortality), as an instrument for sedentarisation. All this overlooks that major recorded killers are usually those that spread exponentially with the increase of population density in poor settlements: TB, malaria and dysentery. In town, people receive costly health care but are said to perform better than pastoralists because of modern culture and education; pastoralists in the bush receive little more than

Figure 6.2 *Ata Lokiru (mother of Lokiru) in Loteere, Turkana district, Kenya.*

sermons on prevention but are said to perform less well because of backwardness and ignorance.

It is true that there are risks and consequences, even serious ones, that are considered acceptable (although not desirable) by the pastoralists in the bush in present conditions. However, the same applies to mainstream society. Catching a disease by drinking dirty water or eating with (visibly) dirty hands is seen as the effect of ignorance and irrationality, but to take a similar risk by living in a highly polluted area or sleeping with a cat on the pillow, both common behaviours in 'modern' settings, is not. McDonalds, the fast food restaurant mega-chain, makes a point of serving all its food and drinks in protective containers for the hygiene-aware modern consumer's peace of mind. But the hands you must use to eat your cheeseburger and fries rub up against bus seats, underground escalators, toilet handles, and money all day. Who checks how many of these modern consumers wash their hands before happily wrapping their filthy fingers around their cheeseburgers? In both Uganda and Kenya, several thousands of people die every year in road accidents, a large proportion of which could be prevented by serious regulation and law enforcement on road safety. Why is a preventable death by dysentery in Karamoja or Turkana considered the result of a backward culture, while a preventable death on a road in the rest of the country is not? Who is to decide which kind of death or health hazard is acceptable and which is not, and on what basis? Behind the pseudo-scientific arguments and the claim for universality, behaviours and practices of pastoral people are rejected and condemned largely on a matter of taste, on the grounds of cultural preferences within 'modern' society.

This section has looked at the way the definition of pastoral culture underpins behaviour by members of the defining group in relation to the defined group. I have shown how pastoral 'culture' is used as an interface and explanatory framework for the understanding of pastoral livelihood and formal interactions between pastoralists and 'modern' society, as for example in the context of service provision or, more generally, of pastoral development. In this role, the public image of pastoralism fosters counterproductive generalisations that only widen social division. The relationship between pastoral peoples and mainstream society is conditioned in a way that leaves no common conceptual grounds, muting the actual situations of integration and exchange. Moreover, the public representation of pastoral 'culture' lends itself, as an explanatory framework, to the legitimisation of inappropriate policies and practices, as well as condoning their reproduction in a void of empirical data or despite them. Instead of increasing pastoralists' chances to expand their own experience of the 'global' world, make up their own mind about it, understand it in their own way, choose what they like and leave what they don't, pastoral development is all too often narrowed down to catechising people into old ideologies of modernisation, where experience is mediated, where understanding means to believe, and where all the choices are already made. Altogether, the way pastoral culture is defined within mainstream culture appears to be a major obstacle to pastoral development and poverty reduction in the pastoral sector.

Conclusions

At the beginning of the chapter, with reference to the dispensary episode in Turkana, I asked what makes an educated health officer think it is alright to give written information on drugs to people who cannot read. The analysis presented in this chapter allows us now to make sense of such behaviour. Firstly, the hierarchical and teleological relation established within the representation of pastoral culture *vs* modern culture implies that, in any interaction, people associated with the first category must adapt to those associated with the second, this very adaptation being understood as development. Secondly, the moral value attached to literacy and modern education, framing the relation between literacy and 'illiteracy' as a battle between good and evil, leaves little room for negotiation or compromise. If illiteracy is *wrong*, pastoral people who desert school education are wrongdoers, who should face the consequences of their behaviour: if they cannot read, it is their problem. Thirdly, the definition of 'pastoral' people through a set of static characteristics also upholds the definition of 'modern' people, by opposition. The static opposition of pastoral and modern inhibits creative behaviour and entrepreneurship, excluding otherwise obvious alternatives to written language, such as for example the use of symbols (objects, drawings). Similarly, 'drugs' and medicinal plants can share no conceptual ground. Supposed to replace people's knowledge rather than interact with it, and locked into the inadequate code of written language, unsurprisingly the new information associated with the administration of drugs remains opaque to people's understanding and experience.

As noted in the introduction, it is not a matter of replacing false with true representations. In Griselda Pollock's words, 'what is at stake in representations is not so much a matter of what is shown as it is who is authorized to look at whom with what effects' (Pollock, 1994: 15). The current representation of pastoralism within mainstream society generates numerous problems without bringing any real benefit. Poverty eradication amongst pastoral groups seems conditional upon a radical review of the way pastoralism and pastoralists are represented within mainstream culture. There is a need for fresh and specific data on the logic of pastoral systems, targeting systematically each of the arguments used to assert pastoralism's structural inadequacy: economic inefficiency, health and nutritional deficit, gender imbalance, etc. At the same time, it is necessary to work to ensure that rich and up-to-date information finds its way into the education system (from primary to higher education), the public administration and the press.

Finally, there is a need to create systematic and structured opportunities for pastoral people (not conditional on literacy and schooling) to increase their experience of the outside world and their capability to challenge effectively the public image of pastoralism and articulate their own view in non-pastoral settings. Outside agencies have an essential role to play in strengthening local capacity while, on the other hand, helping to create the conditions for a change of perspective at the institutional level in the national framework. Seriously committed governments and local administrations will have an excellent opportunity to be instrumental in facilitating and accelerating the process as well as building on its results.

References

Anderson, D. (1999) 'Rehabilitation, Resettlement and Restocking. Ideology and Practice in Pastoral Development'. In: D.M. Anderson and V. Broch-Due (eds) *The Poor Are Not Us. Poverty and Pastoralism*. London: James Currey.

Bonte, P. and J.G. Galaty (1991) 'Introduction'. In: J.G. Galaty and P. Bonte (eds) *Herders, Warriors and Traders. Pastoralism in Africa*. Boulder, CO/San Francisco/Oxford: Westview Press.

Broch-Due, V. and D.M. Anderson (1999) 'Poverty and the Pastoralist: Deconstructing Myths, Reconstructing Realities'. In: D.M. Anderson. and V. Broch-Due (eds) *The Poor Are Not Us. Poverty and Pastoralism*. London: James Currey.

Campbell, B.C., P.W. Leslie, M. Little, J.M. Brainard and M.A. De Luca (1999) 'Settled Turkana'. In: M.L. Little and P.W. Leslie (eds) *Turkana Herders of the Dry Savanna. Ecology and Biobehavioral Response of Nomads to an Uncertain Environment*. New York: Oxford University Press.

Chang, C. and H.D. Koster (eds) (1994) *Pastoralists at the Periphery. Herders in a Capitalist World*. Tucson/London: The University of Arizona Press.

Clifford, J. (1986) 'Introduction: Partial Truths'. In: J. Clifford and G. Marcus (eds) *Writing Culture: the Poetics and Politics of Ethnography*. Berkeley: University of California Press.

Dahl, G. and A. Hjort (1976) *Having Herds: Pastoral Herd Growth and Household Economy*. Stockholm: Department of Anthropology, University of Stockholm.

Economist Intelligence Unit (2001) 'The World in Figures: Industries'. In: *The World in 2002*. London: The Economist Newspaper Limited.

Fabian, J. (1983) *The Time and the Other: How Anthropology Makes Its Objects*. New York: Colombia University Press.

Fratkin, E., E. Abella Roth and K.A. Galvin (1994) 'Introduction'. In: E. Fratkin, K.A. Galvin and E. Abella Roth (eds) *African Pastoralist Systems: an Integrated Approach*. Boulder, CO: Lynne Rienner Publishers.

Galaty, J.C. and D. Johnson (eds) (1990) *The World of Pastoralism: Herding Systems in Comparative Perspective*. New York and London: Guilford Press and Belhaven Press.

Gray, S. (1998) 'Butterfat Feeding in Early Infancy in African Populations: New Hypotheses'. *American Journal of Human Biology* 10 (2): 163–78.

Herskovits, M. (1926) 'The Cattle Complex in East Africa'. *American Anthropologist* 28: 230–72; 361–80; 494–528; 630–64.

Hodgson, D. (ed.) (2000) *Rethinking Pastoralism in Africa.* London: James Currey.

Johnston, D.H. and D.M. Anderson (eds) (1988) *The Ecology of Survival: Case Studies from Northeast African History.* London and Boulder CO: Lester Crook Academic Publishing and Westview Press.

KDC (2004) 'Karamoja Data Centre': < www.karamojadata.org >. Master Plan for the Development of Karamoja, Minister of State for Karamoja Affairs and Italian Co-operation.

Khazanov, A.M. (1984) *Nomads and the Outside World.* Cambridge: Cambridge University Press.

Krätli, S. (2001a) *Education Provision to Nomadic Pastoralists.* IDS Working Paper 126. Brighton: Institute of Development Studies.

———— (2001b) *Educating Nomadic Herders Out of Poverty? Culture, Education and Pastoral Livelihood in Turkana and Karamoja.* A study within the World Bank's Learning and Research Program on Culture and Poverty. Brighton: Institute of Development Studies.

Little, M.L. and P.W. Leslie (eds) (1999) *Turkana Herders of the Dry Savanna. Ecology and Biobehavioral Response of Nomads to an Uncertain Environment.* New York: Oxford University Press.

Muhereza, F.E. and C.E. Ocan (1994) *Report of the Second CBR Pastoralism Workshop on: Pastoralism and Crisis in Karamoja.* Workshop report No. 4. Kampala: Centre for Basic Research.

Nathan, M.A. and E.M. Fratkin (1996) 'Sedentism and Child Health among Rendille Pastoralists of Northern Kenya'. *Social Science and Medicine* 43 (4): 503–15.

National Curriculum Development Centre, Ministry of Education, Uganda, n/d. *Basic Primary Science Course for Uganda,* Harlow: Longman Group U.K.

National Curriculum Development Centre, Ministry of Education, Uganda (1989) *Potentials, Prospects and Problems in World Development* (ed. Henry Lubwama) London: Macmillian Publishers.

National Curriculum Development Centre, Ministry of Education, Uganda, (1995) *Primary Social Studies for Uganda. Pupil Book,* London: Macmillian Publishers.

Niamir-Fuller, M. (ed.) (1999) *Managing Mobility in African Drylands. The Legitimisation of Transhumance.* London: IT Publications.

Okech, A. (2000) *Needs Assessment Survey for Functional Adult Literacy in Karamoja Uganda 2000.* Prepared by Anthony Okech, for the Ministry of Gender, Labour and Social Development, in collaboration with the World Food Programme in Uganda, Kampala.

Pollock, G. (1994) 'Feminism/Foucauld-Surveillance/Sexuality'. In: N.M. Bryson, A. Holly and K. Moxey (eds) *Visual Culture: Images and Interpretations.* Hanover/London: Wesleyan University Press.

Sadr, K. (1991) *The Development of Nomadism in Ancient Northeast Africa.* Philadelphia: University of Pennsylvania Press.

Scoones, I. (ed.) (1995a) *Living with Uncertainty: New Directions in Pastoral Development in Africa.* London: Intermediate Technology Publications Ltd.

―――― (1995b) 'New Directions in Pastoral Development in Africa'. In: I. Scoones (ed.). *Living with Uncertainty: New Directions in Pastoral Development in Africa*. London: Intermediate Technology Publications Ltd.

Scott, E.J. (ed.) (1984) *Life before the Drought*. Boston: Allen and Unwin Press.

Sheik-Mohamed, A. and J.P. Velema (1999) 'Where Health Care has no Access: the Nomadic Populations of Sub-Saharan Africa'. *Tropical Medicine & International Health* 4 (10): 695–707.

Shell-Duncan, B. and W.O. Obiero (2000) 'Child Nutrition in the Transition from Nomadic Pastoralism to Settled Lifestyles: Individual, Household, and Community-level Factors'. *American Journal of Physical Anthropology* 113 (2): 183–200.

Smith, A. (1992) *Pastoralism in Africa: Origins and Development Ecology*. London: Christopher Hurst.

Street, B. (1993) 'Culture is a Verb: Anthropological Aspects of Language and Cultural Process'. In: D. Graddol, L. Thompson and M. Byram (eds), *Language and Culture*. Clevedon: British Association for Applied Linguistics in association with Multilingual Matters.

UNDP-GDI (2003) *Pastoralism and Mobility in the Drylands*. GDI Challenge Paper Series, The Global Drylands Imperative (GDI), Drylands Development Centre, Nairobi, Kenya: United Nations Development Programme.

UNESCO (1995) *Our Creative Diversity. Report of the World Commission on Culture and Diversity*. Paris: UNESCO.

UPPAP (1999) *Kotido District Report*, prepared by Kotido PRA Team, Uganda Participatory Poverty Assessment Project, Kampala.

Wiley, A.S. and I.L. Pike (1998) 'An Alternative Method for Assessing Early Mortality in Contemporary Populations'. *American Journal of Physical Anthropology* 107 (3): 315–30.

Wolf, E. (1982) *Europe and the People without History*. Berkeley: University of California Press.

Wright, S. (1998) 'Politicisation of "culture"'. *Anthropology in Action* 5 (1–2): 3–10.

WTO (2000) 'Agreement on Subsidies and Countervailing Measures' http://www.wto.org/english/tratop_e/scm_e/subs_e.htm#Subsidies

CHAPTER 7

BEDOUIN ARABS IN ISRAEL: EDUCATION, POLITICAL CONTROL AND SOCIAL CHANGE

Ismael Abu-Saad

Introduction

Providing nomadic people with formal education is a major challenge, and as Krätli and Dyer state in the opening chapter of this volume, governmental policies and programmes for the education of pastoralists can be grouped around two major rationales: (1) the full development of the human being as an individual; and (2) the integration of nomadic groups into the wider national context, often on the unilateral terms of the government, and in a manner that appreciably increases governmental control over them. As such, much of the education provision, policy making and planning for nomadic peoples by national authorities has ended up, to varying degrees, creating a threat to their livelihood. The rationales for providing nomads with education, according to Krätli and Dyer (this volume), 'are neither neutral, nor dispassionate; rather, they reflect a set of ideologies about education, nomads and development, and tensions ... emerge when these ideologies reveal themselves to be unshared'.

In this chapter, I will discuss the development of the Israeli state educational system for the Negev Bedouin Arabs, a traditionally semi-nomadic people living in southern Israel, and the governmental rationale for and methods of providing education to this community. While nomadic peoples have often been viewed as 'outsiders' by modern nation-states, whose primary concern has been to control them, this phenomenon has been exacerbated in the case of the Bedouin in Israel, since they are a part of the non-Jewish, Palestinian Arab minority in what came to be defined as a Jewish state. Thus, I will explore the important role of conflicting ideologies in relation to land use and service provision in this particular case study.

Background

The Negev Bedouin are among the indigenous Palestinian Arabs who remained in Israel after 1948 and are today a minority group of Israeli citizens. They have inhabited the Negev desert since the fifth century C.E. (Maddrell, 1990), and were traditionally organised into nomadic or semi-nomadic tribes who derived their livelihood from raising sheep, goats and camels. The majority of the population lived on semi-arid lands and also engaged in seasonal agriculture (Abu-Saad, 2000; Shimoni, 1947). Prior to 1948, estimates of the Bedouin Arab population in the Negev ranged from 65,000 to 90,000 (Falah, 1989; Maddrell, 1990). During the course and aftermath of the 1948 war, the vast majority of the Negev Bedouin fled or were expelled, and became refugees in the surrounding Arab countries/territories (i.e. the Gaza Strip, the West Bank, Jordan, etc.). Thus, by 1952, only about 11,000 remained in the Negev (Falah, 1989; Marx, 1967; Masalha, 1997) (Fig. 7.1).

From the time of its establishment, the Israeli state developed an extensive system for controlling the Arab minority, to which the widely dispersed, semi-nomadic Bedouin population created a special challenge (Lustick, 1980; McDowall, 1989; Seliktar, 1984). This system resulted in the exclusion of the Arab minority, both individually and collectively, from political power, the full benefits of citizenship, and social and economic welfare (Ghanem, 1998; Lustick, 1980; McDowall, 1989; Yiftachel, 1999). One of the primary techniques employed by the Israeli government to control the Arab minority was to make it as dependent as possible upon the majority Jewish economic infrastructure (Seliktar, 1984). This was accomplished through massive confiscation of Arab lands (Gavison, 1999; Lustick, 1980; McDowall, 1989). The loss of so much agricultural land and the displacement of so many communities made Arabs acutely dependent upon the Jewish sector for employment.

Among the Negev Bedouin, the government used land confiscation as a tool for sedentarising the population by depriving them both of the ability to cultivate their lands and the freedom to move around with their herds (Lustick, 1980). Twelve of the 19 tribes were removed from their lands, and the whole population was confined to a specially-designated Restricted Area (*seig*) in the northeastern Negev, which represented only ten percent of the territory they controlled before 1948 (Falah, 1989; Lustick, 1980; Marx, 1967). Furthermore, they were placed under a military administration until 1966. When the military administration over Arabs in Israel was lifted, the vast majority of the Bedouin sought employment in the Jewish sector, primarily as unskilled labourers (Abu Saad, 1991).

Government efforts to consolidate its control over the Bedouin and further reduce their land base were intensified in the late 1960s and early 1970s when it began implementing plans to resettle the entire Negev Bedouin population into seven urban-style towns with no economic

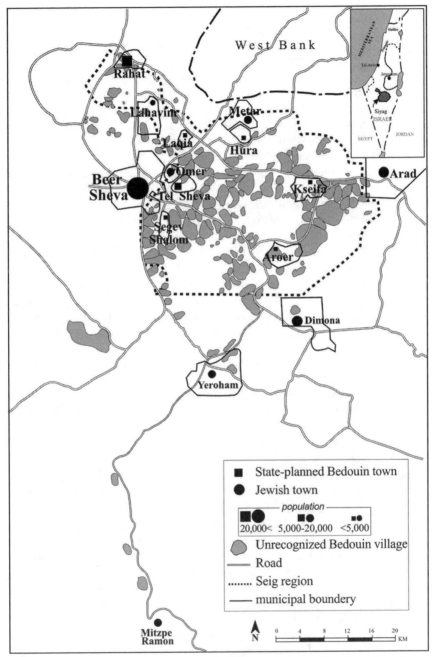

Figure 7.1 Bedouin Settlements in the Negev Desert in Southern Israel.

infrastructure of their own. The Bedouin who move into the towns (onto quarter-acre lots) are completely dependent upon integration into the larger Israeli economy for their livelihoods, since they no longer have land for producing or supplementing their income from animal husbandry and agriculture. While they have access to modern services (such as running water, electricity, telephones, local schools and health clinics, etc.), the associated expenses of these services, local taxes and mortgage payments further increased their dependence upon a regular cash income. Sixty-five percent of the population in these towns lives beneath the poverty line (Hayton, 1998; Ghanem, 1998).

While the planned towns provide basic services, they lack internal and external public transportation networks, active industrial and commercial centres, sewage systems, libraries, sports and cultural centres, and (with the exception of the largest town) banks and post offices, all of which are found in Jewish towns of comparable size (Abu-Saad and Lithwick, 2000; Lithwick, 2000). Due to the socio-cultural inappropriateness of the urbanised settlement plan, and the complete economic dependency it created among the towns' inhabitants, resettlement in the towns has been resisted by the Bedouin who are in a position to do so. As of 1999, only slightly over half of the 120,000 Negev Bedouin lived in the planned towns (most of whom were removed from their traditional lands in 1948–1952), while the remainder continued to live in unrecognised villages and extended family groupings (Abu-Saad and Lithwick, 2000; Statistical Yearbook of the Negev Bedouin, 1999).

Most of the Bedouin living outside the government-planned towns traditionally lived in the 'Restricted Area' to which the government moved the whole Bedouin population in the 1950s, and they are still living on their own lands. Since they have refused to move to the planned towns, they face a different set of pressures and increased levels of legal and political vulnerability. As residents of unplanned (i.e. unauthorised and illegal) settlements, they are denied services such as paved roads, electricity (and in many cases running water), rubbish disposal, telephones, community health facilities, etc. They are also denied licences for building any sort of permanent housing. All housing forms (except for tents, which can be served evacuation orders) are considered illegal, and are subject to heavy fines and demolition proceedings (Maddrell, 1990). Despite these pressures, Bedouin remain on the lands traditionally owned by them (but considered as state lands by the government) to prevent their *de facto*, as well as their *de jure*, confiscation. Most of these Bedouin depend on the traditional occupations of herding and agriculture to supplement or provide their incomes, but this is also restricted by the government through limitations on herd sizes and grazing areas, and most recently, the aerial spraying of wheat and barley crops with herbicides (for a detailed report, see Ibrahim, 2004). Thus, very few of the Bedouin living outside the planned towns can subsist entirely on the traditional sources of livelihood, and must also seek out paid employment in the larger Israeli economy.

In spite of the government's stated aim of 'improving and modernising' the lives of the Negev Bedouin through its resettlement programme, the Negev Bedouin community has the lowest socio-economic status of any group of Israeli citizens (Lithwick, 2000). Compared to the Israeli average, they have twice as many children and only approximately half the monthly income. The average Bedouin family size is 8-10 persons, and 54 percent of the community is under the age of 14 (Statistical Yearbook of the Negev Bedouin, 1999). Their annual birth rate is 5 percent (Statistical Abstract of Israel, 1996), which is one of the highest in the world. The unemployment rate among Negev Bedouin is estimated to be 55 percent of the total workforce, of whom 30 percent are men and 80 percent of women (Shapira and Hellerman, 1998). Those Bedouin who are employed are concentrated in low-status, low-paying occupations such as construction, driving and unskilled labour (Maddrell, 1990; Shapira and Hellerman, 1998).

Development of the Education System

Education has become a basic prerequisite for the Bedouin's successful adaptation to the changes they have undergone, given their need for partial or complete integration into the Israeli economy for their subsistence. The formal Western-style school system represents a new organisation for the Bedouin Arabs in southern Israel. Traditionally, most of Bedouin education was not formalised, but rather acquired through observation and participation in the process of day-to-day life. There was no defined curriculum to be acquired, nor were there any unnecessary drills. Instead, the informal system of education they developed was very efficient in preparing Bedouin youth for the life they were to lead as adults. For boys, this included animal husbandry, heavy agricultural tasks such as ploughing the land and harvesting crops, defence and raiding, hunting, dispute resolution, and oral history. For girls, informal education included cooking, childcare, household management, weaving, embroidery and sewing; lighter agricultural tasks – harvesting crops, taking care of the flock and other domesticated animals; collection, preparation and preservation of dairy and other food products; making household items such as tents, carpets, pillows, mattresses, and quilts; and oral history. Oral history was passed on, as were moral and religious values, through poets, respected elders and storytellers.

In addition to this broad-based informal education, there were limited opportunities available to boys for obtaining formal education. The most common of these were the traditional Muslim schools called Kuttab that usually functioned in a tent around the sheikh's residence. Modest fees were charged for attending these schools, and the services were not utilised by all, but rather by the boys whose labour could be spared and whose fathers/parents saw a value in formal education. Classes usually included about 20 boys, roughly between the ages of five and twelve, who were taught to memorise the whole Quran by sheer repetition. In addition, they learned reading, writing, and the precepts of Islam. The curriculum was primarily religious and moral in content, though later some arithmetic was added. The Kuttab teachers (called Khatib) were elderly males who were literate and known for their orthodox piety. The teachers lived as permanent guests of the tribe to which they were attached and would migrate along with the tribe. They usually lived in the guest section of the sheikh's tent where they were provided with food, shelter and coffee (Tibawi, 1956).

In addition to these traditional forms of education, a few Western-style schools were established in the Negev Desert during the period of colonial British rule from 1918–1948. These were boarding schools which used a standard Western curriculum including maths, science, reading, writing (in Arabic) and English. The vast majority of the Bedouin had no exposure to these schools, since usually only the sons of the tribal sheikhs had access to such educational opportunities (Berman, 1967; Tibawi, 1956).

The Bedouin's traditional forms of education were severely disrupted by the changes that occurred in the process and aftermath of the establishment of the state of Israel (e.g. radical reduction of Bedouin population, loss of lands, transfer to 'Restricted Area', and implementation of military administration). The formal schools were closed or rendered inaccessible when the Bedouin population was moved to the Restricted Area (Maddrell, 1990). In addition, the loss of land and restricted mobility greatly reduced

Figure 7.2 *Traditional Kuttab school.*

the viability of the informal education that had prepared Bedouin children to take on their adult roles in the work of herding and agriculture. Nor was the education provided in the Kuttab schools sufficient to prepare Bedouin youth for integration into the modern, industrialised Israeli labour market.

Under the new Israeli government, a law was passed in 1949 making education compulsory and mandating that every child receive free elementary schooling (from the ages of six to thirteen). The state was obliged to provide trained teachers, salaries, and facilities. It was also responsible for curricula (Abu-Saad, 1991; Al-Haj, 1995). However, the new Israeli institutions were busy with the absorption of Jewish immigrants, and thus, inevitably, schools for Arabs were not a priority (Maddrell, 1990). This was especially true for the relatively widely-dispersed Negev Bedouin population. From the perspective of the Israeli educational authorities, the Bedouin were seen as outsiders rather than an integral part of the society; and consequently, the educational services provided to them were very minimal (Swirski, 1990, 1999). For most of the Negev Bedouin tribes, a whole generation had no access to formal education (Maddrell, 1990). In addition, all Arab schools in Israel which had to be supplied with books in Arabic suffered from a constant lack of teaching materials and textbooks for the first two decades of Israeli rule. So even for the minority who did have access to schools, the quality of education they received was very poor (Swirski, 1999).

At the same time, there was little interest in the new Israeli schools among the Negev Bedouin tribes, many of which had received promises that they would be allowed to return to their lands and former way of life (Maddrell, 1990). In 1956, there were only 350 Bedouin students enrolled in schools, out of a population of 2,000 school-age children. By the end of the school year, only 220 students were still attending school (representing a 37 percent drop out rate within one year), and all of them were boys (Swirski, 1990; Visitz, 1957). During the period of the military administration, the students who wanted to obtain a high school education had to attend schools in the northern Arab villages because there were no high schools for Arabs in the Negev. It was only feasible for a few students to pursue this option because of the high cost and the difficulties in obtaining a permit to leave their area.

Thus, education basically suffered a regression for the Negev Bedouin during this period. Traditional education was either disrupted or lost its efficacy for preparing Bedouin children for adult life in their new context. The Israeli government was slow in establishing public schools for the Bedouin, and the Bedouin themselves initially showed very little interest in this new form of education, since its relevance was not immediately apparent to them.

After the military administration ended in 1966, several developments led to increased demands for formal education from the Bedouin community. First, as the Bedouin were more extensively exposed to modern Jewish society and became involved in its economy, the importance of formal education became more apparent to them. Second, they were able to have more contact with the Arab villages and towns in other parts of Israel, in which the educational system was better established. Furthermore, following the War of 1967, when the Negev Bedouin were able to visit their relatives who had gone to the West Bank and Gaza Strip for the first time since 1948, they found that many of their counterparts were educated and had become teachers, doctors, lawyers, and so on, while they, for the most part, had only had limited access to education, and the vast majority of them remained illiterate (Abu Saad, 1991). Since many women had also attended school in the Occupied Territories, intermarriage between these two previously separated segments of the Bedouin community resulted in educated women from the West Bank and Gaza Strip coming to live in the Negev (Abu Saad, 1997, 1998). These contacts had a tremendous impact on the dynamics of the Negev Bedouin community and led to them sending their children, both girls and boys, to school in greater numbers (Abu Saad, 1997, 1998).

As the demand for education grew, the Israeli government opened more schools and free education became more available to the Bedouin community. However, the value and viability of this education have been gravely affected by a number of policy considerations that have taken precedence over the goal of providing Bedouin students with the knowledge and skills they need to function adequately in the broader socio-economic context of Israeli society.

Politics, Segregation, and the State Educational System in Israel

The Israeli state educational system is subdivided into a Jewish system (which is itself divided into a number of subsystems, e.g. secular schools, religious schools, etc.), and an Arab system. These subdivisions give the system an appearance of educational pluralism, while in fact, the division of the schools into subsystems serves quite a different purpose. Each system contains different students, different teachers and different educational contents (Swirski, 1999). In the Israeli educational hierarchy, secular Jewish schools which primarily serve students of European or American origin (Ashkenazis) form the highest tier. The Arab system forms the bottom tier, with the Negev Bedouin schools ranking the lowest in that system. The schools in the higher tiers of the educational hierarchy (e.g. kibbutzim schools, secular schools serving affluent Ashkenazi communities) provide their students with 'high status knowledge' and 'cultural capital' that translate into better future socio-economic opportunities. Schools in the lower tiers of the educational hierarchy (e.g. schools for the Arab community) provide their students only with partial, restricted and elementary knowledge, which places a ceiling on their future socio-economic opportunities, and maintains current socio-economic inequalities

(Swirski, 1990, 1999). An examination of the structure of the educational system, from goals and curriculum to buildings, facilities and staff, reveals its considerable impact on keeping the Bedouin in their 'proper' place in the social, economic and political hierarchy.

Aims, Goals and Curriculum

The Bedouin schools are a part of the Arab educational system, which differs from the Jewish educational system/sub-systems at the level of aims, goals and curriculum. Despite the fact that Israeli society is heterogeneous, due not only to the existence of the Jewish and Arabic cultures, but also to the existence of a variety of Jewish groups who immigrated from different countries, its educational system has remained monocultural, rather than multicultural (Mar'i, 1978; Al-Haj, 1995). The aim of multicultural education is to equip people of one culture with the knowledge and skills needed to function in their own culture, as well as in other cultural settings within the same socio-political framework (Aikman, 1996; Mar'i, 1978). However, an examination of the educational hierarchy, teaching staff and curriculum in the Jewish educational system reveals a definite bias toward Western, European (Ashkenazi) culture over that of non-Western, North African and Middle Eastern (Mizrachi) Jewish culture. The curriculum in Jewish schools tends to overlook the culture, history and contributions of Mizrachi and other non-Western Jewish groups, and to largely ignore, or provide only minimal exposure to Arabic language and culture.

The same is true of Arab education in Israel. Despite the fact that Arabic is the medium of instruction in Arab schools, the Arab educational system does not represent, in the words of Freeland (1996: 182), an example of 'indigenous control over education and true interculturality'. The Arab educational system has been, and continues to be, directed by members of the Jewish majority and governed by a set of political criteria which Arabs have no say in formulating (Al Haj, 1995; Mar'i, 1978; Said, 1987; Swirski, 1999). The 1953 Law of State Education specified the following aims for education in Israel:

> to base education on the values of Jewish culture and the achievements of science, on love of the homeland and loyalty to the state and the Jewish people, on practice in agricultural work and handicraft, on pioneer training and on striving for a society built on freedom, equality, tolerance, mutual assistance, and love of mankind. (Mar'i, 1978: 50)

No parallel aims have ever been set forth for the education of Arabs in Israel, though some attempts were made by committees directed by Jewish educators in the 1970s and 1980s (Al-Haj, 1995). Instead, the general and specific curricular goals that have been developed for Arab education tend to blur rather than to enhance the formation of Arab identity. The overall aims of the educational system, as well as specific curricular goals, require Arabs to learn about Jewish values and culture, and the results of this are clearly seen in the government-sponsored curriculum for primary and secondary schools (Al-Haj, 1995; Mar'i 1978, 1985; Peres et al., 1970). Arab students are required to spend many class hours studying Jewish culture and history and the Hebrew language (and more in total than they spend on Arabic literature and history). However, the basic goal of Jewish studies in Arab education is not the development of cultural competence in Jewish Israeli society as much as to make Arabs understand and sympathise with Jewish/Zionist causes and to blur their own national identity in Israel (Al-Haj, 1995; Mar'i 1978 and 1985; Swirski, 1999).

In the 1970s, Peres et al. (1970: 151) criticised the curriculum imposed upon Arab schools by the Ministry of Education for attempting to instill patriotic sentiments in Arab students through the study of Jewish history, and pointed out the absurdity of the expectation that the 'Arab pupil ... serves the state not because the latter is important to him and fulfills his needs, but because it is important to the Jewish people'.

Conversely, little attention is given to Arab culture, especially its contemporary political concerns. Nor does it deal with the particular social, cultural and educational needs of Negev Bedouin as they are being transformed into an urbanised population within a modern, Westernised, hi-tech economy. This lack of emphasis on the contemporary social and political concerns of Arabs lowers the relevance of the educational experience for Arab students to the point of seriously estranging them from school (Brown, 1986; Mar'i, 1978).

In 1978, the late Arab educator and researcher, Sami Mar'i described the status of Arab education within the Israeli state school system in the following terms which, unfortunately, still provide an accurate description some 20 years later:

> Arab education is a victim of Israeli pluralism not only in that it is directed and managed by the majority, but it is also a tool by which the whole minority is manipulated. ... [It] is not only an example of the Israeli pluralism by which Arabs are denied power, it is also a means through which the lack of power can be maintained and perpetuated. Arab citizens are marginal, if not outsiders. ... The Arab Education Department is directed by members of the Jewish majority, and curricula are decided upon by the authorities with little, if any, participation of Arabs. Arab participation does not exceed writing or translating books and materials according to carefully specified guidelines, nor does it extend beyond implementing the majority's policies. (Mar'i, 1978: 180)

Reform efforts have repeatedly failed to bring about change, since none of the recommendations of the many committees appointed by the government to study or improve the Arab educational system have ever had any binding power (Al-Haj, 1995, 1996). To give some recent examples, during the Rabin government (1992–1996), the Education Minister was from a 'left-of-centre' political party. In 1994, he appointed a committee of leading Arab educators to develop a plan for restructuring and improving Arab education. The plan was submitted to the Minister in early 1996 and was never heard of again, either to be implemented, or to be used as a basis for further discussion, revision and work. In 1997, the subsequent Minister of Education (from a 'right-of-centre' political party) appointed an investigatory committee to study Bedouin Arab schools in the Negev and produce recommendations for improving their education. The report which was submitted to the Ministry of Education in 1998 (Katz, 1998) contained a five-year plan for improving the material and human resources of the schools, as well as the relevance of the curriculum and educational content. Again, the recommendations were neither accepted nor implemented by the Ministry of Education. In the administration elected in 1999, the Minister of Education is again from a 'left-of-centre' party. He appointed a loyal Bedouin party member to serve as his advisor for Bedouin education, whose only apparent function thus far has been to sign the letters saying, 'there are no funds for implementing these reforms in the current school year'.

Infrastructure and Staffing as Political Tools

In addition to problems with the aims, goals and curriculum of the educational system, the Bedouin schools have inadequate physical and human resources, both of which have been used as tools for furthering governmental policy objectives other than education. With regard to physical resources: facilities and equipment are insufficient, and in some cases, altogether lacking, especially in schools in the unrecognised villages. The schools located in the planned towns, which include elementary, middle and all secondary schools, are classified as permanent. Most, though not all, of these schools are housed in modern buildings and have basic amenities such as electricity and indoor plumbing; but they do not have sufficient laboratories, libraries, sports facilities or teaching materials. In addition, the schools are overcrowded since the developers have not kept up with population growth and increasing enrolment. According to the Katz's report (1998), which was submitted to the Minister in 1998, 730 new classrooms were needed during the next five school years in schools in the government-planned towns just to keep up with the growth in the number of students in the towns themselves. (The needs for the population in unrecognised settlements were left unspecified due to uncertainty over whether government policy would necessitate increased transportation services or more school buildings in unrecognised settlements.) As mentioned above, the Ministry of Education has not allocated funds for implementing this plan.

Twelve elementary schools are located in unrecognised settlements, the vast majority of which were established before the government built the seven planned towns. Since government policy later called for concentrating the whole Negev Bedouin population into these towns, the Ministry of Education classifies the schools dispersed throughout the areas of unauthorised settlement as 'temporary' (Statistical Yearbook of the Negev Bedouin, 1999). As such, these schools are not expanded, have substandard services and equipment, and are poorly maintained (Abu-Saad, 1997). They lack indoor plumbing, and were supplied with generator-powered electricity only in 1998 (despite the fact that many of the schools are near power lines) after a long struggle by the Bedouin community, which culminated in an Israeli High Court decision ordering the Ministry of Education to supply these schools with electricity (*Ha-Aretz*, 1998).

This situation is part of an official policy to encourage the Bedouin Arabs to move into the government-planned settlements (Personal interview with officials of the Ministry of Interior, March, 1980; Maddrell, 1990; Meir, 1986). An education official stated that:

> the government is reluctant to develop schools for temporary settlements because they want the Bedouin to move to permanent areas. The Bedouin tend to move when the schools are relocated. If they don't then the children simply don't go to school. (quoted in Maddrell, 1990: 16)

According to the law, the government is responsible for providing Bedouin children with education; however, it has subordinated this responsibility to its goal of concentrating the Bedouin Arab population in designated settlements. The educational infrastructure continues to be used for this purpose up to the present time. In the 1999–2000 school year,

Figure 7.3 Temporary Bedouin school, 2004.

approximately 6,000 Bedouin elementary, middle and high school students from unrecognised settlements are daily required to travel great distances (up to even 100 km one way) on overcrowded buses to attend school (Arbeli, 1999). A nine-year-old boy, who gets up at 5 a.m., walks 2 km to the bus stop, and then rides on the bus for an hour and a half (one-way), described some of the difficulties of his daily commuting to school:

> The most difficult time is the winter because our mother wakes us up when it is still dark outside. When it's very cold and raining, we rush as fast as we can to the bus stop, but if we're even a little bit late, the bus doesn't wait for us.

These policies continue to take their toll on student retention, especially for girls. Traditionally, females were restricted to the world of the extended family, and took responsibility for many aspects of the household economy (i.e. herding; milking and processing milk products; making animal hair and wool into carpets, tents, mattresses and pillows; harvesting crops; etc.). In addition, they were (and continue to be) considered the 'bearers of the family honour', and thus, their families preferred not to risk their reputations by allowing girls to travel alone and mix with males from other tribes (Abu-Saad et al., 1998; Maddrell, 1990). Therefore, there has been much more reluctance among the Bedouin over sending their daughters to school than over sending their sons to school, especially when schools are far away.

The staffing of the schools is also problematic on several levels. The first is that the hiring of teachers lies completely (at the elementary and intermediate school levels) or partially (at the high school level) in the hands of the Ministry of Education. Since this is a government office, any Arab who is 'blacklisted' by the security services for political activities that are unfavourably looked on is banned from obtaining employment in government agencies, including schools. An advisor from the security services participates with the Ministry of Education in hiring and firing school teachers. Thus, '... a young educated Arab can expect to get and keep a job as a teacher only by staying off the government's blacklist' (Lustick, 1980: 193–94). The refusal to give a teaching position because of security reasons is a widespread phenomenon in the Arab schools, even at the high school level where the local authority plays a major role in the process of hiring and firing teachers. Potential candidates for teaching positions are interviewed by a joint professional committee, which includes representatives of the local authority and the Ministry of Education. The list of candidates, which they select, is then sent to the Ministry of Education for final approval. Al-Haj (1995) found that the Ministry of Education rejected about 10 percent of the candidates approved by the professional committees. According to interviews with Arab mayors, usually the real, but unwritten, reason was 'security considerations'. The mayor of one Arab village described his experience:

Every year we send the list (of selected candidates) for approval to the Ministry of Education. But it is very often that some of the candidates are refused to be given a teaching permission. Then the negotiations start with officials of the Ministry of Education, who inform us, in most cases orally, that the refusal is not connected with them but with the security system. (Al-Haj, 1995: 170–71)

Research carried out by Sa'di (2003) in 2000 indicates that these practices are continuing in the vast majority of Arab communities in Israel. Again, the Ministry of Education's responsibility for providing the schools with qualified teachers comes second to other political considerations, such as the security system's mandate of hiring only teachers who, according to their criterion, are 'politically correct', (e.g. quiescent, uninvolved in Arab student movements or any other struggle for equal rights, etc.) (Al-Haj, 1995, 1996).

While professionally qualified teachers can be turned down for political reasons, the Bedouin schools suffer from a serious shortage of qualified teachers, with the Ministry of Education reporting that 23 percent of the teachers lack basic training and credentials (Melitz, 1994). According to the Report of the Investigatory Committee on the Bedouin educational system in the Negev (Katz, 1998), 978 new teachers needed to be trained and hired by 2002. In addition, approximately 50 percent of the teachers are not local, but come from Arab communities in the central and northern regions of Israel (Abu-Saad, 1997). These teachers are concentrated at the middle and high school levels, since teachers at these levels are required to have a B.A., and not simply a Teachers College education. Teachers from other parts of the country are hired because they have the appropriate qualifications, but this results in high rates of teacher turnover because they generally leave the Negev region as soon as teaching positions open up closer to their home communities.

These problems of curriculum, infrastructure and staffing have affected the capacity of the Negev Bedouin schools to retain and educate students. Approximately 40 percent of Negev Bedouin Arab children drop out of school before graduating from high school, compared with 16 percent and 25 percent in the Jewish and broader Arab sectors, respectively (Ministry of Education and Culture, 2004).

To compound the problem of high drop out rates in the Negev Bedouin schools, the success rates of children who do stay on to complete the twelfth grade tend to be very low. In the 2002–2003 academic year, only 26 percent of Negev Bedouin high school students passed the matriculation exams (compared to 52 percent and 36 percent in the Jewish and broader Arab sectors) a basic requirement for going on to higher education (Ministry of Education, 2004). There are approximately two university graduates per 1000, which is far below the Israeli national average of over 100 per 1,000 (Abu-Saad, 2000). Higher education is broadly recognised as an important tool, particularly for minority groups, for self-development and self-directed integration into the larger society. Despite the fact that faith in education has eroded to some extent in the recent past, it is still expected to play a pivotal role in development. Within education, higher education assumes great significance, for it is through higher education that a community produces the critical mass of 'leader' elements – the entrepreneurs, the intellectuals, the professionals, the managers and political leaders, that it needs for its social and economic development (Gunawardena, 1990). Furthermore, with regard to educational reform, many effective models of indigenous intercultural education have been developed by indigenous teachers' associations, indicating that the development of a core of educated people is a great asset to, and perhaps even a prerequisite for, the development of positive models of indigenous intercultural education and community educational involvement (Aikman, 1996; Freeland, 1996).

Thus, while it is clear that comprehensive change is needed at every level of the Bedouin educational system, higher education may well prove to be an important catalyst in initiating the process, since a community with more educational capital can unite and refuse to accept a substandard educational system, and will also possess the professional educational skills to create something better.

Conclusion

In this chapter, I have discussed the development of the education system for the Negev Bedouin Arabs in relation to their changing social, economic and political context. The Israeli government forcibly ended their semi-nomadic lifestyle and their involvement in pastoralism as a mode of production and a means of subsistence. To further restrict their control and use of land resources, the government made the provision of accessible modern educational services dependent upon their moving into or commuting to government-planned urban-style towns for the Bedouin. Due to the near complete disruption of their traditional pastoral lifestyle and economy, modern education providing the skills to integrate into the Israeli labour market has become essential for the Bedouin community. And, although the government used the full development of the individual and 'modernisation' rationale for its urbanisation and service provision programmes, this seems to have been little more than a façade for the overriding ideological goal of further concentrating the Bedouin, and freeing up their land for the pursuit of Jewish national priorities.

As such, this case study reveals the tensions and adverse outcomes (e.g. high drop out and low matriculation rates, poverty, lowest national socioeconomic rates, etc.) that result from not only *unshared ideologies* on the part of the government and a pastoral people, but a government development ideology that explicitly excludes the pastoral people. However, Israel does formally embrace the liberal humanitarian responsibility of providing educational and development opportunities for all of its citizens, which would enable them to achieve their full potential as human beings, and assure their survival and lifelong development. To fulfill this responsibility *vis-à-vis* the Bedouin community would require re-visioning a development ideology that not only includes the Bedouin, but that the Bedouin are partners in shaping, that entitles them to the use of land and other national resources on a basis equitable to that of all other citizens of the state, and that provides them with multiple educational and development opportunities, including modern pastoralism and agriculture.

References

Abu Saad, I. (1991) 'Toward an Understanding of Minority Education in Israel: the Case of the Bedouin Arabs of the Negev'. *Comparative Education* 27: 235–42.

——— (1997) 'Education in a Society at a Crossroads: an Historical Perspective on Israeli Schooling'. *Israel Studies* 2: 21–39.

——— (1998) 'Minority Higher Education in an Ethnic Periphery: the Bedouin Arabs'. In: O. Yiftachel and A. Meir (eds) *Ethnic Frontiers in Israel: Perspectives on Development and Inequality*, Boulder, CO: Westview Press, pp. 269–86.

——— (2000) 'Higher Education among the Negev Bedouin'. *Notes on the Bedouin* (32) (in Hebrew).

——— and H. Lithwick (2000) *A Way Ahead: a Development Plan for the Bedouin Towns in the Negev*. Monograph published by the Center for Bedouin Studies and Development and the Negev Center for Regional Development, Ben-Gurion University of the Negev, Beer Sheva.

———, K. Abu-Saad, G. Hundt, M.R. Forman, I. Belmaker, H. Berendes and D. Chang (1998) 'Bedouin Arab Mothers' Aspirations for Their Children's Education in the Context of Radical Social Change'. *International Journal of Educational Development* 18: 347–59.

Aikman, S. (1996) 'The Globalisation of Intercultural Education and an Indigenous Venezuelan Response'. *Compare* 26: 153–65.

Al-Haj, M. (1995) *Education, Empowerment and Control: the Case of the Arabs in Israel*. Albany, NY: University of New York.

——— (1996) *Education among the Arabs in Israel: Control and Social Change*. Jerusalem: Magnes Press (in Hebrew).

Arbeli, A. (1999) 'Children Travel 200 Kilometers to School'. *Ha-Aretz*, 19 October, p. A1, A4.

Berman, M. (1967) 'Social Change among the Beersheba Bedouin'. *Human Organization* 26: 69–76.

Brown, S. (1986) 'Two Systems of Education'. *Index on Censorship* 15: 36–37.

Falah, G. (1989) 'Israel State Policy towards Bedouin Sedentarization in the Negev'. *Journal of Palestine Studies* 18: 71–90.

Freeland, J. (1996) 'The Global, the National and the Local: Forces in the Development of Education for Indigenous Peoples – the Case of Peru'. *Compare* 26: 167–95.

Gavison, R. (1999) 'Jewish and Democratic? A Rejoinder to the "Ethnic Democracy" Debate'. *Israel Studies* 4: 44–72.

Ghanem, A. (1998) 'State and Minority in Israel: the Case of Ethnic State and the Predicament of its Minority'. *Ethnic and Racial Studies* 21: 428–48.

Gunawardena, C. (1990) 'Access to Higher Education in Sri Lanka'. *Higher Education Review* 23: 53–63.

Ha-Aretz (1998) 'High Court Order to Supply Temp. Schools with Electricity', 24 August.

Hayton, B. (1998) 'Israel: Beduin', *Simpson's World*. BBC, Documentary Film, London.

Ibrahim, T. (2004) *By All Means Possible: Destruction by the State of Crops of Bedouin Citizens in the Naqab (Negev) by Aerial Spraying with Chemicals.* Arab Association for Human Rights, Nazareth, Israel. (www.arabhra.org/NaqabReport_English.pdf).

Katz, Y. (1998) *Report of the Investigating Committee on the Bedouin Education System in the Negev.* Jerusalem: Ministry of Education and Culture.

Lithwick, H. (2000) *An Urban Development Strategy for the Negev's Bedouin Community.* Monograph published by the Center for Bedouin Studies and Development and the Negev Center for Regional Development, Ben-Gurion University of the Negev, Beer Sheva.

Lustick, I. (1980) *Arabs in the Jewish State: Israel's Control of a National Minority.* Austin: University of Texas Press.

Maddrell, P. (1990) *The Beduin of the Negev.* Report No. 81. London: Minority Rights Group.

Mar'i, S. (1978) *Arab Education in Israel.* New York: Syracuse University Press.

Mar'i, S. (1985) 'The Future of the Palestinian Arab Education in Israel'. *Journal of Palestine Studies* 14: 52–73.

Marx, E. (1967) *The Bedouin of the Negev.* Manchester: Manchester University Press.

Masalha, N. (1997) *A Land without a People: Israel, Transfer and the Palestinians.* London: Faber and Faber.

McDowall, D. (1989) *Palestine and Israel: the Uprising and Beyond.* London: I.B. Tauris and Co. Ltd.

Meir, A. (1986) 'Pastoral Nomads and Dialectics of Development and Modernization: Delivering Public Educational Services to Israeli Negev Bedouin'. *Environment and Planning D: Society and Space* 4: 85–95.

Melitz, A. (1994) *Implementation of the Compulsory Education Law.* Southern District Office: Israel, The Ministry of Education, Culture and Sport, Beer Sheva (in Hebrew).

Ministry of Education and Culture (1998) *Report of Investigatory Committee on the Bedouin Educational System in the Negev.* Jerusalem: Ministry of Education and Culture.

Ministry of Education and Culture (2004) *Matriculation Examination Data for 2003.* Jerusalem: Ministry of Education and Culture.

Peres, Y., A. Ehrlich and N. Yuval-Davis (1970) 'National Education for Arab Youth in Israel: a Comparison of Curricula'. *Race* 12: 26–36.

Sa'di, A. (2003) 'Globalization and the Relevance of the Local: Arab Local Government in Israel'. In: D. Champagne and I. Abu-Saad (eds) *The Future of Indigenous Peoples: Strategies for Survival and Development.* UCLA, Los Angeles: American Indian Studies Center.

Said, E., I. Abu-Lughod, J. Abu-Lughod, Muhammad Jallaj and E. Elia Zureik. (1987) *A Profile of the Palestinian People.* Chicago: Palestine Human Rights Campaign.

Seliktar, O. (1984) 'The Arabs in Israel: Some Observations on the Psychology of the System of Controls'. *Journal of Conflict Resolution* 28: 247–69.

Shapira, H. and J. Hellerman (1998) *The Bedouin in the Negev: a Social Survey.* Unpublished report prepared by the Sampling, Consultation and Research Firm, Herziliya, Israel (in Hebrew).

Shimoni, J. (1947) *Arabs of the Land of Israel.* Tel Aviv: Human Relations Area Files (in Hebrew).

Statistical Abstract of Israel (1996) Jerusalem: Central Bureau of Statistics.

Statistical Yearbook of the Negev Bedouin (1999) Beer Sheva: the Center for Bedouin Studies and Development and The Negev Center for Regional Development, Ben-Gurion University of the Negev.

Swirski, S. (1990) *Education in Israel: Schooling for Inequality.* Brirot, Tel Aviv (in Hebrew).

Swirski, S. (1999) *Politics and Education in Israel: Comparisons with the United States.* New York: Falmer Press.

Tibawi, A. (1956) *Arab Education in Mandatory Palestine.* London: Luzac.

Visitz, Y. (1957) 'Education for Arab Children in Israel'. *Afakim*, 11.

Yiftachel, O. (1999) 'Ethnocracy: the Politics of Judaising Israeli/Palestine'. Paper presented at the International Conference, Challenging the Nation State: Perspectives on Citizenship and Identity, Ben-Gurion University of the Negev, 10–12 January.

CHAPTER 8

WITH GOD'S GRACE AND WITH EDUCATION, WE WILL FIND A WAY: LITERACY, EDUCATION AND THE RABARIS OF KUTCH, INDIA

Caroline Dyer and Archana Choksi

Introduction

This chapter considers literacy and education in the lives of the transhumant pastoralist Rabaris of Kutch, from the state of Gujarat in India. Policy discourses accompanying the national programme for universalising elementary education (Sarva Shiksha Abhiyan) (DEEL 2002) recognise that India's nomadic groups comprise a significant population of those who have been identified as 'hard to reach' communities. Strategies for reaching out to nomadic groups have, however, yet to evolve, and lag behind the interest expressed by such groups in gaining 'education'. By drawing here on the perspectives on literacy and education expressed by one transhumant pastoralist group, the Rabaris of Kutch in Gujarat India, during nearly three years of ethnographic work, we identify some of the salient features to which attention needs to be paid in considering how Rabaris may be included in the promise of Education For All.

This is of particular importance since, as Krätli with Dyer and Carr-Hill (this volume) point out, educational processes play a key role in either valuing and sustaining distinctive nomadic cultures, or in acting as a tool for the domestication and assimilation of nomadic groups into 'mainstream' ways. The evidence in the Rabari case points towards the latter role. We are also particularly interested in the relationship between literacy/education and social power relations (Cook-Gumperz, 1986; Street, 1984, 1987, 2002; Stromquist, 1980; Oxenham, 1980), given that, as many chapters in this volume illustrate, nomads across the globe all too frequently comprise disenfranchised and marginalised groups who tend to be seen as a threat to the established social order.

Our research began as an investigation of possibilities for peripatetic adult literacy, within the wider context of the establishment during the early 1990s of the Indian government's National Literacy Mission (NLM). This national literacy drive was predicated on an entirely sedentary model of educational provision, which thus immediately excluded migrant groups. In India such groups include, along with nomads, the many migrant workers who seek seasonal labour, for example in construction and sugar cane industries, and itinerant groups. Two other aspects of the 'delivery' side of the NLM seemed to us particularly problematic. The first was its reliance on decontextualised primers for literacy source materials, which in Gujarat were transparently used to spread state-sponsored messages of health, hygiene and the small family norm, in an approach to non-literate people that somehow holds them responsible for what the state perceives as society's ills. The second was its use of untrained volunteer labour as the main teaching force, underpinned by an incorrect assumption that teaching literacy to adults is easy if you can read and write yourself, and does not require a specifically trained teacher/facilitator. Both of these tend to be characteristic of mass literacy campaigns around the world (Abadzi, 1994).

The model of adult literacy provision under the NLM falls within what Street (1984) terms the 'autonomous' model of literacy, which sees literacy as a self-standing entity regardless of context that is associated primarily with cognitive development supposedly unattainable in oral cultures (Goody, 1987; Ong, 1982). Our view favoured an approach that Street (1984) terms the 'ideological' model, which speaks of *literacies* rather than a single, monolithic literacy, and of literacy practices and events that occur within social contexts (Barton, 1994). We hope that this chapter provides an illustration of how useful the latter approach is in understanding how literacy fits into the lives of this transhumant group, and how important ethnographic research can be as a tool to inform policy development for 'hard to reach' groups such as Rabaris (see also Carr-Hill's comments in this volume on the practicalities of information gathering if we really intend to achieve Education For All).

Literacy planning, even if predicated on a more appropriate model of literacy education, will inevitably also have to confront another challenge of more general development planning for migrant groups: the paucity of reliable statistical data to provide details of population size or other information that would help planners to identify appropriate financial allocations, placement and staffing of services, and so on. In the case of the Rabaris of Kutch, for example, a 'best guess' of population by community leaders says 90-100,000, but this is not supported by 'hard' evidence. Rabaris tend to be out on migration when Census counts take place and are wary of the motives of persons asking questions about numbers of animals or family sizes. Rabaris are all the more invisible to official sources because they are not officially designated a Scheduled Tribe[1] (ST – Scheduled Tribes are specifically enumerated in the Census). This means that their development requirements, too, are more likely to remain invisible. Not being included under a Schedule means they do not enjoy the protected status under the Indian Constitution that has been extended to other ethnic minority groups (such as the Bakkarwal, see Rao this volume) designated either Scheduled Tribe or Scheduled Caste, and an entitlement to funds or provision for their 'upliftment'. In 1997, the Government of Gujarat rejected the Rabari claim to re-classification. Ironically, Rabaris do feature prominently in Gujarat State's promotional tourist literature – they are physically striking as, in their distinctive clothing, they make their way with flocks of sheep and goats or camels along roads that are now heavy with motor traffic.

Moral and Market Economies, and the Symbolic Significance of 'Education'

Kutch is a semi-arid zone which is almost beyond the reach of the south-west monsoon and suffers from frequent droughts and a shortage of green fodder during the summer months that necessitates the migration of animals such as sheep and goats who cannot survive on dry fodder. There are five sub-groups of Rabaris in Kutch (Fig. 8.1). Broadly speaking, those to the west of Kutch (Gardo and Katchis) are the most sedentarised group and may keep small flocks, unless they still migrate in which case it is possible to sustain larger ones, or otherwise seek casual local employment; those in central Kutch (Dhebars) have often migrated out of Gujarat and tend to be nomadic in other states (such as Madhya Pradesh) while those to the east of Kutch (Vagad and Kanthos) are transhumant, migrating within Gujarat and returning home for the monsoon in favourable years.

Rabaris are devout Hindus. According to their myth of existence they were created by Parvati, the consort of Lord Shiva, who wiped the dust and sweat from Shiva as he was meditating and fashioned the very first camel from the dust balls she collected from his body. Once Shiva had breathed life into this camel, it kept running away, so Parvati fashioned a man, and the first Rabari was given life so he could mind the camel. Keeping animals has thus always been a pious occupation and Rabaris see themselves primarily as custodians of animals during their mortal existence, rather than their owners. It is also their belief that the mother goddess presides over them: her advice is taken about when to set out on migration, and animals are commended to her care.

The establishment of a border with Pakistan in 1947, and the growth of motorised transport, have led to a drop in the demand for camels and only a handful of Rabaris now keep them. Other families have diversified into keeping sheep and goats, and occasionally cows and buffaloes. Some

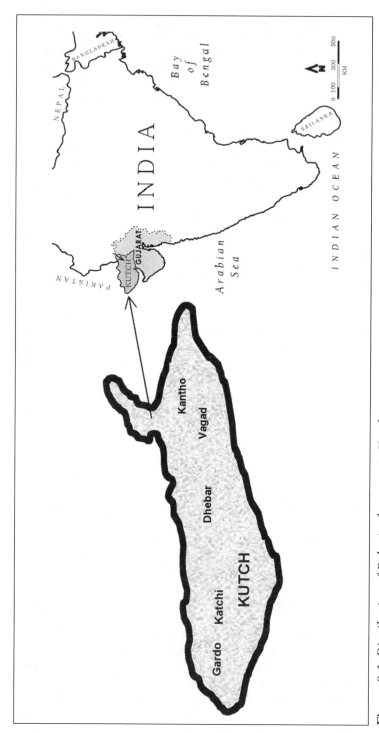

Figure 8.1 Distribution of Rabari sub-groups in Kutch.

protection to those who keep large animals is afforded by the state, which has regulated migratory routes and provides resources in cattle camps in lean years; this is in keeping with the large animal dairy model promoted under Operation Flood (George, 1985). Husbanders of small animals however receive no such support. At both state and national government level, the economic potential of small animal husbandry has scarcely been recognised and although this has been formally noted (GoI, 1987), there are few signs of any significant change to an established policy direction that favours large-scale agri-industries.

Their marginalisation from official agricultural policy, and the absence of any other state development paradigm into which to fit transhumant pastoralists, translates into very patchy outreach services offering veterinary resources and wool gathering centres. But here the ideologies of government and pastoralist groups clash head on. Government services see animal husbandry as a (minor) industry and a commercial enterprise, and assume that pastoralists desire to become more commercially competitive and market-orientated. But for Rabaris, in common with other nomadic groups, values of herd growth outweigh economic means-ends calculations (Gooch, 1998: 43; Galaty et al., 1981). Perhaps more importantly, the religious foundation on which their pastoralism rests is for them a stronger force than the profit and loss values of the marketplace; the basis of their pastoralism is a moral, not a market, economy.

It is this very conflict of assumptions, and the apparent unassailability of the modern market economy over the moral economy which Rabaris have practised so far, that has fuelled Rabaris' interest in 'education'. Over time, growing pressures on pastoralism have encroached upon that moral economy in increasingly unacceptable ways. Rabaris used to sustain migrating animals by offering farmers the dung and urine of their animals as fertiliser in exchange for resting places along migratory routes. This natural fertiliser was highly sought-after and Rabaris also often received payment in kind, such as gifts of *bajro* (millet). Their few cash requirements could be covered by the sale of *ghee* (clarified butter) produced from milking their animals. Gradually, pressures on the land have generated requirements for more and more hard cash. Often, and ironically, this is to a large extent fuelled by the success of the state's agricultural policies for farmers. This has meant that farmers are now able to use competitively priced artificial fertilisers and, availing of heavily subsidised power supplies to agriculturalists, are also often able to irrigate their fields all year round. As a result, there is hardly any time of the year when fields are not full of standing crops and so, for those farmers, migrating animals now represent a threat rather than an opportunity. To offset this threat, they now impose a rental fee to have pastoralists' animals sit on their land during migration.

Another aspect of dwindling pastures which generates a cash demand is the reservation and demarcation of lands which Rabaris could use freely in the past. Common lands around villages are fiercely guarded; the Forestry Department is attempting to address the dwindling tree cover in the country and so is fencing off tracts of land for protection, thus making them unavailable to indigenous users (except perhaps on payment of an illicit 'user fee'); and land that is officially designated wasteland is being acquired by industrial plants that further Gujarat State's industrialising aspirations.

As the cash requirements generated by changing agricultural, ecological and industrial contexts began to escalate, the sale of *ghee* alone was insufficient. Rabaris began by selling milk, even though this was a compromise with the divine purpose of guarding the animals, since to misuse the animal milk which has nourished their children as they grow is seen to be like selling the blood of their sons. In later years, however, Rabaris have had to intensify their efforts to alleviate their cashflow problems, and have taken to selling animals to butchers for onward sale to meat markets in Gujarat, Mumbai and the Gulf. This is a very much worse sin than selling milk:

> This community has its own belief, that if they start selling their own sheep, their name is that of a butcher. He won't do it (kill) with his own hand. If he gazes it, it means he serves the sheep – for him, he is doing this service. (Arjanbhai, community leader, June, 1997)

Rabaris tend, therefore, to try to do this at a step removed, using the services of trusted middlemen, because although it has cost implications:

Figure 8.2 A Vagad Rabari preparing his sheep and goats to leave the encampment in search of fodder.

If you don't sell yourself, but you do give it to others to sell ... they say we just give them to business people, meaning that they aren't actually butchers themselves. This is how they keep their peace of mind. Otherwise they would feel they have killed a life. (Kantibhai, school teacher, Anjar June, 1997)

In such ways, many pressures on pastoralism are generated by changes and developments in the wider market economy in which Rabaris themselves play a miniscule part. Rabaris know little of how and why these pressures are generated, but understand all too well how they force them to transgress their own moral codes. They are therefore inclined to hold themselves and their unpious actions responsible for what they see as their own moral downfall. Rabaris have thus come to believe that their occupation is incompatible with the modern world. The pious basis of their occupation, which is a way of life and not a business, and the moral dilemmas induced by trying to find pragmatic solutions are in sharp contrast with the official discourse of *modernising* the sheep and goat husbandry.

If this were to be tackled by a more proactive government stance, the first requirement would be to develop a policy for small animal husbandry to complement the large animal policy that currently exists. Supporting infrastructure would then have to be considerably developed to offer adequate wool and veterinary services, and support for sheep and goat

Figure 8.3 A Vagad Rabari milking a sheep.

husbanders during lean years, just as there is for husbanders of large animals. Although there is at present somewhat skeletal veterinary and wool outreach, there are no adult education services at all for pastoralists. The provision of the outreach services that do exist implies a modernising project by the state. Yet in the circumstances we have very briefly sketched out above, in the absence of a carefully developed and specific educational component to help Rabaris relate modern veterinary science to their own beliefs and traditions of pastoralism, this modernising project is incompletely conceived.

Three Aspects of 'Education'

As we migrated with a group (*dhang*) of seven Rabari families, some of them extended, we trialled a peripatetic approach to adult literacy. Living and working with these families, our many discussions on this topic allowed us to generate three interlinked categories of education. One was adult literacy; another was schooling for children; and the third was education in a broad sense which was strongly linked with what Bourdieu (1977) has termed 'social capital'.

Adult Literacy

The adult literacy classes we offered were for Rabaris the very first classes that had ever been available to them. It was quite feasible to hold literacy classes on migration: we carried a tent, solar lantern, pens and paper, and some basic teaching learning aids such as number and picture cards. Women came in the afternoons and men in the evenings. This left us time to work with children, whose ages ranged from two to eleven, during the mornings. The 'classes' belied one of the Rabaris' own beliefs – that if you had sheep and goats you would never have time to learn to read and write. Their literacy ambitions were very modest, and related entirely to their immediate needs: they all wanted to learn how to read bus destination boards and tickets; women wanted to learn to read and write letters so they could communicate with daughters married away from home; and it was agreed that they should all be able to read the numbers on currency notes.

The women, used to stitching embroidered symbols of animals and other things from Rabari daily lives onto garments, quickly learned to associate spoken sounds with symbols that were new to them – letters of the alphabet. Since it is women who keep the cash and do all the shopping and accounts, they could all calculate far more rapidly and accurately than either of us, and quickly learned the number symbols. The men focused first on numeracy activities. Used only to handling small amounts of cash to buy *bidis* (local cigarettes) and immediate essentials, they had little experience of handling large amounts of money and some of them could not count sequentially, let alone calculate; a handful also could not recognise different currency notes. This concerned everyone in the *dhang*, as it left them open to being cheated.

En route, we discovered that men never count their animals but, although the smallest flock would comprise at least 350 animals, they know each one by face and name and can immediately tell if one is missing. This made them critical of the readymade picture cards with their generic and inaccurate representations of animals – the autonomous model was after all lurking in the very few, decontextualised, commercially produced materials that we had brought along! All the learners preferred to generate their own drawings; interestingly, these were also highly stylised even when they drew sheep and goats, who do not figure in embroidery.

Figure 8.4 A Vagad Rabari practising her new numeracy skills on migration.

In addition to these self-generated materials, we took cues from the environment, setting adults to find things written down around them. This helped raise their awareness of literacy in their daily lives, and to expand their understandings of its uses. In rural settings that others might describe as 'remote' they could find, and wanted to be able to read, signs and messages painted on bus stops and hoardings, hanging from posts, adverts for films, and so on. Significantly, when we asked about this, they did not associate literacy with potential uses within animal husbandry. For medical problems, for example, they have a comprehensive indigenous system for both humans and animals, which exploits the medicinal properties of the many plants available to them. If they do use modem medicine, they use it sparingly and on the recommendation of trusted others. They seek this resource from a doctor or vet known through their network to be 'good', a term encompassing occupational competence, honesty and a supportive attitude towards them, which includes reading to them instructions for doses and so on, which they commit to reliable memories, so that not being able to read the label is not really a problem.[2]

Schooling for Children

The peripatetic approach to literacy that we were trialling with Rabaris sought to reconcile literacy provision with the occupational imperative of movement. There was, however, mounting evidence that, for the reasons discussed above, Rabaris are becoming uneasy about the future of that occupation itself. This uneasiness has precipitated an interest in exploring alternatives to transhumant pastoralism, both as an occupation and a way of life, and the role that education could play:

> In the past, we had everything. But now the animal husbandry we do today does not give us enough to survive on. God gives us and we are carrying on with it, but truly there is no hope from these animals now. We are still doing animal husbandry because we are illiterate and so we can't find anything else. If we found something else we could change, we are very hard-working, but now pastoralists can't survive. With God's grace; and if education increases, we will be able to find a way, and that will be very good. (transhumant Vagad male, March 1994)

Education, in this respect, means schooling for children. Although Rabaris know that the quality of village schools in Kutch is tempered by teacher absenteeism and corporal punishment; and that children may make slow progress in becoming literate, the 'education' they seek is most likely to be available through this channel. However, this presents logistical difficulties. One solution, which is extreme and may be precipitated by animal disease or misfortune, but is also increasingly a positive choice, is to sedentarise specifically to allow children to gain access to the village primary school. This decision may leave parents dependent on day labouring jobs since the local ecology of Kutch cannot support many pastoralists. This is a risk for which some parents are prepared, as this Dhebar mother explained:

> We returned just for the education of our children. We thought, we are illiterate and if we stay with herding, our children will remain illiterate too. So we came back just for our children.

A related option, which ushers in a more gradual process of adaptation, is to treat schooling as an 'insurance policy' within pastoralism. Typically this involves leaving a son at home in the village with an elderly family member so he can go to school and eventually get a job, and support the family if necessary, should pastoralism cease to be a viable option. This option is less risky from the point of view of parents, who can continue within pastoralism in the mean time, but it too means that Rabaris' aspirations for the future are vested in state schools that have a fragile capacity to retain all children and help them achieve learning outcomes defined with rather different learners in mind.

Another possibility, but given the very limited provision this is for the fortunate few, is to send a child to a private residential school where the teachers, the students and local context of the school are entirely Rabari. Such a school offers Rabari parents peace of mind, knowing that their children are in a safe environment where their socio-cultural norms are respected. Although the formal syllabus, uniform, etc. are all state-prescribed, this is not contested by Rabaris, for whom this is an important aspect of the modernisation project of which education is a part. Before the infrastructure and economy of Kutch were shattered by the earthquake of 26th January 2001, there were three such schools (only one of which, the oldest and largest, was a fully-fledged elementary school for Years One to Eight) and two more were planned.[3] Earlier petitions to the government to establish two more boarding schools in Kutch had failed, as had requests to increase the number of subsidised places in the private schools.

Education and Social Capital

In their discussions about literacy, Rabaris – like other non-literate adults – keenly felt the social stigma of being illiterate. The literacy skills they sought were all linked to retaining independence, and they felt compromised by having to ask the assistance of a stranger – particularly one who, reminding us of the moral code by which they live their lives, might not be 'good' and so deliberately mislead or scold them. It was not, however, a question of simply being able to read and write: rather, literacy is conflated with power, which is described as 'learning how to speak'. Rabaris are very clear that one of the functions of schools is to teach people how to speak, and they seek this power for themselves. They are aware that ascribed status, deriving from their own high position in the caste status, is contested by a new power: the power of being educated. As they migrate, conflict situations for Rabaris tend to involve people in low-level but distinct authority positions within government (police constables, forestry officers and so on) who are stopping them from doing things they believe they have the right to do. These lower level government officials are quite often members of the Scheduled Tribes or Classes, who have benefited from official positive discrimination that has vastly improved their access to education and posts within government service. The rise to positions of authority of those with lower ascribed status as a result of being educated is a further confirmation of the links between education and power.

Farmers, government officers, and shopkeepers with whom Rabaris interact, who are themselves literate, make comments to them about the need to be literate; and while they might intend them positively, underlying their words are many negative messages about the status of those who are not. Unconsciously reflecting the state discourse that links education with development, conceived as universal movement in a direction that represents the state's view of progress, Rabaris associate being 'uneducated' with feeling 'behind' while others go ahead. One Rabari said that he felt like a 'horse stuck in the mud',[4] while others were specific about the problems of not being educated:

> Because we are uneducated, people can put things one way or another. If someone sidetracks or sets us on the wrong way, we won't know. We have got left behind and so we have stayed behind. (Katchi male, March 1994)

Figure 8.5 Young Dhebar boys in camp, using camel and sheep droppings to practise herding sheep and lambs.

Because we have no education we can't speak up. That's why we're beaten. Police harass us, and so do villagers. Forest officers are a problem. If someone writes a letter saying a pastoralist has damaged something a pastoralist can't do anything about it. He may not have any money to feed his children but he has to pay the officers. This is why the community is deteriorating because it has no education. How can it get out of this: they don't know the law so they're stuck in a vicious circle. We get implicated in police cases and because we are uneducated we don't know what to do next. (Vagad male, December 1994)

In these changing circumstances for transhumant pastoralism, Rabaris see as the cause of being behind their way of life, with its cycles of mobility, which has precluded them from gaining 'an education'. It is this mobility, rather than the rigidity of government's sedentary educational provision and the nature of development policies, that is seen by pastoralists, rural communities and educational managers as the reason why Rabaris are 'backward'. The idea of peripatetic teaching was entirely new, as there was no precedent for this in the state, but Rabari community leaders were quick to see its potential: 'We want to study but there is no scheme, no system. If we do want to fit into a system, we can't, because of its timings'.

However, for the pastoralists with whom we migrated, the 'education' they sought was not literacy within pastoralism. Indeed, because of their view that pastoralism itself is outmoded, the very idea seemed to them a retrograde step which would keep them 'backward'. Since the adaptation of pastoralism along the commercial lines advocated by the state did not make any sense to them, what they sought was a way forward, out of pastoralism. They appropriately associated this with the formal schooling of children, since this was seen to be the type of education that conveys social status and the possibility of occupational diversity. That this was almost automatically associated with sedentarisation was not overlooked, but since Rabaris believed that as pastoralism was unlikely to continue to sustain them in the long term, sedentarisation would be a necessity in time anyway.

Rabaris and the State Promise of Education For All

Having denied the Rabari claim to re-classification as an ST community the state is not obliged — as it would be if they were STs — to make residential school facilities available to them. Our work on experimenting with a different model of adult literacy, one that moved with the client group, was viewed as interesting by the Government of Gujarat, with whom policy-related dialogue took place over the life of the project. Despite the wider context of the National Literacy Mission and its ambiguously worded promise of 'total' literacy, this government at that time showed no interest in considering the project's replicability or drawing on the research findings to develop an alternative approach to the education of this or any other migrant group. By not taking any particular action, not only in relation to this research project but, far more importantly, on the demands Rabaris articulated for their own residential schools, the state effectively denies the Rabaris access to education. That denial countermands both Article 45 of the Constitution, and the national and international promise of providing Education For All which India signed up to in 1990 and reaffirmed in 2000. The state's unwillingness to enter into dialogue reflects the phenomenon Krätli with Dyer (this volume) identify: that governments see pastoralism and movement as a lower stage of human development. Klute (1996: 3) observed also that:

> State agents consider nomads in general as belligerent, difficult to control, and see their continuous movement much more as a sort of offence to the requirements of any modern state and its rational administration than as a quest for water and pasture.

The international vision of EFA invokes a notion of education that meets basic learning needs, characterised as 'the knowledge, skills, attitudes and values necessary for people to survive, to improve the quality of their lives, and to continue learning' (WCEFA: 1990: ix). This affirming discourse masks several contradictions for the Rabaris. The research findings presented here underline the difficulties of knowing which knowledge, skills and attitudes are relevant to survival and illustrate the hollowness of decontextualised discourse when it comes to acting on the EFA promise. Rabaris' preferred model of schooling presents a risk to the state that is easily countered by a refusal to grant funds, and so Rabaris' survival needs at the beginning of the twenty-first century are actually making them use, and therefore implicitly legitimise, educational provision that in many respects, both directly and indirectly, contributes to their marginalisation. The small experimental peripatetic model was unable to make much headway in the imagination of education service providers, although one of the project's contributions was extended discussions that raised the profile of the Rabaris' educational demands and their rights.

The idea of Education For All is also not well served by a state approach to minorities' development that sees the official labelling of a minority group as needing specific developmental support as a necessary catalyst for action. Rather, it necessitates the organisation of educational provision that is able to respond flexibly to all users' needs – regardless of whether users happen to be officially categorised or not.

The Government of Gujarat did not accept the Rabaris' claim to more schools of their own, or our suggestion that there is an urgent need to develop flexible and responsive approaches to educational provision. If it had done, it might have run the risk of disrupting the processes of sedentarisation which are quietly taking place as hundreds of individual households reach the conclusion that the future of pastoralism is finite and that an alternative, almost certainly involving sedentarisation, must be found. Had it reacted positively, the Government would have implicitly endorsed pastoralism as a legitimate occupation, and transhumance as a legitimate way of life. The evidence in this case, however, reflects Gooch's (1998: 41) remark, 'nomads simply (do) not fit into the "modern project" of a developing country'. The challenge for the future is to change this perception.

Notes

1. Confusingly, ST status has been conferred on some Rabaris who live in or around areas of Gujarat designated as protected by the Forestry Department, such as Gir in Saurashtra.
2. The labelling itself is problematic, however, since the audience for the label might be expected to read Hindi, Gujarati or English, all of which we found on a sample of medicines at a doctor's.
3. State financial relief was available to rebuild state schools that collapsed: private schools have had to solicit donations and charitable funds to embark on rebuilding educational facilities. Fortunately for Rabaris, the remarkable artistry of their embroidery has attracted international attention and, in the absence of state support, generous donations from external sources have assisted in funding new buildings.
4. This is an interesting analogy as the horse is perceived as a noble animal.

References

Abadzi, H. (1994) *What We Know about Acquisition of Adult Literacy: Is There Hope?* World Bank Discussion Papers, No. 245. Washington D.C.: World Bank.

Barton, D. (1994) *Literacy: an Introduction to the Ecology of Written Language* Oxford: Blackwell.

Bourdieu, P. (1977) *Outline of a Theory of Practice*. Cambridge: Cambridge University Press.

Cook-Gumperz, J. (ed.) (1986) *The Social Construction of Literacy*. Cambridge: Cambridge University Press.

DEEL (2002) *Sarva Shiksha Abhiyan: a framework*. Department for Elementary Education and Literacy. New Delhi: Ministry of Human Resource Development.

Downing, J. (1987) 'Comparative Perspectives on World Literacy'. In: D. Wagner (ed.) *The Future of Literacy in a Changing World*. New York: Pergamon Press.

Galaty, J., D. Aronson and P. Salzman (eds) (1981) *The Future of Pastoral Peoples: Proceedings of the Conference in Nairobi*. Ottawa: International Development Research Centre.

George, S. (1985) *Operation Flood: an Appraisal of Current Indian Dairy Policy*. New Delhi: Oxford University Press.

GoI (1987) *Report of the Task Force to Evaluate the Impact of Sheep and Goat Rearing in Ecologically Fragile Zones*. Ministry of Agriculture. New Delhi: Government of India.

Gooch, P. (1998) 'At the Tail of the Buffalo: van Gujjar Pastoralists, between the Forest and World Arena'. Lund: University of Lund, Department of Sociology.

Goody, J. (1987) *The Interface between the Written and the Oral*. Cambridge: Cambridge University Press.

Klute, G. (1996) 'Introduction'. In *Nomadic Peoples* 38: 3–10.

Ong, W. (1982) *Orality and Literacy: the Technologizing of the Word*. London: Methuen.

Oxenham, J. (1980) *Literacy: Writing, Reading and Social Organisation*. London: Routledge and Kegan Paul.

Rao, H.C.H. (1994) *Agricultural Growth in Rural Poverty and Environmental Degradation in India*. Delhi: Oxford University Press.

Street, B. (1984) *Literacy in Theory and Practice*. Cambridge: Cambridge University Press.

—— (1987) 'Literacy and Social Change: the Significance of Social Context in the Development of Literacy Programmes'. In D. Wagner (ed.) *The Future of Literacy in a Changing World*. New York: Pergamon Press.

—— (2002) *Literacy and Development: Ethnographic Perspectives*. London: Routledge.

Stromquist, N. (1990) 'Women and Illiteracy: the Interplay of Gender Subordination and Poverty'. *Comparative Education Review* 34 (1): 95–111.

Vira, S. (1993) 'The Gujars of Uttar Pradesh: Neglected "Victims of Progress"'. Issues Paper no. 41 Dryland Networks Programme. London: International Institute for Environment and Development.

Wagner, D. (1995) 'Literacy and Development: Rationales, Myths, Innovations and Future Directions'. *International Journal of Educational Development* 15 (4): 341–62.

WCEFA (1990) *The World Conference on Education For All: Meeting Basic Learning Needs – a Vision for the 1990s*. Background Document. New York: Interagency Commission for WCEFA.

CHAPTER 9

THE QASHQA'I, FORMAL EDUCATION AND INDIGENOUS EDUCATORS

Mohammad Shahbazi

Introduction

*I*n the opening chapter of this volume, Krätli and Dyer synthesise a rather scattered body of literature attempting to shed light on the efforts of various agencies to provide marginalised groups with an education for self-actualisation, productivity, economic growth/development, and/or ideological control. They argue that regardless of providers' agendas, the task has not been an easy one, and that the outcomes of schooling have not evolved as planners expected – as many of the chapters in this volume illustrate. This chapter examines these issues with reference to the Qashqa'i case and show the many ways in which providers' assumptions have been challenged. In simplistic terms, if the state officials in Iran had hoped politically to pacify Qashqa'i youth by altering their culture, the tent school unintentionally *facilitated* enculturation of Qashqa'i youths into the culture and values of their own tribal and nomadic societies – an outcome diametrically opposed to the ideological agenda for education set by government officials. What one can learn from the past to enhance present efforts, as the opening chapter explores, is that providers must stop displaying 'expert' attitudes with a 'mission' to recast communities – nomadic pastoralists in this case – into 'better' ones; and do this by working with pastoral nomads to determine what their actual needs are in general and how formal education can facilitate meeting those needs.

The Qashqa'i

The Qashqa'i are approximately half a million Shi'i Muslim Turkish-speaking ethnic tribespeople, living in Fars province (south and southwest

Iran) (Fig. 9.1). State-induced political centralisation among the Qashqa'i emerged in the late- eighteenth century when state rulers encouraged tribal leaders to perform dual functions: to control local and internal problems and to mediate between the tribally organised nomads and the state. This resulted in the formation of the Qashqa'i confederation, which was structurally divided into six large tribes, some smaller tribes, and many subtribes. The confederation was politically centralised and economically independent, and led by paramount leaders who interacted between state officials and their followers. People were connected through commonly shared political figures, cultural symbols, sentiments, and memories. Despite some differences, there has been a repertoire of customs, values, worldviews, and practices – all linked through the Qashqa'i Turkish language – that can be called 'Qashqa'i culture.' Qashqa'i tribespeople migrated seasonally and in groups of households: the activities involved in migration provided meanings for cultural symbols, sentiments and memories. The people reproduced their culture and taught their offspring, and Qashqa'i youth were not subjected to many non-Qashqa'i cultural experiences (Shahbazi, 1988).

The introduction of a state-supported formal education programme in the 1950s altered the cultural experiences of the Qashqa'i people. Although research on the Middle East, Iran in particular, has focused on the connection between the state and its resident tribes and nomads during the past decade, and documented the use of force by state officials to control tribal and nomadic groups (Beck, 1986, 1991; Garthwaite, 1983; Tapper, 1993) much less is known about the state's apparatuses for cultural changes and the ways that tribal and nomadic people respond to them. State-supported formal education has been used as one such apparatus.

This chapter focuses on the educational system provided to Qashqa'i nomadic pastoralists (1957–1979) (see also Shahbazi, 2001b, 2002), and the roles indigenous schoolteachers played in the processes of formally educating Qashqa'i tribespeople, and the extent to which they enculturated them with values held by earlier generations (Shahbazi, 1998). As a Qashqa'i myself, I spent 23 months conducting research in Iran (1993–1995) and another 30 months (1996–1998) in the United States reviewing the literature and analysing and writing up my findings (Shahbazi, 2003). I used three major techniques – archival research, interviews, and participant observation – to collect information to determine how formally educated Qashqa'i people responded to the processes of change occurring in the twentieth century. Most of the interviewees were Qashqa'i individuals, and the rest were members of other non-Persian ethnic groups. Through archival research, I recorded materials relevant to the socio-political interactions of the Qashqa'i with the state and its systems of formal education.

An Historical Overview

An army man, Reza Khan, managed to emerge as Reza Shah (King Reza) in the 1920s, establishing the Pahlavi Dynasty that ruled Iran for over half a century. In an attempt to centralise political power, he put military personnel in charge and ordered all local and provincial leaders to cooperate with his regime. Those opposing his militaristic approach, including tribal leaders in general and Qashqa'i paramount leaders in particular, were removed from their political offices and forced to live in Tehran. In the 1930s, in the absence of paramount Qashqa'i leaders, the regime imposed an enforced settlement policy on the Qashqa'i.

At national level, the regime de-emphasised the traditional Quaranic School (*maktab*), and instead emphasised state-supported secular education. Such education was to function as a means of political socialisation of the students, with an aim of creating in them a national ideology. In the absence of migration, which customarily required active participation of all members of Qashqa'i households, many settled Qashqa'i families sent their children to either state-supported schools or the *maktab* (most villages did not receive modern schools until the late 1950s). Many elite Qashqa'i families already had their children formally educated by privately hired teachers (*mirza*) or sent them to study in towns and cities.

The Second World War forced Reza Shah out of power in 1941. His son, Mohammad Reza, succeeded him. Since the young son lacked full control over the nation's affairs, the Qashqa'i could return to nomadic pastoralism – and with much enthusiasm, most of them resumed their seasonal migrations. This helped re-establish the Qashqa'i as a political entity. The political establishment, with its capitals moving between summer and winter quarters, needed literate people to serve the leaders effectively and represent them outside the tribal confederation. Those who had earned some formal education during the forced settlement were hired as *mirza*, account keepers, or secretaries. More than the income these literate individuals received, their elevated social status attracted Qashqa'i attention.

With well established socio-political organisation and nationally recognised leadership, the Qashqa'i lived independent of state impediment for over a decade. This picture changed when a coup d'état against the shah failed, in the face of American support for him, which led to the collapse of Iran's national government in 1953. The shah dissolved the Qashqa'i confederation in 1957 and exiled paramount Qashqa'i leaders to Europe when they declined to support the regime.

A Qashqa'i man, Mohammad Bahmanbaigi, who had majored in law at Tehran University in 1943 and provided secretarial services to the paramount Qashqa'i leaders during the late 1940s and early 1950s, emerged as an innovative educator in the late 1950s. He established a modern literacy plan for Qashqa'i tribespeople and was able to convince Iranian state officials to support it. Bahmanbaigi's involvement facilitated provision of a state-supported literacy programme for Qashqa'i tribespeople (Shahbazi, 2001a). The regime saw him as a cultural broker, and he was able to mediate between state officials, who saw formal education as a mechanism with which to create unity, promote nationalism, and gain greater control over the ruled, and the receivers, such as tribally organised ethnic groups, who were suspicious of any kind of services offered by the state. He had also gained American political support and technical assistance for developing and implementing the initial phase of the literacy programme for the Qashqa'i.

Bahmanbaigi introduced several teaching and training institutions between 1957 and 1979. They included the Teacher Training School (from 1957), the Elementary School (from 1955), the Middle School (from 1973), the High School (from 1968), the Technical School (from 1973), and the Carpet Weaving School (from 1973), all in and near Shiraz. He also co-sponsored, through the literacy programme, midwife and paramedic training and veterinary training at Pahlavi University in 1975. I discuss briefly here the Teacher Training and the Elementary Schools (see Shahbazi 1998 for a detailed discussion of all these institutions) because they played major roles in exposing Qashqa'i tribespeople to cultural changes.

Elementary Schools (Grades 1–5) for Nomads

Qashqa'i schools, known as Schools for Nomads (*madaris-i 'ashayiri*), consisted of cone-shaped white canvas tents, each equipped with a blackboard, chalk, and a teacher trained to teach grades one to six. (After 1966, teachers taught years one to five.) Unlike most other Iranian schools, this school system was co-educational. The tent accommodated 15 or more students and protected them from heat and cold. School equipment was transported between camps and schoolteachers, often members of the camping groups, travelled with them.

Qashqa'i students who completed elementary education gained different opportunities. A few of these graduates were admitted to the boarding high school in Shiraz established expressly for the children of nomads; others entered the Teacher Training School and became schoolteachers. Some parents managed to send their male children for further education in towns and cities in the region but many students discontinued formal education after completing the elementary level because their families could not afford to support their education in towns and cities. Becoming a teacher remained the top priority of the Qashqa'i young generation, so the Teacher Training School played a significant role in meeting their job priorities.

Teacher Training School

Beginning in September 1957, teacher training for nomads began for 60 teacher trainees. It was the core of the literacy programme for nomads.

During 22 years of activity (1957–1979), during which there was no change to the regulations under which applicants were admitted, it trained 8,921 schoolteachers (7,818 males and 1,103 females) (Sohrabi, 1995; Shahbazi, 1998). Applicants were required to have a nomadic and tribal background, be at least 17 years of age, have at least an elementary-level education (five years or more), pass a written examination, and be interviewed by Bahmanbaigi.

Believing that applicants from socio-economically poorer families could better carry out the programme's goals, Bahmanbaigi inspected the interviewees' clothing, facial expressions, and hands to determine their eligibility. He was reluctant to admit individuals from élite or financially well-off families, even if they were well qualified. Bahmanbaigi and other formally educated tribespeople confirmed in personal communications to me that he encouraged élite or high-status families to send their daughters to school and to his teacher training programme; indeed, his own daughter was among the first group of tribeswomen to become schoolteachers. He capitalised heavily on role modelling, for Qashqa'i tribespeople had practised this concept previously. At first reluctant to send their daughters to school, Qashqa'i non-élite families did so when they saw élite Qashqa'i women as teachers.

Figure 9.1 Qashqa'i children attending a tent school.

Throughout its operation, the Teacher Training School for Nomads remained a boarding institution. From the time trainees were admitted until they graduated 12 months later, they were provided with free food, housing and tuition. There were no female trainees during the first four years. Once female trainees were admitted to the programme, they lived in Shiraz with their relatives and friends of their families. The increasing numbers of female candidates required officials to arrange a dormitory for them, which occurred after 1965. The dormitory was in Shiraz, with Bahmanbaigi's daughter as its headmistress until 1979.

In sharp contrast to teacher training programmes elsewhere in Iran, the trainees in the Teacher Training School did not receive certificates upon completion of the programme. They were given only a tent, some chalk, a blackboard, a Persian dictionary, and a box that contained materials for basic scientific experiments. During the early years of the programme, each schoolteacher also received a white canvas tent. Some of the teachers resided in the same tent. As the programme's financial condition improved, each teacher received two tents: one for personal use and the other to be used for classes.

Cultural activities have always been important to Qashqa'i tribespeople. Most formally educated Qashqa'i I interviewed mentioned two key cultural activities of the training programme: circle dances performed by Qashqa'i female trainees and stick games played by male trainees. Both these activities were part of tribal wedding celebrations. Dressed in multicoloured clothes, women danced in a circle to rhythmic music. In the men's game, one man attempted to hit a defender on his legs with a metre-long stick, while the defender protected himself by holding a two-metre-long pole vertically. Such occasions appealed to the participants' cultural and educational sentiments, and they played out such emotion through artistic skills, which in turn became entertainment. Aware of this interest, Bahmanbaigi arranged a weekly cultural programme for trainees and often lectured prior to such activities, telling them they were warriors who would use their literacy skills instead of guns against the tribe's common enemy, ignorance. These activities provided a culturally familiar and entertaining framework. They also reinforced the trainees' tribal passion and emotion, creating in them a feeling of belonging and a desire to help their fellow nomads.

To promote trainees' future teaching performances, officials bussed in students from successful schools. Teachers from these schools demonstrated for the trainees their approaches and methods of teaching, and sometimes the trainees were asked to teach these students. They received immediate feedback to improve their skills. There was also an annual gathering entitled *ordu* which usually lasted several days, and had both political and educational aims. Government officials were invited and entertained during the course of the *ordu*, and students were examined in the presence of these officials, teachers, and the teacher trainees. Teachers from successful schools were rewarded, while those with poor performances were sometimes humiliated in public. Some of the Qashqa'i schoolteachers I interviewed told me that the excitement at these gatherings was so high that right there and then they decided to work as hard as they could in order to become successful schoolteachers. Educational activities were followed by music to which students and teachers danced and played. Several interviewees said that these interludes were similar to the memories their parents had from the time when paramount Qashqa'i leaders would gather the best fighters from among the tribesmen to prepare an attack on a target.

While some interviewees said that Bahmanbaigi played down Qashqa'i culture, cultural activities promoted through the literacy programme for nomads indicate otherwise. The teacher-training programme for nomads admitted applicants from different ethnic backgrounds in the 1970s. Male candidates were required to own a complete set of their ethnic dress upon registration. Female candidates were required to dress in their ethnic attire, but trainees gradually replaced their heavy clothing with thinner fabrics to the extent that some Qashqa'i did not feel comfortable seeing their daughters in such clothes.

The cultural impact of these activities (*ordu*, ethnic dress, weekly cultural activities) was enduring. Some of these trainees, particularly males, had grown up watching their fathers replacing their ethnic dress with urban-style clothes. Some Qashqa'i teacher trainees, becoming more conscious of their tribal and sub-tribal identities, wore ethnic dress in the schools for nomads and encouraged their students to practise their culture.

Views of Qashqa'i Schoolteachers

A total of 609 current schoolteachers (some had been students, but most were Qashqa'i schoolteachers in the pre-1979 period) were asked to list roles that schoolteachers performed and the impact that these teachers had on their own society. Their responses can be categorised by social, economic, political and cultural factors.

Social Factors

Qashqa'i schoolteachers and their students, through schools and other educational programmes, linked their immediate families to a world quite different from the one in which their ancestors had lived. Qashqa'i Turkish was (and remained) the medium of statement, social groups were reproduced, pastoralism combined with dry farming provided a subsistence economy, and a political hierarchy prevailed. Even at the household level, age determined position and elicited respect and recognition. The introduction of formal education and social mobility through education, coupled with integrated socio-political and economic changes, significantly affected Qashqa'i society.

Teenagers with elementary-level formal education emerged as social actors, cross-cutting the existing hierarchical structure at the family and tribal levels. Parents and older siblings depended on younger members whose literacy skills qualified them to lead. Qashqa'i teachers mediated between group members and outsiders: in the absence of paramount Qashqa'i leaders, educators stood between tribespeople and government officials. Qashqa'i youth were exposed to civil laws and procedures.

Teachers taught their relatives enthusiastically, hoping that their students would in turn serve their society. To attend school, Qashqa'i children had to gather at one place, share space, compromise on differences, and work toward the same goal. This process was a uniform socialisation, new to the Qashqa'i. While state officials were under the impression that such an approach would eventually produce co-operative citizens and distance the participants from their socio-historical past, it actually benefited the Qashqa'i in several different ways. The state-supported educational programme brought together children from scattered families and exposed them to an unfamiliar environment, new school subjects, and a new language. Facing all these, Qashqa'i students sought and received help and support from one another and from their Qashqa'i teachers, and they shared a culture and a language. Such unintentional development reinforced a sense of unity among the students and others.

If in the past, this collectivity and sense of unity was transmitted through Qashqa'i leaders, in the new era such unity was conveyed through teachers, the ultimate trusted leaders. A whole generation not only learned the national language they needed to elevate their skills to the level of many other Iranians, but also learned a political language and civil laws and practised individual development. The entrance of thousands of youths into teacher training and high school provided them opportunities to learn about one another and to exchange views. Many formally educated Qashqa'i reported that it was during teacher training, the annual gatherings of students for inspection, and high school that they truly felt that the Qashqa'i culture was larger and more powerful than they had known:

> I felt I was among my siblings. In the past twenty years, I have maintained friendships with many Qashqa'i I met at high school. Some thirty of us meet on a regular basis and discuss issues related to change and continuity among our people (a former Qashqa'i schoolteacher).

Literacy provided the skills Qashqa'i needed to read and write about their society and culture. The literacy programme in the 1960s and the 1970s created a sense of belonging and peoplehood in Qashqa'i youth. It brought together children of scattered families and gave them a professional direction. 'We learned about our past, a past that was about to be forgotten,' a Qashqa'i professional claimed.

Another development that helped interest Qashqa'i youth in their culture was the interest in Qashqa'i dress shown by other tribespeople. Members of some ethnic groups attending educational institutions for nomads adopted Qashqa'i clothing. For instance, Lor tribeswomen dressed like Qashqa'i women, and some Kurdish men showed interest in the Qashqa'i felt hat.

When a conflict arose, students learned to apply state-supported civil laws instead of tribally based customs. They learned to defend their individual and social rights through legal channels. Some took government jobs, particularly after 1979, through which they facilitated some services to other Qashqa'i. Primarily because of the literacy programme for nomads and the role teachers played, Qashqa'i tribespeople no longer lived in isolation. They, along with other tribespeople, were by 1995a clearly defined sector of Iranian society with specific needs.

Literacy helped to reduce both internal and external tensions. While helping formally educated Qashqa'i reach their goals, literacy also promoted a national mainstream culture and a sense of nationalism. If in the past people talked about love for one's homeland (*vatan*), in the new era love for one's country (*mehan*) was being prompted through schooling. Media and published materials exposed the Qashqa'i to current developments and events – as they did other Iranians.

Formal education profoundly altered Qashqa'i behaviour towards one another and towards non-Qashqa'i. It created some trust and a certain level of understanding between and among the Qashqa'i and other citizens: for instance, formally educated Qashqa'i learned that not all non-Qashqa'i disliked them, as state officials, particularly army officers, had indicated through unkind interactions with tribespeople. Non-Qashqa'i interacting with the Qashqa'i for the first time learned that they were not the 'wild mountain people' whom they had learnt about through the state-controlled media. Formal education also prepared Qashqa'i tribespeople to be better informed politically; and to be more tolerant of others, particularly state officials. It promoted understanding of other societies and introduced skills adapted to the rapid changes that were taking place. The Qashqa'i learnt where to go for help and how to develop a common goal of preserving and promoting their culture; and to see their socio-political and socio-economic problems objectively.

In my field interactions (1993–1995), I noticed that Qashqa'i families who lived in cities fell into two categories: families whose members lacked literacy skills at the time of residence there, and families who had at least one member who was formally educated and possibly had a salaried position. Most families in the first category had tried to assimilate into the larger city culture but, having failed, became part of a growing subculture of emigrants from villages. These Qashqa'i tribespeople tried hard to disconnect themselves from their socio-cultural past, but because of their parental enculturation they did not fully assimilate into urban society. These families have a mixed feeling about their identity, and have as much difficulty identifying themselves as others have in identifying them. The second category of Qashqa'i families was clear about their identity. They willingly and sometimes proudly identified themselves as Qashqa'i, and the older generation in the family wanted to make sure that the younger generation knew Qashqa'i culture and that they spoke Turkish at home. Other cultural markers in these families included the way they organised their belongings, the way they sat, the tone of their voices, the playing of Qashqa'i music, participating in Qashqa'i cultural activities and festivals, enthusiastically watching videos about Qashqa'i weddings and cultural festivals, and in intermarrying with other Qashqa'i.

Economic Factors

One early and visible economic impact of the literacy programme for nomads was the income schoolteachers brought home on a regular basis, since many were from poor families. Because these families did not possess many animals and consequently had less need for the labour of their young children, they were able to invest part of the income earned by a teacher in the education of other members of their household. Most interviewees said that their income somehow supported the training and education of younger members of their households. Some of these families also started investing in farming, orchards, and livestock. Such activities, often economically successful, encouraged other Qashqa'i parents to show interest in literacy.

The preoccupation of a whole generation of Qashqa'i with formal education left wealthier Qashqa'i lacking the relatively cheap labour that many poorer Qashqa'i had provided. Previously many of the poor were dependent on rich families. In the new era, many Qashqa'i became dependent on a stable state and regular pay cheques. Prior to the introduction of formal education, the main source of income was pastoralism and limited agriculture. Once schoolteachers and eventually other formally educated Qashqa'i started bringing in cash, families diversified their economic opportunities. Despite a rapidly declining subsistence economy for the Qashqa'i in the 1970s, the pay cheques issued to schoolteachers provided an easier and economically better life for Qashqa'i than some neighbouring villagers had.

But the literacy programme did not benefit all Qashqa'i, nor did it benefit them equally. It did help expose the Qashqa'i to the world outside and to other available occupations. Some tribespeople found jobs that did not require advanced literacy skills: drivers, staff at the educational institutions for nomads, cooks, weaving instructors, and so on. Such occupations also led to additional income flowing from urban to nomadic sectors. Teachers and other formally educated Qashqa'i also helped other Qashqa'i to find paying jobs in cities.

Some formally educated Qashqa'i found better markets for their products. Some mechanised pastoralism and farming. Because they had acquired a better understanding of the national economy and were influential among the tribespeople, they could and often did help others economically. For instance, if wool dyeing in the customary way, using organic herbs, was not cost-effective, then formally educated Qashqa'i convinced people to use methods that were. 'Literacy gifted us with a better understanding and application of tools and techniques that were required for success in economics', said a Qashqa'i schoolteacher. Some who received government salaries received loans from private and state financial institutions. 'Literacy helped us to use our mental rather than physical powers to improve our economic conditions' (ibid.).

Political Factors

Asking respondents about politics was more controversial than gaining information on economics or culture. The world views and ideologies of teachers born in the 1970s were influenced by the post-revolutionary era, and some teachers did not want to jeopardise their teaching jobs by talking about politics. However, the overall theme of their statements is that formal education and the presence of schoolteachers elevated the political awareness of Qashqa'i tribespeople. Many teachers said that Qashqa'i tribespeople had lived under the control of tribal leaders and had learned, through literacy and formally educated Qashqa'i, that they did not have to obey tribal leaders. One former Qashqa'i schoolteacher wrote on a questionnaire: 'We received education so as to have the understanding that we should not follow the khans blindly. We learned not to support people who exploited our ancestors. We learned from our educators and in turn taught our students that they should know their foes and friends'.

Another teacher reported that Qashqa'i youth did not support the leaders who returned from exile during the revolution and said, 'Our literacy had something to do with this'. Another said that some formally educated tribespeople managed to enter government institutions and reach decision-making positions in the post-revolutionary era: 'these people have been helping the rest of us. In a way, we all have benefited from literacy'. Some teachers also said that a major factor promoting a mutually respectful political relationship between some formally educated Qashqa'i and officials of the Islamic Republic was the fact that formal education and the print media had given tribespeople a clearer understanding about the state and its institutions. Non-literate Qashqa'i, particularly prior to the 1960s, sometimes lacked such understanding and believed then, as some still said in the 1990s, that state officials cannot be trusted. One teacher, a Qashqa'i university student, said that he appreciated my research, but he wanted me to know that although literacy, formal education, and the revolution might have changed many issues, one thing remained unchanged: 'No matter what, a Turk is still seen as a Turk and a Tat [non-Qashqa'i] as a Tat'.

Some may argue that matters between the Qashqa'i and non-Qashqa'i improved, yet political tension continued to exist for practical reasons. One reason is that all educational institutions and facilities of the literacy programme for nomads prior to the 1980s were taken under control by non-Qashqa'i people in the post-revolutionary era. A note in one questionnaire read, 'In my view, the Qashqa'i do not exist politically. Formal education dismantled the Qashqa'i political institution'. Another questionnaire comment read: 'The literacy programme for nomads was a wolf dressed like a sheep. This way, it kept the Pahlavi ruler happy by announcing that the programme intended to benefit the regime, but in reality the programme taught freedom and bravery to the Qashqa'i'. Another teacher claimed that the programme indeed solved the state's problems once and for all, as, 'Formally educated Qashqa'i served state officials rather than their people.' Another said: 'Education made Qashqa'i youth realize right from wrong. It taught them to think and then act, to make informed decisions. We think in political terms, understand political language, so we must exist politically' (a Qashqa'i university student).

The feeling among professionals was that formally educated Qashqa'i were the political hope of the tribespeople: 'Our parents were used by *khans* and rulers. We will not let this happen to our children. Our power is now our education. We need to know our rights and learn legal channels to practise and defend them' (a former Qashqa'i schoolteacher). Formally educated Qashqa'i learned about the mistakes their ancestors made. They seemed to want to apply past socio-political and cultural experience to unite their community through culture rather than politics.

The Qashqa'i lived in remote areas distant from the application of civil laws and regulations and carried out instructions from tribal leaders. They were, for the most part, armed, and fought against central authority because their leaders wanted them to. They benefited by gaining access to allocated pastures and grazing lands. Could they have had the same access without challenging state authorities? People developed the idea that co-operation with state officials promoted literacy skills and replaced the *khans'* formula with what schoolteachers were preaching. 'Give me the gun; I will give you literacy.' In the past, the Qashqa'i had used guns to secure their safety and continuity of lifestyle.

It is difficult to reach a consensus as to what political impact formal education has had. Formally educated tribespeople learned to see their social, economic, political and cultural problems. Some said that seeing a problem is halfway to having the solution. Formally educated Qashqa'i, and for that matter tribespeople as a whole, were more politically alert and seemed to know more about what was going on in local, national, and sometimes international politics. Most formally educated Qashqa'i seem to have a political vision. Many tribespeople read newspapers, listen to the radio, and interpret politics on their own.

Cultural Factors

The literacy programme for nomads emerged when many Qashqa'i families debated about settling, mainly due to economic and political pressures. Economically, it helped by creating jobs, and Qashqa'i educators began mediating between tribespeople and state officials, a process that eventually lessened economic and political pressure. Reduction of these pressures delayed the rate of settlement, which proved beneficial in cultural terms. Many Qashqa'i families continued their lifestyle, and some of them settled years later when they had a more developed sense of their Qashqa'i-ness. Unlike many non-literate families who settled and accepted unsatisfactory jobs in villages, towns and cities, some Qashqa'i families who received formal education and then settled enjoyed better jobs and relatively easier lifestyles.

The literacy programme brought together in the same tent children of the rich and the poor, élite and non-élite, and taught them the same subjects. This created a sense of equality, togetherness, and mutual respect. As one formally educated Qashqa'i explained, the school tent was viewed as a tent with an ever-burning hearth. Children from residential tents came to the school tent and walked away with the light they needed to move on in life. 'No child was discriminated against because of his or her family background,' said a teacher. Once they learned this lesson, the teacher concluded, 'The darkness of the whole world could not put out the light these children carried away from the school tent.' Because part of the knowledge that Qashqa'i children attained through the tent school was, in fact, Qashqa'i cultural knowledge and values, I argue that the tent school unintentionally facilitated enculturation of Qashqa'i youths with the culture and values of their own tribal and nomadic societies – more so than the ideological agenda that government officials had hoped to achieve. But formally educated Qashqa'i also noticed the negative cultural impact of the literacy programmes for nomads. Tribespeople lost a relatively independent economic status and became state-supported and dependent consumers. 'Our children learned literacy skills and forgot how to herd.'

Teachers and students shared their knowledge with the rest of their community, through the use of their indigenous language, and so not only conveyed information but also reinforced their language and culture. The programme promoted interest in literacy and reading, which in turn exposed Qashqa'i to diverse schools of thought. Some formally educated Qashqa'i followed different ideological directions, such as socialism, communism and Islamicism.

Formal education also facilitated cultural adaptations. When a person developed chicken pox or other infectious diseases, the whole population expected to suffer from them too – many Qashqa'i viewed such suffering as unavoidable. But with the introduction of formal education and other changes in Iran in general, tribespeople understood that some diseases could be prevented or cured. Parents were informed by some educators that it was important to treat their male and female children equally. This resulted in opportunities for some Qashqa'i girls to enjoy social mobility, respect and prestige, as did some Qashqa'i boys. Qashqa'i tribespeople also adjusted their concepts of time and planned for future needs and new developments, engaging increasingly in long-term planning and cost-effective alternatives.

Schoolteachers and the Mechanism of Enculturation

Schoolteachers taught and also observed, mediated, and reflected ongoing issues and events in and around the camps, and advised their kin and group members how to interact with outsiders. They were among the first group of systematically trained government employees, so their presence was as visible as their white cone-shaped tents. Because tribespeople tended to trust teachers, they followed the guidelines teachers gave them. Teachers witnessed engagement ceremonies, wrote marriage contracts, and attended other events such as business transactions, rituals, religious ceremonies and burials. Teachers dealt with internal and external tribal affairs. Just as students saw teachers as their role models and copied them, teachers viewed Bahmanbaigi as their ultimate role model. Because Bahmanbaigi repeatedly instructed teachers that they had to respect their elders and work with them co-operatively, most teachers performed accordingly.

Prior to the 1960s, Qashqa'i tribespeople, influenced by tribal leaders, viewed state officials as enemies. Tension existed among the Qashqa'i, the state officials, and non-Qashqa'i villagers who lived on Qashqa'i migration routes. In the absence of paramount leaders, teachers were influential in minimising these tensions and promoted peace by implementation of elements of civil societies. Qashqa'i students trusted, believed in, and followed schoolteachers who were viewed as the vanguard in literacy and culture. A teacher was viewed as a socio-cultural manifestation of the Qashqa'i. Female schoolteachers were required to wear Qashqa'i dress all the time and played important cultural roles. Their female students and the mothers saw them as people whose clothes did not keep them from success. Their male students, siblings and fathers also developed the idea that people can succeed without having to strip themselves of their identities.

Students saw their teachers as role models with two distinct sides. On one side, there was a common cultural base for teachers, students and parents. Teachers had physically moved away from this base for training and returned with some knowledge. Teachers became icons whose hidden powers were speculated upon, appreciated and desired. In a more visible way, they gained a salary. Many parents wanted their children to visit this other side and return victorious. For many students who wished to realise their parents' dreams, the only way to do so was through the teachers. Students mimicked the way their teachers talked, walked and behaved in both public and private – but did not always discriminate in registering what they observed about their teachers. Teachers could imprint their students with a Qashqa'i culture pattern during the elementary-school years while exposing them to another culture. This imprinted cultural pattern gained strength in the post-revolutionary era.

Most of the sources of information schoolteachers had access to were in Persian. They shared this information with colleagues, parents and students in Turkish. Parents showed great interest in what their school-attending children communicated to them from school. These children sometimes translated the information they wanted to relate to their parents into Turkish. Because efforts go into making a translation meaningful to an audience, this process affected both teachers and students, particularly students whose Persian vocabulary was minimal. Therefore students had to draw on their Turkish skills to explain Persian words, a process that reinforced their indigenous language skills. Language has been the most significant element of Qashqa'i culture in a predominantly non-Turkish province.

Because teachers knew that students and others closely watched their activities and behaviour, they avoided conduct that would give a bad impression. A teacher reported to me that his official title was teacher. But 'I did everything in my capacity to lead my group. They were dependent on me. I tried to connect, in social terms, my small group to the larger Iranian society.' Another teacher said, 'I, as a teacher, burnt like a candle so my students and other members of my group could find their way to success.'

Most schoolteachers were reliable and trustworthy people, according to a Qashqa'i educator who worked as a school inspector during the 1970s. Qashqa'i children had internalised the rule of obeying parents, older siblings and kin. It was a cultural value to respect and obey the learned members of one's society. Because teachers were viewed as wise, educated, cultured, and experienced relatives, students saw them as more important than even their parents did.

Students, Teachers, and Elders: Concluding Remarks

Rapid changes, primarily through the introduction of the state-supported education programme, could lead to cultural discontinuity, and students were the ultimate target of any significant cultural alteration. Bahmanbaigi applied cultural knowledge and experience to promote the educational programme, and elders came to support it. The mechanisms transforming the community through culturally constructed social meanings led to further cultural awareness in the post-revolutionary era.

The older generation, who had lived under the socio-political structure of the Qashqa'i confederation and internalised the social meanings that set them apart from other Iranians, passed on the internalised social meaning discursively. Customarily age, respect and credibility went hand in hand in the Qashqa'i socio-cultural system. Any matter concerning a Qashqa'i sub-tribe that had to be presented to a headman or other tribal leader was handled first by the elders of the group. From the inception of the literacy programme for nomads, Bahmanbaigi practised this same principle. He assigned a teacher to a group only if an elder personally requested. Despite standard procedures for admission to the Teacher Training School, elders who wished their daughhters or sons to apply for teaching positions always approached Bahmanbaigi and expressed their need for his help. On occasion an elder could influence Bahmanbaigi in securing admission for an otherwise qualified applicant whose entrance exam score was low.

Elders were important and influential in several other areas that reinforced their position in social and cultural terms. For instance, an unmarried teacher assigned to a group of families, but whose own family lived elsewhere, usually stayed with the elder of the group if there was no headman. The family provided him or her with food and other logistical support, such as transporting the teacher's belongs during the migration. Usually the elder who had asked Bahmanbaigi for a teacher was responsible for such matters. Reinforcing the elders' position in the community, when government officials, teacher-inspectors, or other outsiders visited the teacher, they were usually invited to the elder's tent, served meals and entertained generously. Elders on behalf of the group asked the teacher to write letters of request for governmental services or letters of complaint. They also watched schoolteachers closely for behaviours that they considered 'moral corruption' (*fisad-i akhlaqi*). Under the influence of city culture, some teachers liked to play cards, consume alcohol, or listen to popular Persian music. The elders would warn teachers who were so involved. Teachers knew that if Bahmanbaigi learned about such matters from elders, he would humiliate them in public or transfer them to less desirable places. Elders also were concerned about the way teachers dressed, how they styled their hair, and even with whom they associated.

Students interacted with teachers as they did with their siblings and kin. They sat crossed-legged in a tent at home as well as at school. They respected older household members and their kin and could expect to be respected by those who were younger. Qashqa'i started their daily chores at dawn and continued until and even past dark; Qashqa'i schools followed the same kind of pattern of activities (but for a shorter duration). Members of households attended to chores according to gender and age, as the task required. Schools for nomads followed a somewhat similar pattern. There were no school bells, no clock hanging from the tent pole, no syllabus, no timetable as to what subject should be studied and when, and no order as to which grade received lessons from the teacher first and which one received them last. All subjects were studied and practised all day, every day. I do not mean to imply that teachers did not know what they were doing. My aim is to demonstrate that schools operated in a similar fashion to Qashqa'i households and Qashqa'i society in more widely.

Knowing that the students' labour was needed at certain times, teachers permitted students, indeed encouraged them, to help their families. When teachers work with students in a fashion that encourages their attentive participation, there is an 'accommodative' effort, which fosters positive feelings toward school. In the Qashqa'i case, teachers were accommodating, both by culture and by their training, which created interest in the students and made them feel positive towards the teachers, and wish to follow in the teachers' footsteps.

Ogbu (1987, 1992) discusses 'oppositional identity' or boundary-maintaining mechanisms adopted by a group subjected to a culturally or ethnically dominant power. Through these mechanisms, minorities reject the values and symbols associated with the dominant group. In the Qashqa'i case, although the textbooks were the same as in any Iranian school, teachers and students were both Qashqa'i, and schooling took place in Qashqa'i geographical, physical and cultural environments. Rather than *oppositional identity*, complementary identity was formed, hence reinforcing Qashqa'i identity. Simultaneously, elders filtered out many values and symbols that were non-Qashqa'i, processes that transformed culturally constructed social meanings for the students. In other words, the paramount Qashqa'i educator, Mohammad Bahmanbaigi (1920-), applied his cultural knowledge to replicate the Qashqa'i confederation's political structure through the literacy programme he developed. The influence of Bahmanbaigi on teachers and the influence of teachers on several hundred thousand Qashqa'i students facilitated the transformation of meanings within Qashqa'i society and culture.

Acknowledgement

I gratefully acknowledge the National Science Foundation (NSF), Sigma Xi, the Social Science Research Council (SSRC) and the American Council of Learned Societies (ACLS) for supporting my research. I am also thankful to Washington University in St. Louis for awarding me the Dissertation and Teaching Fellowships, which facilitated my work on campus residency (1996–1997) while my doctoral dissertation was in progress. Dr Caroline Dyer's encouragement and Dr Zahra Sarraf's ongoing and unconditional support made this work possible. I thank them both.

References

Beck, L. (1986) *The Qashqa'i of Iran*. New Haven: Yale University Press.

———— (1991) *Nomad: a Year in the Life of a Qashqa'i Tribesman in Iran*. Berkeley: University of California Press.

Garthwaite, G. (1983) *Khans and Shahs: a Documentary Analysis of the Bakhtiyari in Iran*. Cambridge: Cambridge University Press.

Ogbu, J. (1987) 'Variability in Minority Responses to Schooling: Nonimmigrants vs. Immigrants'. In: G. Spindler and L. Spindler (eds) *Interpretive Ethnography of Education: At Home and Abroad*. Hillsdale, New Jersey: Lawrence Erlbaum Associates.

———— (1992) 'Understanding Cultural Diversity and Learning'. *Educational Research* 21 (8): 5–14.

Shahbazi, M. (1998) Formal Education, Schoolteachers, and Ethnic Identity among the Qashqa'I of Iran. Unpublished Ph.D. Dissertation thesis. Washington University in St. Louis: Department of Anthropology.

Shahbazi, M. (2001a) 'An Anthropological Study of the Paradoxical Nature of Literacy for an Ethnic Minority in Iran'. *The Jackson State University Researcher: An Interdisciplinary Scholarly Journal* Vol./XVII/ (4): 37–53.

Shahbazi, M. (2001b) 'The Qashqa'i Nomads of Iran (Part I): Formal Education'. *Nomadic Peoples*: 5(1): 37–64.

Shahbazi, M. (2002) 'The Qashqa'i Nomads of Iran (Part II): Formal Education'. *Nomadic Peoples*: 5(2): 98–126.

Shahbazi, M. (2003) 'Anthropological Fieldwork Endeavor and Indigenous Researchers'. *Nomadic Peoples* 7(2): 97–106.

Sohrabi, A. (1995) *Amuzish va parvarish dar 'ashayir-i Iran* (Education among the Nomads of Iran). Shiraz: Shiraz University Press.

Statistical Center of Iran (1986) Census Books vol. 1–3. Tehran, Iran.

Tapper, R. (ed.) (1993) *The Conflict of Tribe and State in Iran and Afghanistan*. London: Croom Helm.

CHAPTER 10

EDUCATION AND PASTORALISM IN MONGOLIA

Demberel and Helen Penn

Preamble

This chapter was originally conceived as a joint endeavour to describe the history and present state of education in Mongolia between a pastoralist, Demberel, who was Director of Education in Gobi Altai region in Mongolia, and Helen Penn, an English academic. Tragically, Demberel was killed in an accident after he provided an initial draft. This chapter therefore provides a first version of what he wanted to say. As the remaining author, I have drawn on my notes of our conversations to edit his contribution, and I may well have distorted some of his nuances. Although unfinished and unchecked by him, the chapter is also intended as a tribute, a published record of his work and concerns. He was a very humane, sophisticated and well-educated pastoralist.

Demberel was brought up in an utterly remote herding community in Gobi Altai. He progressed through the Mongolian education system and read for a degree in physics – many pastoralists took advantage of tertiary education in Mongolia – and then returned to his native region, as a teacher, a headteacher, then as Director of the region. Recently he had participated in a Danaid project (Holst et al., 1996) to develop a more liberal education system in Mongolia, and as part of this project had travelled to Germany on a study tour, which had raised important issues for him, particularly about the role of communism. He was interested in and open minded about the intellectual as well as financial contribution donor agencies could make to Mongolian education, particularly the education of pastoralists.

He accompanied me when I was contracted to work for the Mongolian Ministry of Education and Culture by Save the Children U.K. He was the chief informant for my fieldwork in the Gobi Altai region and we travelled together throughout the mountainous desert region. We discussed education issues and the problems of transition a great deal, despite my inability to speak Mongolian. (We should also thank our translator Tsendseren.) Demberel's comments were so insightful that with this chapter in mind, I persuaded him to write an autobiographical account of his own experiences of education both as a pastoralist, and as someone who had become responsible for delivering a modernised education system to pastoralists.

His account is in two parts, first his autobiography, and his reflections on the history and present state of education in Mongolia. Then I add my own comments to contextualise his account for readers who may be less familiar with this context.

Demberel: a Biographical Account

As my own biography is closely connected with the history of education in Mongolia, I would like firstly to tell you something about myself. My father, Lodoi, was a typical herdsman, and my family is one of the many families that live year round in *gers* (a circular felt tent covering a flexible wooden lattice frame, a typical pastoralist dwelling) in the crests, valleys, and pastures of the Khar Azarga mountain chain in the Altai mountains in Gobi Altai, in the west of the country (1200 km away from Ulaanbaatar, the capital of Mongolia). My parents lived a nomadic style of life, as do the overwhelming majority of Mongolians.

My father gained experience handed down from generation to generation, and at the age of 20 he was called up for military service. After five years' service he returned to his homeland and got married. He was literate and had considerable practice in husbandry and felt making and could cure sick animals. He could as easily apply first aid to an animal with a broken leg or to a person made sick by a poisonous plant. He was respected and honoured by his fellow countrymen. As part of the social organisation and development under communism he took care of his allocated herds. In 1959 he enrolled as a member of the herdsmen's union. He died before reaching old age.

My mother, Khumbaan, has lived in Khalian *sum* (district) all her life. She can read, and do mental arithmetic. She has raised six children. Khumbaan makes dairy products, such as curd and skimmed milk, and preserves the food so it can be eaten all year round, especially in winter. She sews clothing and makes footwear from felt and animal skins.

The lives of my parents are typical of ordinary Mongolian herding life. I was born in 1949, the second son. Until the age of eight I lived with my parents herding the flock of sheep and goats. I helped them with the daily work, I played with my siblings, and enjoyed the beauty of the land.

One sunny summer day a representative of the *sum* headquarters came and gave us an enrolment paper. Later I identified it as a letter of invitation for me to study at the school. My mother began to prepare food and sew some clothes. I was very excited. I put two notebooks and two pencils into a cloth bag my mother had sewn for me. We headed off 20 km away to the *bag* (the commune or sub-district, the smallest administrative unit) accompanied by father and my sister Tserendolgor, who was going into the third grade. As everyone rides a horse, we would race. Commonly, a Mongolian child at the age of five would be expected to ride fast.

The beginning period of studying was unusual for me, as someone generally used to living in a solitary *ger* in the mountain pastures. My first school was in a little settlement in the semi desert. There were about ten people working there: a teacher, doctor, guard, stoker and some other workers. The school consisted of two little white houses: a school and a dormitory. It was especially strange to be among contemporaries in a room with strange smells and colours, and to apply myself to lessons. It has left precious, unforgettable recollections in my memory. I studied there for four years. My sister and I lived with my uncle for the first two years. When I was living with relatives, in my free time I used to carry water, herd the flock, collect fuel and dung, and prepare food. The days passed quickly.

The following two years, from September until May, I spent in the school dormitory. In the dormitory children would play and study, so the days seemed longer and boring. Occasionally for the weekend, or for holidays we would go home. Homesickness was one of our big problems. A few among us would be discouraged and run away. The main thing that enabled us to survive was our knowledge that the teacher, the cook, the guard, and the president (of the commune) were all doing everything possible for us. In the dormitory we were well provided for – even bed clothes and sanitary facilities. They made our food and even the stoker and cook bathed us and washed our dirty clothes. Gradually through those people's love we became accustomed to the school. It is not an easy thing to be away from home during one's childhood. Every countryside child must overcome this.

After graduation from the first school in 1961, I continued studying at the centre of our *aimag* (the region). Our *aimag* centre was 120 km away across the desert and it took two days to get there. After graduating from my secondary school in 1967 I entered the Pedagogical Institute of Ulaanbaatar. During these periods of secondary and tertiary education I continued to live in the dormitory or with relatives. After graduation in 1971 I went to work in my homeland, Khalian *sum*, as a teacher of Physics and Mathematics. I was working there as a teacher, then as a headmaster. In 1974 I took a higher degree as a pedagogical manager in Ulaanbaatar, and continued my work as a teacher, headmaster and methodologist at the *aimag* Education Centre, as its Principal. My autobiography is in effect a historical document, which shows how the Mongolian educational system worked.

Demberel: a Historical Perspective on Education

Educational policies covered almost all the countryside people. But its effects were not always predictable.

State Policies on Education

At the beginning of this century a number of Mongolian scripts such as *'Tod'* and *'Somboyo'* were taught in religious schools. In the 1910 Manji period there were many thousands of monks in Buddhist monasteries whose task was to prepare unimpeachable officials. Some of these monks established independent schools where Manji, Mongolian, Chinese, Arithmetic, and Kunzi doctrines were taught. During the Bogdo Khaan empire in 1911–1921 a fair degree of attention was paid to culture and education and there were some attempts to broaden schooling, and to enlighten [note: Demberel uses 'enlighten' and 'educate' interchangeably in this account] the population. Mongolia was not an entirely illiterate country.

On October 2 in 1921 in the former capital, Niislel Khuree, under communism, the first elementary school was established. It had 40 students and was guaranteed a state budget for three years. The primary goal of the communist state was to maintain and develop public literacy and prepare teachers to work in the system. So in 1922–23 a temporary school was established to re educate existing teachers to work in the new system. In 1925 this temporary school became a teacher training school for new students. Through such activities the number of teachers was increased and made it possible to establish many schools in the provinces. In 1923 in Niislel Khuree at the elementary school both sciences and languages were taught – Mongolian, Arithmetic, Geometry, History, Geography, Physics and Chemistry.

In 1924 the Ministry of Enlightenment was established to train managers and officials responsible for schooling procedures, and to make sure every *aimag* was covered. In the period 1921–30 many religious schools where only boys studied, of necessity, co-existed along with state schools. These religious schools mainly instructed in Buddhist doctrines, philosophy, astrology and medicine. In 1924–34 the number of state schools increased and five secondary schools were opened for a total of 600 pupils. By the end of this period, 59 schools were established for a total of more than 3,100 children. Technical schools were set up to train specialists. In 1925 the School of Finance, the School of History, and the Central Party Political School were established. In 1926 a School of Veterinary Studies, a School of Communication, and a School of Nursing were opened. From 1930 Mongolian children were able to study in Russia to further their education.

To educate children not enrolled into schooling and for others who were illiterate, traditional home tuition and study circles were set up. These tuition circles also aimed to enlighten the poor and middle level monks. During 1930 the infrastructure for study circles – materials and courses – was developed.

By the 1940s a decision was made to enlighten (offer universal education to) every child under 18 years old, with opportunities for all children to take their education further if they chose to do so. In 1942 the Mongolian State University was founded. In 1945 the Evening School Pedagogical Institute was established, and by the end of 1950, the Agricultural and Economic Institutes were fully established.

A comprehensive state governed (communist) educational system was therefore established within 20 years. The policy was developed by the State Great Khural (Parliament) and Party as a coherent, concrete, comprehensive programme. This policy fell into three stages.

During the Revolution of 1921 only one percent of the population was educated and 1.5 percent of the children enrolled into schooling. So the first stage was to try to address widespread illiteracy. In 1926 at the Great Khural, cultural and educational issues were discussed, and it was agreed as a major priority, to adopt a ten-year plan to develop culture and education for 1926–36 and to budget for it on an annual basis. By 1963 the problem of illiteracy was virtually eliminated. We had moved from one percent literacy to 90 percent basic literacy (this included enlightenment about communism). From 1940 the second stage was to achieve elementary public education for everyone. Again this was achieved within a generation. From 1960 the third stage was to aim for secondary education for most children. Again we managed this. By 1990 most children received a minimum of eight years' schooling.

Strict laws were implemented which required detailed planning to introduce the state programme. At all levels of the state, national, regional and district, party organisations and officials had to prioritise education and literacy. We tried to develop an inclusive system, so that everyone was fully involved in the education process.

Pastoralist people deeply respect Mongolian traditions and nationality, and their cultural upbringing bred a strong sense of collective obligation. These two factors, respect for traditional ways of life, and the sense of communal obligation, were understood and incorporated by the state, which considerably helped towards the successful adoption of the education programme. Now people criticise this state centralism. I consider it a humanitarian policy done for the well-being of the country, right for people at that specific time, when we were so behind in culture and education. This education programme succeeded phenomenally in a short period of time, because it earned the support of the people.

Methods of Eradicating Illiteracy

As indicated above, there were many strands to the programme to eradicate illiteracy. For pastoralists the study circles, local tuition and targeted courses were particularly important. Every literate person was asked to teach at the study circles, and everyone who was literate was set a task to teach a certain number of people. Husbands taught their wives, students their parents and neighbours. I used to teach my mother and the children of my neighbourhood. We would gather in someone's home and study together. Everyone's attention had to be focused on becoming literate.

At the level of formal schooling, an important principle was that education was free at primary, secondary and tertiary levels. Universities and colleges provided scholarships, and gave additional grants to successful students. Fees for the use of libraries, courses, and any in-service training were paid by the state.

For pastoralist children dormitories were established by the schools. A dormitory was a big economical unit with a sufficient supply of bedclothes and fuel, rooms to live and sleep and cook in and a cellar to store food. Usually they provided for all children in the region. Everything in these dormitories was free, too. Teachers would be on duty at all hours, eat with the children at mealtimes, wake children up, put them to bed. These teachers were responsible for all aspects of discipline, including paying attention to health, hygiene and wellbeing of the students.

The teachers were regarded as key players in the implementation of educational policy. Every school had an outreach area for which it was responsible. Teachers would update their roll of students from 0 16 year olds every year, inform the parents whose children should begin school, and enable them to prepare their children for school. These teachers took their duties very seriously and paid a lot of attention to enrolling every child into studying. Some parents were not willing to let their children go to school, so teachers had to propagandise and bring the children back. The salary of teachers was relatively high, compared with the wages of the population generally, and they earned their salary taking on the extra jobs.

Adults also had opportunities for education and could take courses at evening shift schools, and correspondence courses, so they did not have to leave work in order to study. These education courses were linked to secondary education qualifications.

The educational system had a unitary purpose and an organised programme, and the methods of delivery ensured that there were no differences in the quality and outcomes of education between urban and rural schools. When I was in the fourth grade in our *aimag* there was a competition in arithmetic. I represented my school and won. When I was in the tenth grade I became a champion in arithmetic in our *aimag* and won the 6th place in the state arithmetic competition. I remember how I trained for an international competition and was so proud because pastoralists had the same opportunities and the same chances of success. One proof of this is that from among my pastoralist contemporaries, people achieved success in many different professions such as scientists, doctors, teachers, economists, engineers – and if not academic success, then awards for being labourers of the first rank.

In addition to public education institutes and universities, colleges were established. Lots of young people were sent to Russia and to other socialist countries. This was also a good strategy for valuing literacy. Pastoralists were actively enrolled into activities such as going abroad and taking part in wider social life.

In summary these education changes were very successful, and they were paralleled with changes in health and other key services. Every pastoralist in the remotest parts of the country had access to these services. UNESCO rewarded us with a special international decoration entitled '*Krupskaya*' for working successfully for the eradication of illiteracy and the development of a culture of education. Most of the state laureates and leaders of the country were the children of herdsmen. Their names might not be well known outside Mongolia, but they were distinguished people – Ts. Damdinsuren was three times awarded the state Prize for outstanding achievement; J. Gurarigchaa was a cosmonaut; and there were notable politicians such as Tsedenbal, Ochirbat and Bagabandi.

The effects of the education system were cumulative. The more education there was, the more people respected it. It became evident that people with education had a better standard of living, yet one which did not necessarily mean abandoning herding. Parents became more interested in educating their children. The desire of pastoralist children to study was as keen as that of urban children. This was evidence for pastoralists like myself that the education process was a fair system. But in retrospect the system also generated problems which were not fully recognised, but which have become sharpened under transition.

The Difficulties and Shortages

Mongolian pastoralists who live in the vast steppes and who live nomadic lives face lots of difficulties in the education process. It is not altogether natural to separate young children from their parents and their home. Homesickness was a constant pressure and some children could not concentrate on learning and do well. But as well as being away from their parents' love, the children missed out on daily work routines. They became used to living a ready-made life where everything was provided without effort. They grew soft and were tempted by the easy way out. They lost that sense of sturdy independence that characterises a traditional Mongolian childhood. They became passive, and lost their sense of initiative and the ability to take an overview and find innovative solutions. On the other hand, parents would become worried and despair, because they could not influence their children, instill traditional virtues, or even help them to do their homework.

So on both sides, that of the children, and that of the parents, there were some reservations about the processes of education. It was offset by state investment. To meet the costs of education, food and dormitories for hundreds of thousands of children, the state spent lots of money. Since transition in 1990, the state has had to introduce charges. Parents whose children stay in dormitories have to pay for half of the food (food costs in Mongolia are very high, now amounting to half the school budget), and for other educational expenses other than tuition fees. They must also pay for tertiary education. This causes difficulties for families with many children and for poor families, and makes education not only less attractive, but in many cases impossible.

We cannot at present change the charging system. But in order to mitigate problems of homesickness and alleviate parents' fears of softness, we have been trying to put into practice such ideas as rooming together children of one class, or of one family. Little children are put together with bigger children, and dormitory rooms equipped like a home. But children do need their parents' attention as well as our care.

As I have indicated, teachers of pastoralists carried out lots of other duties alongside educating children. They took them for outings, and oversaw dormitory life. Without the first pioneering enthusiasm, and as the relative value of their salary has decreased, the teachers inevitably pay less attention to these duties.

The education system is now much more unequal. An additional reason, besides the introduction of charges, is the introduction of new technology. In urban areas we have educational programmes geared to the needs of urban children, who in turn have access to radio, television, periodicals and study materials. This inequality of provision leads to different outcomes for urban and rural children.

Education after Transition

The Democratic Revolution began in 1990 and the mode of life of the country has been completely changed in a short period of time. Since we have realised that democracy, human rights, liberty, and the principles of a free economy are the ultimate goals of humanity, we abolished the former communist political and economic system of social and intellectual life. Now we are trying to establish a new political system which takes a different view of democracy and economically we are working towards a market economy.

As part of this process, the Government is revising educational law. Despite the successes of our 70-year experiment, education in our country has been too ideological. The study process was based on the needs of society rather than on the interests or desires of the individual. It was too theorised and removed from practice and usage, and its management was very centralised. We are trying to change these aspects at each of the stages of education.

The present stages of Mongolian education can be summarised as follows.

- *Pre-school*: There are 667 kindergartens where 67,900 children are being educated. In Mongolia usually 0–2–year-old children are educated at home, and children from 3–7 years old in kindergarten. Kindergartens are the basis for systematically organising pre school education for children under school age. The purpose of pre school education is to develop the ability to express oneself, to understand others and to help oneself, to teach rituals and traditional approaches, and to prepare children for their future elementary education. In order for pastoralists to benefit from pre-school education, we organise some specific outreach work and tuition.
- *Elementary education*: In the 1996–1997 academic year 234,100 children were studying at elementary education schools, and 7,587 teachers were employed in them. The curriculum of elementary education continues to use proven practices and methods. Children study for four years at elementary school. The elementary education curriculum, the physical condition of buildings and qualifications of the teaching staff will soon be set as minimum educational standards.
- *Secondary education*: Mongolian secondary education consists of eight years (incomplete) or ten years (complete). Usually the first eight years can be obtained at *sum* level, and the final two at *aimag* level in technical or professional high schools. 184,000 students are now studying at *sum* level secondary schools or at high schools. (Informal secondary education is available through the programmes of various education organisations.) The purpose of secondary education is to give people general technical knowledge and professional skills. This includes aesthetics, humanities and citizenship. We try to foster healthy attitudes, and produce socially active citizens who will go on developing their talents. We want to equip children to find ways of living and working in this new democratic climate.
- *Higher education*: In 1997 1998, there were 10 universities, 18 colleges, and 56 private educational institutes, employing 1,400 teachers. 40,000 students are studying in them. A further 17,000 students are studying in various technical colleges. Higher education should aim to follow through the policies of the state education system, and be available for all people. In practice, the introduction of charges make this difficult for poor people who cannot obtain scholarships.

Helen: Education in Mongolia

My particular brief in Mongolia was to undertake a situation analysis of the education system, in particular focusing on the kindergarten system, as part of a joint SCF/Ministry of Education project. As part of this analysis, I reviewed a number of official documents and data sets (e.g. Mongolian Demographic Survey, 1994; Mongolian Household Income and Expenditure Statistics, 1995–1996; Mongolian Education Statistics, 1995–1996; Mongolian Programme of Action for the Development of Children in the

1990s). I visited Mongolia in 1997, 1998 and 1999. Because of Demberel's death and changes in the project team at SCF, I have not been back since, although I have spent time recently in neighbouring Kazakhstan, where I was also carrying out an educational review. Some of my information about Mongolia may now be dated. In a sense this is an historical account, a snapshot of change at a particular moment.

Pastoralist Life in Mongolia

Pastoralist and nomadic communities are often regarded as among the most geographically, economically and politically peripheral in the world. In fact their integration with broader socio-political and economic forces is consistently underestimated, and they have always had to adapt to survive and prosper (Chang and Koster, 1994). Here, I briefly explore how in Mongolia in the last century, the survival and development of pastoralism, and pastoralist education in particular, has been closely linked to the ethos and ideology of external aid programmes, first from the Soviet Union, and subsequently from Western aid programmes. Demberel's account describes the impact of communism and market ideologies from the inside, as the lived and considered experience of an educated pastoralist; I attempt to contextualise those experiences for a wider readership, and to locate them more widely. As I explained in the introduction to this chapter, our dialogue is an incomplete one, and is bereft of development, due to Demberel's untimely death. I would have much preferred to discuss and revise my comments with him before offering them up to a wider readership.

Mongolia covers an area roughly equivalent to half of Western Europe. Most of the country consists of steppes at an elevation of around 2000 metres, although there are also desert and mountainous regions. Only one percent of the land is arable. The climate is hostile and the temperature ranges from -40°C in winter, to + 40°C in summer. The total population is around 2.5 million. The capital city, Ulaanbaatar has a seasonally fluctuating population of around 700,000.

Mongolian nomadic society was at its peak in the thirteenth century under Chenngis Khan, when mobility became a decisive asset in warfare (Wolf, 1997). In subsequent centuries Mongolia became very isolated, and in Chinese-ruled Inner Mongolia, pastoralists became mainly sedentarised several centuries ago (Onon, 1972; Lattimore, 1941). In the early twentieth century, Outer Mongolia became a satellite state of the USSR. Unlike other pastoralist communities within the USSR, and especially in contrast with neighbouring Kazakhstan which has an overlapping population with Mongolia, pastoralism survived and flourished. Religious institutions, mainly a form of Buddhism, were, however, brutally suppressed. There is debate about the extent to which monasteries and other Buddhist institutions and activities were regarded as corrupt and parasitic by the majority of the population, and overlaid an earlier shamanism. Shamanism was also firmly suppressed, but post-transition has been revived. There are no obvious signs of a Buddhist revival. On my trip with Demberel, we were met on the outskirts of most settlements by local leaders at an *oba*, a shamanistic shrine. Everyone circled the *oba* and tossed offerings. When I discussed it with him, Demberel did not appear to attach any particular significance to this; he saw it as a ritual of greeting rather than as a spiritual event.

Under the communist regime, a relatively sympathetic collective system was evolved. From the 1930s, the herders were organised into *Negdels* or collectives; they continued to be pastoralists and to move in search of grazing, but the number and type of animals they herded were negotiated within the *Negdel*. Moreover, the *Negdel* were organised into *sum* or district level centres. A number of free (at the point of use) *sum* services were provided – basic medicine and veterinary services, emergency fodder supplies for harsh winters, sales outlets for animal produce (almost all meat sales were contracted to the Soviet Union), gully and bridge maintenance; and, in particular, kindergarten, primary and secondary schooling and adult education services. A substantial number of people were employed at *sum* and *aimag* level in providing these services, and the services in turn offered reasonable job opportunities to skilled and unskilled alike. (Sovietisation did, however, mean the introduction of unsustainable urban policies in the *sum* and *aimag* centres – for example inappropriate sewerage programmes, or, incredibly, a piano in every kindergarten!) The combination of collectivity, independence and minimisation of risk that these arrangements offered to pastoralists were relatively unique under a communist regime (Goldstein and Beall, 1994). At the time of transition in 1990, the majority of Mongolians were pastoralists, or were within a generation of being so.

Figure 10.1 School at sum settlement, Gobi Altai.

In theory at least, pastoralism is still a highly respected as a way of life, viewed as economically productive in a hostile terrain, and producing a sturdy, adaptive and resilient people. Demberel took pride in the moral and intellectual characteristics of Mongolians that he considered were fostered by a pastoralist life; an ability to work hard and endure hardship, taking events in their stride and not fussing; and a sense of initiative, and the ability to take an overview and find innovative solutions.

But without the support of the *Negdels* and the services they provided, pastoralist life has become harsher. Families still own herds of animals – sheep, goats, cows, horses and camels – and move around with them, on prescribed routes and in prescribed arcs, to find suitable grazing. In the Gobi, where the climate is still more extreme, winter habitations are semi-permanent, whereas in spring and early summer herders may need to move every three to ten days to find suitable grazing and water. A viable number of animals cannot fall much below ten cows and thirty sheep plus horses and/or camels for transport; but richer herders will have up to 2,000 animals.

The disbandment of *Negdel* services post-transition meant that herders have become more vulnerable in many ways. Veterinary services have become harder to obtain; transport has become more difficult as roads fall into disrepair; and sales of produce more difficult to arrange as Soviet meat markets have disappeared.

Figure 10.2 The Gobi Altai in the winter months.

Figure 10.3 Spring comes to the Gobi Altai.

These changes have meant considerable unemployment in the *sum* and *aimag* centres. Some families have stayed in the *sum* centres and barely survive. Those that have had the resources to develop viable herds have left to become full-time herders again. (On the trip with Demberel, we visited a *ger* where the woman of the household was an unemployed veterinary surgeon. She now just administered to her own herd and occasionally assisted neighbours.) On my visit to the Gobi, there had been a dramatic increase in the number of animals, possibly unsustainably so, but very recent harsh winters have decimated some animal populations. The new herds needed looking after, and herder children had become a critical source of labour. Children who previously might have expected to go to school are now kept at home to herd the animals. The drop out rate from school has been considerable, for boys rather than girls. Many of the boarding schools now have ten to twenty girls for every boy. Other children stay away from school simply because of the costs of education.

Education in Mongolia under Communism

Although it is one of the world's poorest and most thinly populated countries, within two generations Mongolia achieved a literacy rate of around 95 percent. As Demberel has described, Mongolia was strongly influenced by the USSR, and the remarkable changes in literacy levels owe a great deal to the communist ideology that pulling together was the only way to succeed; all for one and one for all. Without that kind of ideological thrust it is unlikely that such high literacy levels would have been achieved, and indeed, since transition, literacy rates have been falling badly (UNDP,

2003). The literacy rates also owe a great deal to Soviet financial support. About 30 percent of the country's income came as direct or indirect subsidy from the Soviet state, and much of this went directly into education, as Demberel describes. Teachers were well-paid and schools were well-supplied. Any child who showed aptitude or talent had the opportunity for rapid progression through the system to tertiary level. (These expectations still persist amongst some herders. We visited a herding family, several generations gathered together in a small *ger* camp on a very inaccessible mountainside. The mother of one of the families had had 15 children, all of whom had become herders except the fifteenth, a girl, who was studying English at university in Ulaanbaatar – although the change from Russian to English was also a sign of the times.)

Mongolian pastoralist childrearing practices tend to be strongly collectivist, as opposed to individualistic (Penn, 2001). Like other nomadic societies, Mongolian pastoralists place great emphasis on the well-being and harmony of the immediate group (Briggs, 1970; Humphrey, 1996). In addition, there is a familiarity with animals and landscape, and a physical robustness that is more or less unimaginable in contemporary urbanised Western societies (Lattimore, 1941). Demberel completely unselfconsciously referred to these aspects of daily living in our conversations: for example the expectation that young children would be able *to ride a horse (or camel) fast*; or to the job usually given to young children of collecting up weak newborn animals in springtime and corralling them. Demberel took enormous trouble with a stray kid that decided to hide under the wheels of our jeep, walking some distance across the desert to find a boy with a sack who would care for it and take it back to the *ger*; and the occasion led him to reminisce about some of his own youthful herding experiences. He himself had four teenage sons, and when I asked if they gave him any difficulties as a parent, he looked puzzled and said *no, why would they?* Children are expected to be responsible and dutiful, and to contribute to the household to the best of their skill and ability; in return the household values their contribution and respects their autonomy. (An interesting example of this is the recent film about pastoralist life made in Gobi Altai, *The Weeping Camel*, which portrays experiences in a herding family.) Writing about Central Asia more generally, Falkingham (2000: 21) points out that 'In the Central Asian region children take pride of place within the family and, culturally, are prioritized within the family's hierarchy of needs'.

As Falkingham and others have pointed out (UNESCO, 2000), these expectations of children and their place in society, as contributors and as responsible agents within the households, but also as obedient and supportive of household harmony, chimed well with communist education principles. In particular, the pastoralist culture of respect and obedience towards elders transferred to school settings. The relative didacticism of the communist education system and the apparent lack of questioning within it went unchallenged, since it also delivered a self-evidently sound education (Alexander, 2001).

The sheer achievement of the communist educational policy in a country as poor, remote and difficult to traverse as Mongolia deserves recognition, particularly since it appears to have been achieved without the deliberate repression and denigration of pastoralism that marked education policy in neighbouring parts of the Soviet Union, like Kazakhstan or Siberia. The curriculum did not particularly reflect the needs of pastoralist life and many, if not most, of the texts used were of Soviet origin. But as Krätli and Dyer suggest in the opening chapter of this volume, curricular appropriateness may not necessarily be a critical issue if the wider culture is truly supportive of pastoralism, as in Mongolia. Many teachers in rural areas drew on their own experiences of pastoralism continually, as Demberel did.

Demberel argued that communist education had succeeded amongst pastoralists for a number of reasons. It was part of a national endeavour involving very committed and well-paid teachers; it was both formal and informal in approach; it dovetailed with the needs of herder families for labour, and it was perceived as fair and egalitarian towards pastoralists. It was both carrot and stick. It conferred tangible benefits, but all families were firmly and persistently pursued to ensure the attendance of their children. Above all, education was free, and part of a wider package of health and other services.

Mongolia Post-transition

Post communism, Chenngis Khan is revered as the nomadic founder of the nation and sacred texts concerning his origin are now reprinted (Cleaves, 1982). His image is repeated endlessly on medals, carpets, and other memorabilia. This reification of a halcyon nomadic past is also taking place in Kazakhstan, where all schools are required to have a small corner dedicated to pastoralist lifestyles, for instance a *ger* containing tribal artefacts (Kazakh Ministry of Education, 2004). But whereas in Kazakhstan there is little relationship between this pseudo-historical past and contemporary life, in Mongolia the past is everywhere present. Seeing horsemen in traditional costume in the Mongolian steppes, one could be looking at a picture from the thirteenth century.

Economists have argued that a comprehensive welfare system in a country as poor as Mongolia is not affordable or sustainable without external aid, and services have to be paid for by increased productivity in a world market if Mongolia is to stand on its own feet (World Bank, 1996). (This chapter does not address the future sustainability of pastoralist lifestyles in Mongolia. There seems to be some evidence of overgrazing, and recent very harsh winters have illustrated the extent to which herding life may have fared better under the collective organisation and risk management once offered by the *Negdel* such as winter fodder supplies or meat sales.) Generally, structural adjustment, in Mongolia as elsewhere, has led to sharper divisions between rich and poor, and to a downgrading of public services (World Bank, 1996; Woodward, 1997). In Ulaanbaatar, on each of my successive trips there were more night clubs and bars, more signs of consumerism on the one hand; and on the other, a rise in the number of street children being reported.

But ironically, 14 years after transition, Mongolia is still heavily supported by external aid (UNDP, 2003). Western donors now provide around 23 percent of GDP in aid compared to the 30 percent provided by the USSR. However, aid policies and aid income are now much more fragmented. There is competition among donors, lack of co-ordination between donor agencies, bands of roaming consultants, prospectors from global businesses in search of mineral concessions; and fundamentalist Christian sects – much like the aid industry generally (Penn, 2005).

Education in Mongolia Post-transition

As elsewhere in the Soviet Union poverty has increased sharply since transition. It is now the poorest children, whether or not they are children of herders, who have most problems at school; and conversely the schools in the poorest areas that have most difficulty in meeting educational objectives (Penn, 1998). Apart from tuition fees, obtaining even the most basic schooling materials – pencils and paper – being clean, unscabby, dressed and shod (an absolute necessity for Mongolian winters), being able to afford the school food, all present insuperable problems for the poor. Similarly, paying teachers and maintaining school buildings, especially heating, present problems to authorities in poor districts as education budgets become progressively decentralised. The downward turn in school enrolment is similar in most transitional countries (UNICEF, 1998). Herder children in Mongolia at present tend to be slightly better off than the children of the unemployed in *sum* and *aimag* centres, who cannot manage to sustain even the basic necessities of a herding life. Pastoralism is after all not yet looked down upon, and may even be seen as an enterprising solution during transition. On the other hand, as already pointed out, the demands for herder labour mean that among pastoralist communities, girls are far more likely to be at school than boys.

There are revisions taking place in the curriculum, which Demberel was piloting. Up until then the first stages of the curriculum were formal, with considerable emphasis on writing an immaculate script, reading and basic arithmetic. Some of the reforms of the curriculum, particularly at primary school level, are intended both to introduce more relevant material for herder children, and to try to promote a child-centred style of education that gives more autonomy to children. Herder children certainly appeared very shy and tongue-tied in school settings (Penn, 2001). A more child-centred and individualistic approach seemed to me, as to Demberel, somewhat problematic to introduce. Demberel accepted the need for a market economy but the competitiveness, ruthlessness and range of choices of the market were aspects with which he was unfamiliar. He wanted children to be better equipped to be part of a market economy, but he still saw children as being necessarily subservient to communal traditions and mores. I very much wish we had been able to continue discussing conceptions of childhood and how various traditions and ideologies might shape such conceptions.

Before transition about 30 percent of children attended kindergarten, which were provided for working parents in the cities and in the *aimag* and *sum* centres. The kindergarten system was particularly vulnerable after transition, as it was regarded as a peripheral education service, but Demberel was concerned to build on and extend its benefits, even in so remote an *aimag* as Gobi Altai. In Gobi Altai many of the *sum* kindergartens were encouraged to develop outreach tuition, and teachers would regularly visit outlying *bags* and *ger* settlements by whatever transport was available, usually camel or motorbike. Also there were intense one-week summer schools organised at the end of summer term for children who would not otherwise attend.

Discussion about the education system revolved around both micro level issues (the relevance and appropriateness of the curriculum and teacher training) and macro level issues (universal access and affordability) but at neither level did Demberel view the education of pastoralists as particularly problematic. His view was not altogether shared by many development agency staff, importing experiences from elsewhere in the world, and problematising pastoralism more than he considered appropriate. But whether or not Demberel underestimated the issues facing pastoralist education, there was undoubtedly an official, more than tokenistic, respect for pastoralist traditions. Pastoralism has a unique place in the conceptualisation of the state in Mongolia (Scott, 1998).

The major contemporary challenge for educationalists has not been to include pastoralists, but to recognise and address the needs of the new poor, whether they live in urban, semi-urban or rural poverty. Under communism, gross poverty tended to be regarded as a self-inflicted wound and somewhat disgraceful: no-one needed to be very poor; everyone could take advantage of the opportunities offered. But coping with structural poverty is a different matter. Poverty is now almost inevitable for certain groups of people, for example single parents, or the relatively unskilled unemployed, and cannot be avoided merely by personal effort. Such structural poverty impacts harshly on children (de Vylder, 1996; Waddington, 2004). Poor children miss out on schooling, or may be bullied if they do attend, or may run away from home and join the swelling numbers of street children (DfID, 2000).

The admittedly unusual experience of Mongolia suggests that education can be practically organised for pastoralists. It can become valued among pastoralist communities without necessarily conflicting with their cultural and collective identity. The more pertinent question is whether such success is possible in a market economy where other values strongly prevail.

References

Alexander, R. (2001) *Culture and Pedagogy*. Oxford: Blackwell.

Asian Development Bank (1995) *Escaping the Poverty Trap, Lessons from Asia*. ADB no. 010394.

Briggs, J. (1970) *Never in Anger*. Cambridge, MA: Harvard University Press.

Chang, C. and K. Koster (1994) *Pastoralists at the Periphery*. Tucson: University of Arizona Press.

Cleaves, F.W. (1982) *The Secret History of the Mongols*. Cambridge, MA: Harvard University Press.

de Vylder, S. (1996) *Development Strategies, Macro-economic Policies and the Rights of the Child: Discussion Paper for Rädda Barnen*. Stockholm: Rädda Barnen.

DfID (2000) *Towards Responsive Schools: Supporting Better Schooling for Disadvantaged Children: Case Sudies from Save the Children*. London: Department for International Development.

Falkingham, J. (2000) *Societies in Transition: a Situational Analysis of the Status of Children and Women in the Central Asian Republics and Kazakhstan*. Almaty: CARK-UNICEF.

Goldstein, M.C. and C.M. Beall (1994) *Odyssey: Mongolian Nomads in the Gobi*. London: Hodder and Stoughton.

Holst, J., U. Kruchov, U. Madsen and Norgaard, E. (1996) *School Development in Mongolia 1992–1994*. Copenhagen: Royal Danish School of Educational Studies.

Humphrey, C. with U. Onon (1996) *Shamans and Elders: Experience, Knowledge and Power among the Daur Mongols*. Oxford: Clarendon Press.

Kazakhstan (2004) *Concept Paper: Ministry of Education*. Astana: Ministry of Education, Kazakhstan.

Krätli, S. (2001) 'Education Provision to Nomadic Pastoralists', *IDS Working Paper 126*. Sussex: Institute of Development Studies.

Lattimore, O. (1941) *Mongol Journeys*. London: Jonathon Cape.

Mongolia Demographic Survey (1994) Main Report. Mongolian National University: Population and Teaching Research Centre.

Mongolia Household Income and Expenditure Statistics 1995–6. Mongolia: National Statistical Board. (Sample data only.)

Mongolia Education Statistics 1995–6. Mongolia: Ministry of Enlightenment.

Mongolia's National Programme of Action for the Development of Children in the 1990's. (1993) Government of Mongolia (with the help of UNICEF).

Onon, U. (1972) *My Childhood in Mongolia*. Oxford: Oxford University Press.

Penn, H. (1998) *Mongolia: Situational Analysis for SCF/MOSTEC*. Ulaan Baatar: SCF/MOSTEC.

—— (2001) 'Culture and Childhood in Pastoralist Communities: the Example of Outer Mongolia'. In: L. Alaanen and B. Mayall *Negotiating Childhood*. Lewes: Falmer, pp. 86–100.

—— (2005) *Unequal Childhoods: Young Children's Lives in Poor Countries*. London: Routledge.

Scott, J. (1998) *Seeing Like a State: How Certain Schemes to Improve the Human Condition Have Failed*. Yale: New Haven.

UNDP (2003) *Human Development Report 2003*. New York: UNDP/Oxford University Press.

UNESCO/MoE (2000) *Case Study: Kazakhstan Preschool Education System at the Doorstep of the 21st Century*. Astana: Ministry of Education.

UNICEF (1998) *Education For All?* Regional Monitoring report no 5. Florence: ICDC/UNICEF.

Waddington, H. (2004) *Linking Economic Policy to Childhood Poverty: a Review of the Evidence on Growth, Trade Reform and Macro-economic Policy*. CHIP report no. 7. London. SCF/Childhood Poverty Research Centre.

Wolf, E.R. (1997) *Europe and the People without History*, 3rd edn. Los Angeles: University of California Press.

Woodward, D. (1997) *Economic Aspects of Education and the Role of the World Bank*. Cyclostyled paper for the U.K. NGO Education Forum.

World Bank (1996) *Mongolia: Poverty in a Transition Economy. Draft Report April 1996*. World Bank: Rural and Social Development Operations Division, Chinese and Mongolia Dept, East Asia and Pacific Regional Office.

CHAPTER 11

BOARDING SCHOOLS FOR MOBILE PEOPLES: THE HARASIIS IN THE SULTANATE OF OMAN

Dawn Chatty

Introduction

Modern, Western-style education for people who move or have no fixed abode has always been problematic. At the beginning of the twenty-first century, as in earlier times, formal efforts to provide education for migratory or mobile peoples has been difficult to plan, implement and sustain (see Krätli with Dyer, this volume; Sandford, 1978; Swift et al., 1990; Bonfiglioli, 1992; Lambert, 1999; Semali, 1993; Dyer and Choksi, 1997). Recent reports in Africa, the Middle East and South Asia are replete with projects that have failed (e.g. Rybinski [Algeria], 1981; Hendershot [Iran], 1965; Udoh [Nigeria], 1982) while studies highlighting success have been sparse. In Iran experiments with boarding schools and tent schools going back as far as the 1920s have had some limited successes (Varlet and Massumian, 1975; Shahshahani, 1995). In Mongolia where the majority of the population are nomadic pastoralists and where education has been compulsory for every child between eight and eighteen since 1940, dormitory schools are reported to be only a qualified success (Demberel and Penn, this volume).

For the most part, educating children of marginalised and mobile communities has proved difficult due to three principal political, economic and structural factors. The locally perceived purpose of state education is recognised as unsympathetic to mobile communities. Its underlying aim is often to establish political hegemony over a disparate set of communities, and to integrate and assimilate minority groups (see Krätli with Dyer, this volume). Political leaders often use education systems to inculcate certain ideas such as the acceptance of a state identity and citizenship as well as the duties of the individual to the state. Many governments 'use schools as a vehicle for creating a strong national identity, and deny children from ethnic minorities the opportunity to learn about and to value their own culture' (Ogadhoh and Molteno, 1998: 30). With mobile peoples, the unwillingness to be so drawn in, 'modernised', settled or transformed is often expressed by moving away and keeping out of reach of the state's long arm.

School curricula often reflect the mainstream government's vision of life and cultural aspirations. The issue of cultural relevance often only emerges in times of crisis. When real life pressures overwhelm a community through complex political emergency, or natural disaster, then children and their parents dismiss school learning which does not relate to their way of life. With mobile peoples, such rejection of an 'irrelevant' curriculum which denigrates and undermines the mobile way of life is also prevalent and is usually expressed by high primary school dropout rates and by the physical moving away of the family and community from the reaches of government and school authority (see also Carr-Hill, this volume).

A simple economic factor is often also at the heart of mobile communities' initial willingness to keep their children in school. This is the hope that such education will provide the youth with the tools and skills required to get well-paid jobs in industry (often petroleum and other large-scale extractive industries) and businesses of the surrounding areas (Abu-Saad et al., 1998). This hope is generally dashed as the national curriculum is nearly always geared toward the sedentarisation and modernisation of the mobile community through an urban or agrarian based 'liberal arts' secondary education. The mobile peoples' desire for education which allows new knowledges and technologies to become part of their learned skills is rarely available.

Finally, the administrative and infrastructural demands of setting up school facilities in remote parts of a state are often overwhelming and many such efforts begun with a blaze of publicity become neglected and are often abandoned shortly thereafter. Not only is there difficulty in keeping such units staffed by state-educated teachers, but linguistically, there is often the problem of language. Many mobile and pastoral communities have a mother tongue which differs from the national language. For the most part, the latter is required throughout state education. Certainly in secondary and higher education, the sole way for a child of a mobile or pastoral community to progress in life is through learning to communicate in the national language. But in the earlier years, the child's mother tongue is a more successful conduit for learning to read than a second language (Ogadhoh and Molteno, 1998: 34). The unwillingness of most state education systems to recognise or use local languages in the early years of education contributes significantly to the high numbers of children from marginal and mobile communities who drop out of state-run education (but see Edwards and Underwood, this volume).

The case study presented in this chapter highlights why, as much through design as by accident and serendipity, a boarding school in the middle of a vast extensive tribal area succeeded in the face of the kinds of problems which so often spell defeat. Here the political underpinning of the 30-year-old state education was clearly evident in the state's messages about Omani citizenship and the duties and obligations of its people. A lack of relevance of the urban and agrarian based state curriculum for the desert-based communities of Oman was equally evident, but this was balanced by a desire on the part of the local community to take advantage of all that was on offer. Last, but not least, the government's determination to make the desert school a 'flagship' and model for other future efforts in similar regions meant that some commitment to move beyond the normal level of support for a government school was implemented.

Boarding Schools for the Pastoral Nomads of Oman

Late in the 1970s, the young ruler of Oman, Sultan Qaboos bin Said, embarked on an innovative and ambitious plan to bring government social services to the remote, central regions of the country. Less than a decade into his reign, he had already revolutionised governance in Oman. Taking over from his ultra-conservative father in 1970, he set out to modernise the state as rapidly as possible. Working concurrently outwards from the capital of Muscat and the southern city of Salalah, he rapidly set up primary and secondary schools, clinics and hospitals, where before there had been none. He built roads, ports, created a physical infrastructure, and extended electricity and sewerage. He also set about establishing a modern institution of governance to replace the semi-feudal system that had operated before 1970 under his father's reign. In 1979, he decided the time had come to extend these services to the central desert areas of Oman, home to nomadic camel and goat-raising tribes. His directive was to extend services to these mobile communities, without forcing them to become settled.

Background

The Harasiis is a small mobile community of about 3,000 people inhabiting the edge of the Empty Quarter in south-eastern Arabia. Organised along kinship lines, each tribal section is made up of extended family groups. The male members of a household own and manage the far-ranging camel herds and female members own and look after the more close-ranging herds of goat, and occasionally, sheep. Their recognised tribal territory is called the Jiddat-il-Harasiis (referred to here as the Jiddat), a largely flat plain of rock and gravel which extends across the middle of Oman from the Empty Quarter to the edge of the escarpment which drops down to the Arabian Sea. This remote territory of approximately 40,000 square kilometres effectively separates north Oman from the southern region, Dhofar. It is in the middle of this tribal territory that the first experiment in delivering government services was to take place (see Fig. 11.1).

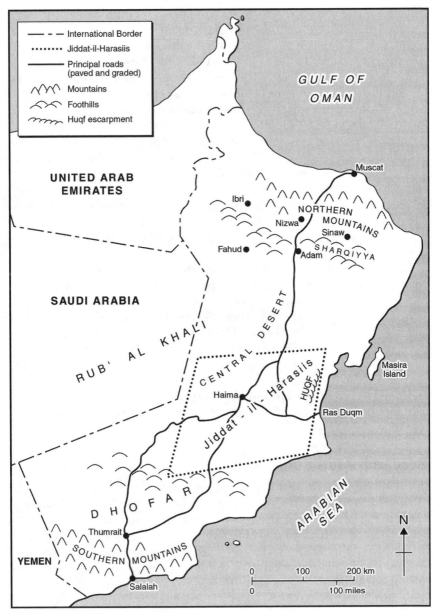

Figure 11.1 Jiddat-il-Harasiis.

The ministries of Social Affairs and Labour, Education, Health, Interior and the Border Police Force all worked together to create a development plan for tribal community centres. These were built upon the then popular development paradigm of comprehensive community centres. Such units had already been set up in remote areas of Dhofar for transhumance pastoral communities. These centres served as magnets drawing the adjacent population to them in the search for health care, schooling and other government services. In the mountains of Dhofar, the population spent most of the year in remote village settlements moving cattle down into the plains for only three or four months before returning to their villages. In the central desert of Oman, there were no villages, a reality government administrators found – and still find – hard to accept. Notwithstanding this very different population base, the government commissioned the first of six desert centres to be built, each at one of the few existing wells. By 1980 Haima, previously only a water well, was a vast construction site with an emerging office complex for the local governor, the *Wali,* which included four rooms for a school, two rooms for a health clinic, and a reception room to receive visiting tribesmen. Also under construction were a mosque, a petrol station, a reverse osmosis water plant, a border patrol police station, and six villas to house the future government employees.

In order to support this building programme and encourage the local community to make use of this modern complex, a team of social workers from the Ministry of Social Affairs and Labour and from the Ministry of Education set out late in 1980 to interview the local community. After a long and arduous journey across the Jiddat looking for families to interview, the team returned to Muscat and prepared a report. This study showed that most of those interviewed wished to use the government facilities, and in support of this finding, the names of 127 boys and 25 girls had been registered as potential school pupils. September 1981 was set as the official date for opening the school, but this deadline came and went without any sign of teachers or pupils.

Research Methodology

In 1981, I began a two-year action-oriented study of the needs and problems of the Harasiis tribe funded by the Voluntary Fund for the Decade of Women, the precursor of UNIFEM. This project, run by the UNDP, had been designed with a two-fold objective: to collect anthropological data on the needs and aspirations of the Harasiis tribe; and to design practical programmes in collaboration with the local community which addressed their needs without forcing them to settle in order to access government services (Chatty, 1984). After selecting a representative sample of extended families, I began intensive anthropological fieldwork with the help of two field assistants and two local guides. A purposive sample of 17 extended families out of a total population of about 250 households was selected, on the basis of the size and age structure of the unit, the family livestock holdings as well as their location across the various grazing and browsing areas available that year on the Jiddat-il-Harasiis.

Week after week, we visited and camped with these families, collecting socio-demographic data, conducting semi-formal interviews, group interviews, focused topic discussions, and participant observation. Once we had developed a clear idea of the services the community envisaged, we reviewed the services the government intended to extend to this population. It soon became clear that the provision of education services would be the most problematic. Community members could be expected to travel to the government centre occasionally for curative and preventative health services, but they would be unable to make the journey on a daily basis which schooling as envisaged by the government would entail. With only the one tarmacked road running from north to south and connecting Muscat to Salalah, every journey to Haima for the local inhabitants was across open rock and gravel desert. Journeys of two, three or four hours were not unusual, and were not undertaken lightly. Only a medical emergency, a dispute over water, a requirement for petrol or some other supplies, might be sufficient cause to make the long and costly trip to Haima.

The Administrative and Infrastructural Problem

The government plan had been to open a primary school of mixed classes. It had set aside four rooms for the school, three of which were intended to be classrooms. Consideration had also been given to the housing requirement of the teachers who would have to be imported from abroad. The few Omani teachers with the requisite training were not prepared to serve in such a remote area. No adequate consideration, however, had been given to how the Harasiis children would be able to get to the school. The planners in the Ministry of Education were unable to conceptualise that communities of no fixed abode existed in Oman. Hence their plan had been to organise a fleet of busses to collect children in the morning and return them to their homes each evening.

Within three months of commencing the study, we were able to map out the trends of the ever–fluid household locations as families and herds were moved to make best use of available graze and browse. A superficial analysis of our findings regarding camp locations over the past five years revealed an erratic, but predictable, pattern of movement. Although families could be found camped in all of the major valleys (*wadi*) of the Jiddat, the density of family groups always followed the rainfall. Good precipitation in one year would mean that a large number of families would set up their camps in that location over the next four to six months. On average, families tended to move major distances three or four times a year, and short distances to access natural graze for their herds every few weeks. Every family had access to a four-wheeled drive vehicle. The half-ton truck had rapidly replaced the camel as the beast of burden and contemporary pastoral life depended upon the increased mobility which motor vehicles offered.

The tribal centre at Haima had been built on a salt flat (*sabkha*). There could never be any grazing in the vicinity, and hence families could not camp near Haima. At the time of our study the closest family groups were camped in a small depression or (*wadi*) 75 kilometres from Haima, a drive across rocky terrain that often took two hours or more. Many others were camped three or four hours drive away. We realised that over a number of years, Harasiis family groups tended to cluster in one *wadi* or another depending upon the previous few years rainfall or lack of it. This constant short-term and long-term unpredictability in location within the vast tribal territory did not seem a very promising point from which to organise the bussing of students to a permanent school at Haima.

Alternative Solutions

Through our interview and discussion group work, a number of alternative suggestions emerged from the community. Some families wanted teachers who would move around with them in vehicles and tents. Others wanted an intense, four-month-a-year school which operated in a fixed location during the very hot summer months. And a small number wanted a permanent school built near a known source of sweet water several hundred kilometres south of Haima in an area that had year-round browsing, if not grazing, for their livestock. These alternative solutions took on a life of their own and the community elders began to campaign to have their way accepted by the whole. Traditionally, community disputes were settled in council meetings attended by the elders of the tribe. Discussions often raged for days and weeks until finally unanimity or exhaustion prevailed and one lone position was accepted by all. This was followed by discussion of the organisation and details of the schooling, which were conducted in the same fashion.

One group, made up of the more mobile herders with large camel numbers that required quite substantial migrations each year, strongly supported the idea of seasonal schools. This suggestion – never fully developed – appealed to many because it supported the Harasiis notion of migration and mobility. The government would be asked to supply a number of teachers, provide them with four-wheel drive vehicles and tents and send them off to camp wherever a concentration of families could be found. During many of the late night discussions which were held to discuss schooling, I gently tried to interject a sense of the difficulties that such a solution would create. Where, for example, would the Ministry be able to recruit teachers who were prepared to live such a peripatetic existence? How would they move the required books, papers and other teaching materials around? The model that some Harasiis had in mind was that of their traditional religious teachers, the *shuyukh*, who were occasionally hired by a family to accompany them on their migrations and to teach their children to read the Koran. In such cases, there was only the one book to take and most of the learning was by rote memorisation.

Another group, mainly made up of the 20 percent of the population who owned date gardens several hundred kilometres to the north of the Jiddat at the foothills bordering the agricultural communities of northern Oman, had other ideas. This group argued for an intense, four-month-long school which would operate in a pre-planned, fixed location during the very hot summer months. Such an idea grew out of what they were convinced was an intractable problem; finding teachers who would be prepared to move around the Jiddat. The Harasiis appreciated that their way of life, with its constant movement, and scarce water resources, would be difficult for others. They regarded, their ability to go days without drinking water with great pride – managing to keep their thirst controlled by taking long, deep draughts of camel or goats milk in the early morning or evening before or after a long day's work. Many members of these families generally spent the four hottest months of the year, when temperatures regularly ranged between 45 and 50°C, in their date gardens to the north in the villages surrounding Adam – the last major market town on the border with the central desert of Oman. During these months the family members helped with the date harvest, which took place during the *Qaidh*, the hottest season of the year when the dates are traditionally said to ripen. The Harasiis and other pastoral tribes with date holdings in the area constructed palm frond huts in which to live during this season. These temporary huts encircled the date gardens and the permanent mud houses and protective walls of the indigenous townsfolk.

Increasingly over the past decade, various units of government services had used this season, the *Qaidh*, to reach out to the Harasiis and other nomadic pastoral people. In some years, a carnival atmosphere prevailed with government social workers trying to spread various social and health messages, such as the importance of nursing infants instead of bottle feeding them, or the benefit of vaccination. Often these promotional campaigns were accompanied by the handing out of gifts, toothbrushes, soaps and other accoutrements of modern Western life. The Harasiis were genuinely puzzled by these government handouts. They did, however, recognise that there were great differences in their appreciation of desert life and by those who had never lived it. Since they could recognise how an urban-raised teacher might not find the constant moving around in the desert appealing, they suggested a special intensive period of schooling during the *Qaidh* in the date gardens. A teacher, they argued, could be found who would remain in the date gardens during the period of their residence, teaching their children at a time of the year when there was little else to distract them.

Yet another faction of the Harasiis, representing a small but outspoken lineage, wanted a permanent school to be built, not at Haima, but several hundred kilometres south near a source of sweet water. The push for this alternative was orchestrated by an influential and outspoken Harasiis man who had strong vested interests in the area. Already hired as the 'liaison' officer to mediate disputes between the national oil company operating in the area and local tribesmen, he saw his future very much tied to a narrow circle of movement at the oil camp of Rima (see Fig. 11.2). He knew that over the coming years – for as long as he held on to his job – he would not be able to move his family far. Paid employment at Rima would be more important than the subsistence income which his and his wife's herds provided. In all the discussions in which he took part, he would consistently push his solution. Unlike the etiquette of consensus over most tribal affairs, he could not be dissuaded, even though his was the lone voice supporting such a proposal. The Ministry of Education did eventually agree to his request and a number of years later (in the late 1980s) supplied two teachers and two portacabins to his extended family unit near Rima to set up a temporary school.

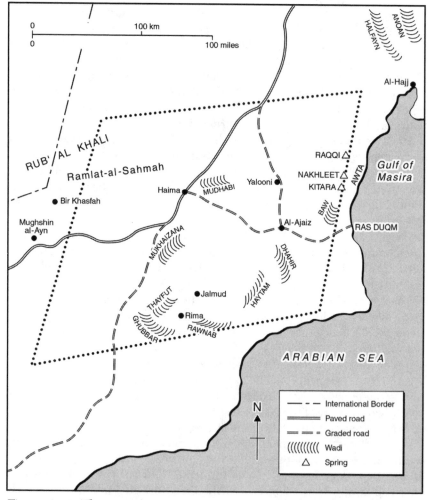

Figure 11.2 The area of movement around the oil camp of Rima.

Negotiating a Compromise

By the early winter months of 1982, the Ministry of Health, as well as the other interested agencies began to feel some concern about the apparent lukewarm welcome the tribal centre seemed to be receiving. The Health Centre was hardly used, the school was not functioning, and other official offices had few visitors. The issue of the school was being handled directly by the office of the Minister of Education. This immediate access gave my team the opportunity to put forward the alternative solutions which the Harasiis were considering. The Harasiis elders – many of them prospective parents – were petitioning the Ministry of Education through the offices of the *Wali* at Haima. Occasionally when other business brought them into Nizwa, the regional office for the Ministry of Education, or Muscat, Harasiis tribesman would visit the Ministry's office and lobby their views.

In due course we were able to draft several papers representing the various alternatives the Harasiis were considering. My own preference was for a semi-mobile school – as in a portable cabin – which could be moved to different locations as the population density shifted from one valley to another with changes in rainfall. This opinion was partially derived from my cautionary interpretation of the limited successes of residential schooling for the children of nomads in Israel (Meir, 1990: 771; Abu-Saad et al., 1998), Iran (Barker, 1981), India (Rao, 1987) and other parts of the world. Either the schools ultimately failed, or the students became totally alienated from their parents, culture and eventually left nomadic life. I did not want to see the same story repeated in Oman.

Although the Ministry was prepared to listen to our arguments in support of a mobile school, it soon became clear that our starting point had to be the existing four rooms in the *Wali*'s offices earmarked as a school for the Harasiis. The interesting proposal for a seasonal school during the hottest summer months, which was also supported by the *Wali* of Haima, had to be put aside, as did our proposal for a portable school. With the existing structure at Haima accepted as the physical base for schooling, we began to negotiate how to meet the needs of the Harasiis people and the requirements of the Ministry of Education. The Ministry gracefully accepted that bussing the students to the school daily was not a feasible option. Reluctantly we found ourselves arguing for the construction of a residence for the students at Haima.

All of the Harasiis elders accepted the Ministry's decision to construct a residence for the prospective students. Another round of discussions was held with the tribal elders, and a new set of concerns were raised. It was understood by the Harasiis that the Ministry expected children as young as seven to attend the school. By law this was the official nationwide age for beginning primary education. For the Harasiis this was too young. Their own understanding of the process of socialisation put nine years of age as one when full rational cultural understanding could be expected. Few parents were prepared to consider letting their children live away from them before this age. Their concern was that the children were in danger of being culturally alienated. One Harasiis mother told me: 'How can we let our children go before they know their language (Harsuusi) and they understand the desert'. After looking at a number of alternatives, the elders of the tribe decided that they would have to select a few of their own number to camp out near the tribal centre to supervise the young boys and girls and thus act as cultural guardians. Respected older Harasiis men and women were approached and asked to take on this task at least until the Harasiis children were well settled in the school.

A further expression of this concern was raised in the guise of an administrative issue. No family wanted its children to be away from home for months at a time. The Harasiis knew of the one other boarding school run by the Ministry of Education in the Jebel Akhdar (Birkat-il-Mooz) in northern Oman and understood that its dormitory was run on a termly basis, children spending only a few months away from home at any one stretch of time. The Harasiis wanted to see their children more regularly, ostensibly in order to have the boys and girls help out with the herding of livestock and the regular collection of water for the family. Initially arguing for a very short school week of four days, they eventually reached a more realistic compromise of a five-day, Saturday to Wednesday school schedule. The Ministry of Education accepted this suggestion as it fitted quite neatly with the *de facto* five-day work-week of many government employees, despite an official six-day work week in government. Such a schedule, ministry officials felt, would make the task of recruiting teachers to take up such a remote post a little more attractive.

Cultural issues continued to dominate the concerns of the Harasiis households. The Harasiis wanted to know what food the children would be eating. The worry was that the students would no longer have access to camel and goat milk and would end up being served a permanent diet of Indian curry with rice. The concern was easy to understand since nearly all the eating establishments in the interior of Oman were run by Indian expatriate workers. This issue was never resolved adequately and other seemingly more pressing concerns emerged. The Harasiis parents learned that the students would not remain at school all day. The standard period of schooling per day varied in Oman from four to six hours. What would the students do after school hours, the parents wanted to know? Would there be any supervision of the students in the afternoons and at night? Would there be any organised sports activity? Already the border police officers regularly played soccer with the local government workers running the water purification plant. Would something similar be developed for the boys? These issues were taken up and presented to the Ministry of Education, where all efforts were being made to establish what would be a 'flagship' school – indeed a model for further schools in the desert interior.

Figure 11.3 *The Wali, and community elders visiting classroom at the boarding school.*

After nearly a year of petitioning and negotiations, the Ministry of Education agreed to open a residential school at Haima for the Harasiis. It agreed to run the school on a five-day week, to hire one Harasiis elder at a time to look after the welfare and cultural concerns of the students, to set up catering which would not be dominated by an expatriate cuisine, to recruit a sports coach to keep the students busy after the regular hours of instruction and to set up some civic organisations like a boy scout troop. However, girls would not be permitted to be resident at the school.

The Compromise: Residential School for Boys, Day Schooling for Girls

The Haima School opened in December 1992 with forty boys and two girls. The boys were temporarily accommodated in an abandoned army barracks on the edge of Haima until the dormitory building could be completed. Tribal elders, taking their shepherding roles to heart, drove the boys the short distance of perhaps 500 metres from the barracks to the school each morning and afternoon, remaining with them in the afternoons and evenings. The girls were daughters of Harasiis tribesmen employed by the *Wali* as guards and thus they remained with their fathers out of school hours and returned to their campsites each night. They took an active part in all the school-time activities, and were not discriminated against in any way – and generally outshone the boys in their eagerness to learn.

Figure 11.4 *Harasiis boys use a truck to travel to weekly boarding school.*

The first two teachers were Egyptian nationals hired by the Ministry of Education under a bilateral agreement which resulted in the import of nearly 5,000 Egyptian schoolteachers each year into Oman. Most of these Egyptians were from the Delta or oases settlements along the Nile. Being posted to Haima, a desert outpost in the middle of the country, when they were expecting the charms of the cosmopolitan urban centres in the Arabian Gulf, caused problems. Their didactic teaching style was reminiscent of the small primary schools of Egypt described so poignantly by Taha Hussein in his *Al Ayam*. Straightforward rote memorisation of the alphabet and verses of the Koran were the order of the day. For children whose mother tongue was not Arabic, but rather *Harsuusi* (a South Arabian language which predated Arabic in origin), this was a gruelling introduction to modern Western-style education.

Harasiis parents began to arrive in Haima regularly on Wednesdays to run their errands, visit the various government offices and collect their children from the school. Wednesday afternoons quickly took on a holiday atmosphere as tribesman gathered around the petrol station, Harasiis mothers congregated outside the health centre and children milled about waiting for their parents or kinsmen to make the drive across the desert to their campsite.

Within a few months, complaints about the cultural divide between the Egyptian teachers and the Harasiis boys surfaced. These complaints were serious enough for the Ministry to consider carefully the future placement of teachers in Haima when their current two-year contracts ended. In 1984, the Ministry appointed a Jordanian as head teacher. This was a very popular decision as he showed himself to have significant understanding of nomadic pastoral culture, being of Bedouin origin himself. He was able to flag areas which the Ministry needed to consider with care – issues such as curriculum relevance, personal and group hygiene, and sleep and study arrangements.

Girls continued to attend, but only as day students. They were never separated from boys in class, and often shared the same two-seater benches with them. But when their fathers moved on to other jobs or their mothers' homesteads were moved too far away, they would be pulled out of school. After a few years, the only girls at the school were those of the local *Wali*, and the Sudanese veterinary doctor. Their urban Arab parents, unlike the Harasiis, were not comfortable with the lack of segregation between boys and girls in the school and put significant pressure on the Ministry of Education to have girls separated from boys, at least as they got into the intermediate levels of education. A number of the Egyptian teachers eventually became uncomfortable instructing the young adolescent girls in mixed classes and succeeded in having the girls withdrawn from late primary school. Instead, the Ministry of Education offered the older girls 'adult literacy classes' – taught by the same Egyptian teachers – in the afternoons at their mothers' campsites near Haima.

The most dramatic clash to emerge in the early years of the school's history was superficially about food. On one level it was a tribal statement concerning their cultural integrity, but at another deeper level it was about control and empowerment and the violation of the compromises negotiated

Figure 11.5 Harasiis girls and boys together in the classroom.

with the state. A few years after the school opened, the kitchen of the dormitory came under non-violent 'protest'. Most of the schoolboys had grown up drinking litres of camel and goat milk supplemented with bread and rice. They refused to eat the daily diet of rice and curry served up by the Indian catering staff, which was increasingly perceived as unpalatable, and took instead to using their R.O. 20 (about £30) monthly allowance from the Ministry of Education to buy snacks of crisps, chocolates, soft drinks and sweets each day. Some boys put on significant weight, enough to alarm a visiting dietician who was conducting another study in the region. Particularly worrying was the weight gain of the one polio victim Harasiis student, who had previously managed on wooden crutches, but had to be provided with a wheelchair and finally a motorised tricycle.

In spite of these teething pains, the school continued to grow and by the end of the 1980s, it had nearly 100 students. In 1990 the school's first intake of boys received their intermediate school diploma (grade nine). Four decided to leave school and join the border police. They were accepted at the Police Academy and later returned as junior officers serving in the desert regions. All the parents had wanted to keep the boys in school until they completed their secondary schooling, but this original group resisted with good reason. In 1982, these boys had entered school with a mean age closer to 12 than to 7. Hence their age upon reaching grade nine was probably more like 20 or 21 instead of the normal age of 16 or 17. These young bearded youths were no longer able to bear being treated like children in classroom and they took what education they had acquired and converted it into the first skilled job training of any generation of Harasiis.

Figure 11.6 *Harasiis boys studying at the boarding school.*

By 1994 the Haima school had 120 boys and 22 girls enrolled. The sudden climb in female enrolment was due to the efforts of the women who, having grown tired of petitioning year after year for a residence for girls, took matters into their own hands and set up a system of boarding girls in a makeshift dormitory in the sand on the edge of Haima (see Chatty, 1996: 158–63 for a full discussion). Plans had been drawn up several years earlier to build a separate school and dormitory for girls in the nearby *Wadi bu Mudhabi*. This girl's school was up and running in 1994, but few regular female students at Haima shifted to it. The Harasiis did not consider it necessary to segregate the girls from the boys; such ideas came from the Egyptian schoolteachers and government officials who were uncomfortable with older adolescent girls attending classes with boys.

Also in 1994, the first high school graduates, seven young men, took their high school diplomas and became eligible for recruitment into the Army and the national oil company as skilled workers. For the Harasiis this was a major achievement. At last their youth could compete for the higher paid jobs that had until then always gone to rival tribesman. Having been the most remote and most difficult to reach community in Oman, the Harasiis had been the last to have access to education and other government services. Whereas rival tribesmen had acquired access to education in the 1970s, the Harasiis had had to wait until the 1980s. By the end of the 1990s a few boys were graduating with high school degrees each year. Some were succeeding in winning government scholarships to go on to higher education and especially technical training relevant to the oil and gas industry. In 2000, two young Harasiis youths graduated from Haima High School and took qualifying exams to enter the prestigious technical training college in Muscat run by the national oil company. In 2002, these young men were enrolled in the technical training college in Muscat and others were awaiting their opportunity to benefit from this specialised training as a road into employment in the gas and oil industry.

Conclusion

The Haima School has continued to function and, despite a high dropout rate in the first two to three years of attendance, its overall enrolment has continued to increase. It has brought formal, state education into the heart of the desert, providing girls with basic numeracy and reading skills, and boys with some of the necessary tools to seek skilled employment. The aspirations and wishes of many of the elder generation of Harasiis, who could only find work as watchmen, trackers, or well guards, have come true. The Haima School, by providing education from primary level to secondary level, has become an instrument for limited success, providing a select few youths with potential access to well-paid and skilled jobs in the desert. For the households these youths belong to, family livelihood security is improved by increasing its potential for economic differentiation.

Conventional educational measures of evaluation might not regard the Haima School as a success. Only a small percentage of the total population of Harasiis children are selected by their parents to attend school. The dropout rate remains high, indicating that universal literacy, a state goal, is unlikely to be achieved. However the school continues to operate. The question needs to be asked why this educational experiment has been allowed to continue in the face of limited success. How was it that a top-down decision by government to build a 'flagship' school in the middle of a salt flat, inaccessible to the nomadic pastoralists' livestock and hence to family units, turned into such an ongoing and partially successful venture?

My interpretation of the data revolves around three major themes: political goals, cultural hegemony, and economic opportunity. The school at Haima was established with the backing of the Minister of Education himself. It represented the government's determination to reach out to the most remote and marginal segments of Oman's population and hence draw the community into the national 'fold'. The realisation of this political goal required considerable negotiation and, in some cases, compromise with the local Harasiis community. The Harasiis parents and elders wanted a school and were prepared to accept whatever the government would provide. The fact that the school was built without any consultation in an unsuitable location gave the Harasiis a strong bargaining point. If the Ministry wished them to use the physical premises they had already built, they would have to help the Harasiis children to get there. Hence the compromise over the school hours and days of attendance, over the welfare of the resident students, over the supervision of the students out of school hours and over the admission of girls into the school. The protracted period of negotiations meant that multiple voices were heard. These included our own regular reports and suggestions, those coming from the Ministry of Interior through the office of the local *Wali*, and the direct intervention of Harasiis elders when they were in Muscat.

The state's desire to integrate the Harasiis into the Omani state as citizens and its effort to inculcate a national cultural hegemony among the student body was only partially successful and hence acted to keep Harasiis parents interested in taking the risk of sending their select youth to the school. The combination of deliberate holding back by local parents of children from entry into the school until they were considered 'reasonable' and well aware of their own culture – about nine or ten years of age – as well as the inability of the Ministry of Education to persuade any Omani teachers to accept assignments at the Haima school, meant that there was no one overarching cultural identity dominating the school community. It also meant that the pastoral way of life, although inevitably denigrated by the foreign teachers, was not seriously undermined by those Omanis who mattered.

With the school representing no particular cultural threat, Harasiis families came to regard the institution as providing a special economic opportunity for a select few. Families with large numbers of children – five or six – were able carefully to choose those to support and encourage to remain in school. Sometimes this was the oldest son, but as often it was the child identified as the 'brightest' or 'cleverest' in a family. There was never any idea of universal education among the Harasiis. That would not have been possible as the labour of children was, and still is, required to manage the family's herds of camel and goat. A well-established family with half a dozen children would typically select one or two to send to school. The rest would remain at the campsite or in the desert helping with the family herds. Nevertheless, this generation has options the parents never had; to remain in the desert as subsistence herders or to go into other professions in the Army, Police or oil and gas industry while keeping herding as a secondary economic and cultural activity. This power of choice has meant that, for some pastoral families, a greater multi-resource base is now possible because of the way in which state formal education provision has been taken on and adapted by the local community. A few select pastoral households with youth who have succeeded in completing the education offered by the state are now able to tap into links with wider society through the employment potential of their young. Throughout the world, pastoralists strive to develop multi-resource household economics. In the Jiddat-il-Harasiis formal state education has made that aspiration a reality for a select set of households.

References

Abu-Saad, I., K. Abu-Saad, G. Lewando-Hundt, M.R. Forman, I. Belmaker, W. Berendes and D. Chang (1998) '"Bedouin Arab Mothers' Aspirations for Their Children's Education in the Context of Radical Social Change"'. *Journal of Educational Development* 18 (4): 347–59.

Barker, P. (1981) 'Tent Schools of the Qashqa'i: a Paradox of Local Initiative and State Control'. In: N. Bonine and N. Keddie (eds) *Modern Iran, The Dialectics of Continuity and Change*. Albany: State University of New York.

Bonfiglioli, A.M. (1992) *Pastoralists at a Crossroads: Survival and Development Issues in African Pastoralism*. NOPA (UNICEF/UNSO Project for Nomadic Pastoralists in East Africa), Kenya, Nairobi.

Chatty, D. (1984) *Final Report: Pastoral Community Assistance and Development*. UNDP, DTCD New York and Muscat.

—— (1996) *Mobile Pastoralists: Development Planning and Social Change in Oman*. New York: Columbia University Press.

Dyer, C. and A. Choksi (1997) 'Literacy for Migrants: an Ethnography of Literacy Acquisition among Nomads of Kutch'. *Compare* 27 (2): 217–29.

Hendershot, C. (1965) *Report on the Tribal Schools of Fars Province. WhiteTents in the Mountains*. Washington, D.C: USAID.

Lambert, R. (1999) *Perspectives on Pastoralism and Education: Some Thoughts and Issues*. Background paper prepared for the project Towards Responsive Schools, Save the Children Fund and DFID.

Meir, A. (1990) 'Provision of Public Services to the Post Nomadic Bedouin Society in Israel'. *The Service Industries Journal* 10, 768–85.

Ogadhoh, K. and M. Molteno (1998) *A Chance in Life: Principles and Practice in Basic Primary Education for Children*. London: Save the Children.

Rao, A. (ed.) (1987) *The Other Nomads: Peripatetic Minorities in Cross-cultural Perspecitve*. Cologne: Boehlau Verlag.

Rybinski, A. (1981) 'Expériences français en matière de l'education des pasteurs nomades'. *Africana Bulletin* 30: 159–76.

Sandford, S. (1978) 'Welfare and Wanderers: the Organisation of Social Services for Pastoralists'. *ODI Review* 1: 70–87.

Semali, L. (1993) *The Social and Political Context of Literacy Education for Pastoral Societies: the Case of the Maasai of Tanzania*. Paper presented at the Annual Meeting of the National Reading Conference (Charleston, SC, 1–4 December 1993).

Shahshahani, S. (1995) 'Tribal Schools of Iran: Sedentarization through Education'. *Nomadic Peoples*, 36–37: 145–56.

Swift, J., C. Toulmin and S. Chatting (1990) *Providing Services to Nomadic Peoples: a Review of the Literature and Annotated Bibliography*. UNICEF Staff Working Papers No. 8. New York: UNICEF.

Udoh, S. (1982) 'The Problem of Administering Mobile Schools'. In: C. Ezeomah (ed.) *The Problems of Educating Nomads in Nigeria*. Proceedings of the First Annual Conference on the Education of Nomads in Nigeria. University of Jos, 5–6 February 1982, Jos, Nigeria.

Varlet, H. and J. Massumian (1975) 'Education for Tribal Populations in Iran'. *Prospects* 5 (2): 275–81.

CHAPTER 12

ADULT LITERACY AND TEACHER EDUCATION IN A COMMUNITY EDUCATION PROGRAMME IN NIGERIA

Juliet McCaffery, Kayode Sanni, Chimah Ezeomah and Jason Pennells

Introduction

This chapter reflects on successes and tensions in an education project with the Fulani pastoralist nomads in Adamawa and Taraba States in Nigeria. The project formed part of the Community Education Programme (CEP), funded by the British Department for International Development (DfID) in Nigeria from 1997 to 2001. The chapter focuses on adult literacy and teacher education, the two major project components. The adult literacy component adopted a participatory and pragmatic methodology which draws on the experience, knowledge and skills of the participating communities to enable men and women to develop the literacy and numeracy skills they require for every day life. The teacher education programme developed a model of building teacher capacity in marginalised communities, addressing, but not necessarily resolving, some of the issues inherent in providing education to pastoralist nomadic communities. We present both the tensions and successes of this project, and hope that reporting our experience will contribute to a wider understanding of ways of working together with marginalised peoples to assist them to achieve their learning goals.

Our experience reflects a range of the key issues highlighted in Krätli and Dyer's opening chapter. In Nigeria, the debate about the underlying purpose of efforts to make educational provision available to nomadic pastoralists closely mirrors the fundamental issue of whether education is to integrate nomads into the wider national context, and if so whether this should be through cultural assimilation or through enabling the nomadic communities to engage more successfully, and on their own terms, with the wider economic, legal and social context while supporting the maintenance of a distinct cultural and social identity (Ezeomah, 1993). The possible (intended or unintended) effect of formal education as a force for 'reproduction' of modern society within the traditional and hitherto distinct nomadic culture, as captured in the opening chapter, is central to this debate. This provides the national background to the project, in terms of policy, provision and academic discussion concerning nomadic education, as the literature makes clear (Tahir, 1998).

Within this context, related issues – again as touched on in Krätli and Dyer's introductory chapter – play important parts as background to the project, informing the intentions behind the project interventions and the directions it took. These issues include the assumption in the Nigerian education sector of an evolutionary progression from mobile, nomadic life to settlement (Ezeomah, 1987); education as a means of modernising nomads' means of livelihood; and facilitating nomads' fuller integration into the national market economy (Ezeomah, 1983). Issues of educational content and delivery reflected in this project are the high turnover rate of teachers posted to nomadic schools; the relevance of curriculum, who determines the curriculum and how to balance relevance to nomads' current life against exposure to wider experience and encouragement of aspirations beyond nomadic pastoralism; the availability of suitable materials for adult literacy and for primary education in the nomads' mother tongue; and whether education can and should be provided on a mobile basis to follow the nomadic migrations or in fixed locations.

The Cultural Context

Fulani pastoralists live across the savannah belt of West Africa from Senegal to Cameroon, with higher concentrations in the major river valleys. Although found throughout Nigeria, there are greater concentrations in the north, on and over the borders with Niger, Chad and Cameroon and along the Benue river. Pastoralist Fulani in Nigeria are predominantly Muslim. Their language is Fulfulde but many also speak Hausa, the dominant language in northern Nigeria. Cattle rearing is the main occupation of men; selling milk and dairy products in the markets, along with household maintenance, is the main occupation of women. Though some nomadic Fulani own very large herds of cattle, up to 2,000 head, they own very little else. The dependence on, and close relationship with cattle is well recognised: two cultural elements are central to the identity of Fulani nomads: *n'ai* (cattle) and *pulaaku* (the essence of being Fulani). *Pulaaku* comprises a strong moral code which derives from the struggle in the physical environment, a path which guides one to be just, moral, virtuous, well mannered, dignified, compassionate and with a certain reserve (VanEcke, 1991). It is distinctive and segregates members from non-members, and in many ways is a birthright. Women symbolise qualities such as kindness, compassion, peace, unity and sympathy.

Fulani nomads have been categorised according to their characteristic pattern of movement. 'Total movement' pastoralists have no base camps or areas of semi-settlement, and the whole clan moves with the animals. 'Partial movement' groups have semi-permanent sites, and men and boys go with the herds leaving women, children and the elderly in base camps. Some clans move on a particular route annually from the dry season pastures to the wet season pastures. Dwellings are temporary shelters made of corn stalks bent and strengthened by saplings tied around them to form a dome structure, which is often covered with a tarpaulin.

Providing accessible and relevant education to nomadic pastoralists was and remains a major challenge to education providers in Nigeria. Literacy rates among the pastoralists are low. A survey of 900 nomadic pastoralists in Southern Borno State found only four percent of the men had either Western or Koranic literacy. The literacy rate for nomadic women is estimated at less than one percent (Sa'ad, 2000). However, men and women receive instruction in the Koran from traditional community religious teachers and learn to recite the Koran in Arabic.

Educational Initiatives

The DfID-funded project developed from and built on a history of nomadic and educational policy formulation, research and activity in Nigeria. The policy objectives of the National Policy on Education in 1981 were agreed:

1. The inculcation of national consciousness and national unity.
2. The survival of the individual and Nigerian society.
3. The training of the mind in the understanding of the world around him[1] (training in scientific and critical thinking).
4. The acquisition of appropriate skills, abilities and competencies, mental, social and physical as equipment for the individual to live in his society and to contribute to its development.

A comprehensive research programme on nomadic matters was undertaken at the University of Jos between 1976 and 1988. This research addressed issues relating to the educational, social/cultural, economic, language and communication, demographic, psychological, human and animal health aspects of nomadic pastoralists. The research (Ezeomah, 1988) furnished information and insights about:

• accurate demographic statistics on the nomadic population in Bauchi, Gongola and Plateau States
• nomadic values and beliefs, family and clan structures
• the philosophical constructs in which the nomads' educational needs and aspirations are rooted

- the major economic activities and the work roles of nomadic families
- the various modes of information gathering and dissemination among the nomads and between them and sedentary people
- major causes of mental illness and the traditional methods of treatment
- the health status of nomads and prevalent common diseases
- animal health and the importance of livestock to nomads.

In addition, and to address the educational needs of nomadic communities, the Federal Ministry of Education commissioned a statistical survey of nomads in ten northern states of Nigeria in 1988. The study provided data on the estimated population of nomads in the affected states, their settlement and annual migration patterns. The findings resulted in far-reaching recommendations to develop suitable curricula, and to plan, organise and administer appropriate educational, health and settlement schemes for nomads. Its findings were used to develop policy guidelines for the education of nomads, spelling out the objectives and approaches of an education programme designed to integrate nomads into national life.

Drawing on these sources, between 1990 and 1999, the Federal Government of Nigeria in collaboration with donor agencies (UNESCO, UNICEF and DfID) made explicit efforts to equalise educational opportunities for nomads in Nigeria to enable them to develop appropriate skills, knowledge and competencies to both develop their communities and to contribute to national development.

In 1990, the National Commission for Nomadic Education (NCNE) was established to handle implementation of nomadic education. Its specific roles included adapting and developing relevant curricula in eight subjects for nomadic primary schools, training and paying teachers' salaries and hardship allowances. Prompt payment was seen as essential for teacher retention. Major achievements included construction of permanent and collapsible classrooms, increased enrolment of pupils and employment of 2,000 teachers (Ezeomah, nd). According to a report by NCNE (Umar and Ardo, 1998), adult education was also encouraged during this period. A survey in eight states reported 65 active adult education centres, exclusively for nomads, in which 3,400 men and women were enrolled, as well as 82 co-operatives assisting the nomads to operate loan schemes drawing on funds from banks and the government-run Family Economic Advancement Programme (FEAP).

The Context and Development of the Community Education Programme

The increased concern over the education of nomadic pastoralists and the initiatives undertaken by Nigerian and Fulani educators and researchers in the 1990s coincided with a reassessment of support to education by the Overseas Development Administration (forerunner to DfID), and the policy shift from supporting tertiary to supporting basic education. The British

Council assisted with the design of a three-year pilot programme of support to basic education in four geographically and culturally separated Local Government Area (LGA) project sites in Abia, Akwa Ibom and Borno States and with Fulani total and partial movement clans in Adamawa and Taraba states.

Target communities were selected in each LGA, following a consultation exercise to ascertain their educational goals and economic aims, and their ability to contribute to and sustain an educational programme. The programme was operationalised as the Community Education Programme (CEP) in April 1997. The project was designed to improve and develop new models of training teachers and adult literacy facilitators and to increase attendance in primary school and in adult literacy and numeracy classes. Appropriate management infrastructure was established in the four LGAs. The prevailing political situation – military dictatorship and concern over human rights – necessitated channeling inputs directly to the four communities through locally appointed project managers and Educational Project Committees rather than through the federal or state governments. However, there was good communication and support from government institutions.

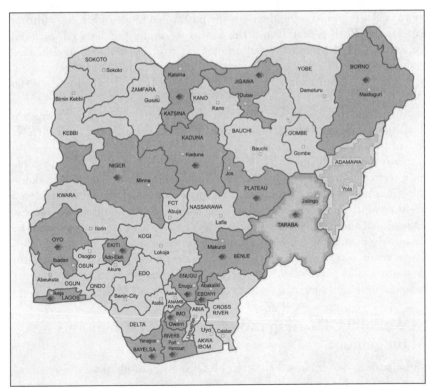

Figure 12.1 Nigeria showing Taraba and Adamawa States.

The broad goal of the CEP was to

enhance economic and social development at community level through improving the quality of education (specifically primary and adult education). (ODA, 1996)

The stated purpose was to

enhance learning among primary age and adult learners, particularly girls and women, by improving quality and increasing access to basic education in a number of target disadvantaged LGAs and for nomads in the north east of Nigeria. (ODA, 1996)

The criteria for selecting the target clans were educational marginalisation and a demonstrable commitment and capacity to work with the project for improvement. The focus was on Adamawa, Taraba and the eastern part of Bauchi state, where the total nomadic population was estimated to be 1,300,000 in 1989. Four clans were selected initially: they were deeply religious, had very low levels of literacy, and had identified illiteracy as one of the major factors excluding them from the decision-making process. There appeared to be no women with even minimum primary education.

In designing and implementing the nomadic project of the CEP, there was a real attempt to value the nomadic pastoralist mode of life and cultural expression. Both research and the failure of many previous educational initiatives demonstrated the importance of involving nomads in decision-making processes relating education to both pastoralism and nomadism, otherwise the result is a defensive reaction (VanEcke, 1991; Tahir, 1991). ODA was clear that the project should not be an agency for settlement, but should assist pastoralists to develop their abilities to make their own decisions about the future, and support them in maintaining their distinct way of life on their own terms.

However clear the donor's objective, there were different views on possible long-term outcomes among stakeholder communities, policy makers, implementing agencies and project personnel. Some stakeholders considered eventual settlement inevitable; some envisaged partial settlement to access educational and health services; and others believed these services should be designed so that they could be utilised by total movement communities. These issues were rarely discussed and never resolved. While this allowed for flexibility and nomadic self-determination, this failure to address fundamental issues created an underlying tension within the project.

Stakeholder Participation in Project Design and Management

Participation was catalysed through initial consultations with the National Commission for Nomadic Education, a participatory project design workshop, establishment of Education Project Committees with beneficiaries as members, inception workshops, annual workshops to agree annual plans and participation in the project mid-term review. A key factor in the design of the programme was a gender sensitive participatory consultation process using Participatory Rural Appraisal (PRA) techniques, aiming to

> generate discussion among the stakeholders to identify the achievements and problem areas in their educational provision, consider the ramifications and implications for their social and economic development and proffer solutions. (Ezeomah, 1995a)

Policy makers, education professionals, beneficiaries, including women, children and clan heads (*Ardo'en*), were asked for their views. Important issues for men were 'life' problems such as land, grazing reserves, provision of water for humans and animals and safe migratory routes – areas where the government was perceived to have failed. Settlement was not an expectation. Contrary to the expectations of many policy makers and educators the clans perceived the acquisition of education as important for a variety of purposes, including interacting with government bureaucracy, involvement in political and decision-making processes and providing modern knowledge on treating animals and humans. Women and children wished to become veterinary doctors or nurses. All wanted education adequately funded including improved school facilities, teachers' allowances and means of transport. Clan members were aware they had not made serious efforts to acquire literacy skills, and they held this responsible for some of their present difficulties.

The policy makers and professionals identified ignorance, suspicion, a lack of co-operation and 'landlessness' among nomadic clans as contributing to 'backwardness'. They tended to view nomadism as a culturally and materially deficient way of life that could be improved through education.

An important feature of the project was the development of local ownership in order to sustain the programme beyond the three-year funding period. The concept of partnership was stressed from the beginning. During consultations and at the project design workshop, nomads committed themselves to promoting education for both males and females, providing teacher accommodation and transport and providing other practical assistance

Education Project Committees (EPCs) were established to co-ordinate the planning, implementation, monitoring and accountability of the project at LGA level. A proposal by officials that only one or two nomads be on the EPC was firmly rejected with the response: 'We are not educated. If there are only one or two of us on your committee, you educated men will be able to trick us'. The *Ardo'en* received 50 percent of the places and a senior *Ardo*, who was not literate, chaired the Committee. To assist the EPC at community level, Community Education Committees (CECs) were formed and committee members and leaders given training. The programme policy was that a third of the representatives on all committees should be women.

Adhering to this on the EPC necessitated including non-nomadic and non Fulfulde speaking women, which raised cultural and linguistic difficulties. Female representation was not possible at community level. PRA consultation continued during the project and effective community development became an increasingly important third element.

Adult Literacy: Ensuring Relevance through Participatory Learning

Adult literacy programmes have proved hard to deliver and the outcomes hard to measure: Abadzi (1994) estimated a success rate of only 12.5 percent. A methodological framework that would enable the pastoralists to acquire literacy and numeracy skills in the most effective way possible was required. Nigeria inherited a formal and traditional model of British education that has also been adopted for adult literacy. As the experience of education was formal, the instinctive demand was for ready-made reading primers in the dominant regional language. The previous experience of the adult education team, however, was that participatory learning methods are more effective and arouse more interest among those learning.

Different models of literacy provision have been developed at different times and these can be placed on a continuum between traditional formal programmes and learner centred contextually focused community programmes. The learner oriented community approach to adult literacy and the traditional programmes are at opposite ends of the spectrum (see Fig. 12.2). When non-formal, learner centred approaches in the local language are used the curriculum can be responsive to the desires of the potential learners and informed by the social, religious and economic context of the community, its literacy practices and events, and linguistic heritage.

Drawing on past experience of literacy programmes, the theories of 'New Literacy Studies' (Street, 1984: 93, 95; Barton, 1991), Freire's psycho-social methodology and the then emerging ActionAid REFLECT[2] approach (Archer and Cottingham, 1996), the team adopted a contextually sensitive participative and eclectic learner oriented approach to adult literacy. This was termed Learner Oriented Community Adult Literacy (LOCAL) to emphasise the two key foci, the learner and the community.[3] Facilitators were required to move away from a model of knowledge transmission and dependence on rarely available centrally produced material to developing their own materials from their own and community resources, based on the literacy and numeracy practices and events prevalent in the communities. Barton's comment about people's purposes in reading and writing (1991:8) was adapted and became a slogan to aid the understanding and acceptance of this new method of teaching and learning:

> People learn to read in order to read something.
> They learn to write in order to write something.

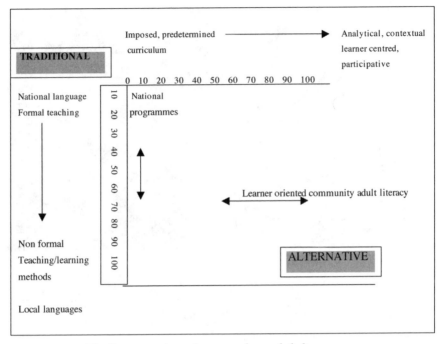

Figure 12.2 The learner oriented approach to adult literacy.

This quotation enabled both experienced and new facilitators to conceptualise the approach, thus helping participants learn the literacy and numeracy skills they required to function in their communities, and in the case of the nomads, in their interactions with the 'external' world, and to create lessons directly related to the learning objectives that the participants themselves defined.

Although one of the criteria for a facilitator was basic training in adult education and some teaching experience, the majority of Fulani trainee facilitators were completely new to the experience. They were not merely being introduced to a new methodology but needed to acquire the whole range of skills necessary for the successful teaching of adults. They needed considerable guidance in identifying the literacy and numeracy skills the nomads required, assisting them identify their learning objectives, framing these into lesson plans and delivering them in a coherent way. 'New Literacy Studies' provides a conceptual framework now widely accepted, but there is less documented experience of how to apply this conceptual framework in the practical teaching and learning situation. The project developed a simple nine step framework to help facilitators implement the LOCAL approach (see Table 12.1): it describes activities for identifying literacy events and practices in the nomadic communities and translating these into specific learning objectives (McCaffery, Obanubi and Sanni, 2000).

Figure 12.3 Locally contextualised learning.

1. Establish learning aims with participants

2. Prioritise aims with participants

3. Conduct a survey of community literacy and numeracy events with participants

4. Assist participants chart their economic activities and daily routine

5. Match prioritised aims (2) with related events and activities (3 and 4) and collect real everyday materials relevant to the aims

6. Identify specific learning points in the materials collected

7. Identify the teaching task required for each learning point

8. Develop clear objectives for each session

9. Develop and deliver practical and participatory teaching activities to engage participants in their own learning

Figure 12.4 The LOCAL Framework

Source: McCaffery et al. (2000).

Recognising and validating learners' life experiences was a key component of the methodology. It was not only the basis for learning but also the arena in which problems might be raised and solutions found. This is important in all literacy teaching and learning. With the nomadic Fulani it has a special significance in view of the way their life style is denigrated and because their

Figure 12.5 *Small books produced locally.*

lack of formal western education classifies them as ignorant. An important result of the LOCAL approach of merging the world of literacy with the real world was the production of learner-generated materials (LGMs). Participants told their stories in their own words and these were written up, typed or printed and became the textual material for literacy learning. The main language of learning was Fulfulde, though many pastoralists also spoke Hausa. Seventeen such small books written in Fulfulde, Hausa and English were printed and distributed, and were immensely popular among the clans. A notable example is 'Why We Move', an informative piece complete with illustrations tracing the annual migratory route of one of the clans. The book production process enabled participants to explain their way of life, express their frustrations and share important information with others.

Training Programme for Adult Literacy Facilitators

The training drew on theories of experiential learning (Rogers, C., 1974; Habermas, 1978; Kolb, 1993; Rogers, A., 1996) in which new knowledge is assimilated into past experience. The agency and the autonomy of the learner are paramount and the learning process is seen as one of taking control over one's own life. The strategy was to train local facilitators to work in their communities, drawing on their skills and resources and those of the participants and their communities. The most effective facilitators were then trained as local trainers. The objective was to first phase out the international trainer and then the national trainers, leaving self reliant and experienced trainers and facilitators in each project area who could sustain the literacy programmes established by the project in their communities and also work with federal and state adult literacy providers who expressed interest in the methodology.

The initial training was carried out predominantly in Hausa and Fulfulde, but also with English. The majority of facilitators were from partially settled clans or neighbouring communities and initially all male. Only a few were from total movement clans – one of these was exceptionally talented and also acted as translator on the training course. All training was gender-integrated. There were four stages of training:

1. Initial training of facilitators for two weeks.
2. Practical experience in the field.
3. Monitoring visits by the national trainers to observe facilitators.
4. Follow-up training for ten days.

Second level training available to selected CEP facilitators consisted of specialised workshops on producing and using learner-generated materials, on quality control through supervision, monitoring and evaluation and methods of training community facilitators.

Four local facilitators completed the second level training and successfully co-facilitated training new facilitators. The training was active, dynamic and popular. Participants were prepared to leave their cattle, farming activities and communities for up to two weeks at a time; attendance was 100 percent. A key feature of the courses was the use of training techniques used by community development workers to change attitudes and develop self-reliance.[4] Training guidelines were produced to provide a framework for local trainers (McCaffery et al., 2000).

Assessment and Evaluation of the Adult Literacy Programme

In its original period, from April 1997 to March 2000, the project trained 24 adult literacy facilitators, 10 female and 14 male and ran classes in 20 literacy centres with a total of 371 participants, 162 female and 209 male. Monitoring visits in February 2000 revealed that the LOCAL approach was in use in one form or another in all 20 centres. The following markers of progress were in evidence:

- A variety of learning methods and materials were in use, including individualised attention to learners, use of concrete materials like counting sticks, use of real materials such as immunisation records, drug bottles with manufacture and expiry dates, empty packets, tax receipts and voter cards.

- Seventeen learner-generated small books in three languages on a range of subjects were in use.
- A number of handwritten small books for individual and class use had been produced.
- There were posters and other relevant information on walls, e.g. the lifecycle of a mosquito and pictorial manuals of economic activities such as rope making.
- There were charts of participants' economic and daily routine activities.
- Facilitators had pre-planned lesson notes.
- Participants were able to identify specific learning achievements.
- Participants were able to identify specific impacts of literacy activities on their lives.
- Participants were observed writing their names on blackboards, reading from the LGMs they produced and reading posters about dams and farming.

Achievements can be divided into enactive, personal, social and socio-economic (Charnley and Jones, 1979). Interviews revealed that participants preferred to measure their progress by the uses to which they put their literacy and numeracy skills, their enactive achievements rather than what they did in the literacy centre, and could now perform real life tasks that included:

- reading manufacture and expiry dates of drugs to avoid being sold outdated stock
- reading road signs like 'Welcome to X city' sign boards
- reading signboards in both Fulfulde and Hausa, e.g. 'No Parking', 'Do Not Urinate Here'
- checking figures on receipts
- identifying amounts correctly on receipts and forms
- recording profit and loss in trading transactions.

The last three statements have economic implications though it would not be possible to state that such a short project had a significant impact on raising incomes.

A significant project outcome was the introduction of adult literacy classes for women, and this in itself affected the personal and social dynamics of the communities. The importance of the clan leaders in encouraging men to allow their wives to attend and leading by the example of sending their own wives must be stressed. Literacy centres for women began to serve as meeting points for young married women, providing them with regular opportunities to socialise.

Generally, women were not as forthcoming as the men on their reasons for attending literacy centres or the benefits they gained, and their ability to identify their uses of literacy was less specific. However, responses included a new ability to buy things in the market at actual cost rather than inflated prices, to read number plates on cars in order to retrieve lost luggage from taxis, to read marriage certificates and hospital cards and the ability to write children's ages.

Both men and women stated they gained further knowledge of how to 'follow religion', and were more confident when speaking in public. At one centre, participants enacted a drama demonstrating how the literacy programme had improved their ability to interact confidently with the police to show the right papers and avoid fines.

The data gathered suggests the social outcomes on both individuals and the communities could be significant. The psychological and the practical impact of developing literacy skills are expressed in the comment of one clan leader:

> As recently as a few years back, not one single person in the community could read a letter. They had to take it to Kunini to be read for them. Now there are many people around who can read letters for us!

Perhaps one of the most interesting and significant comments from a clan leader was: 'They talk to each other more now and co-operate better'. This was echoed by an individual who said 'I talk to people more now'. The considerable skills, abilities and communicative practices of nomadic communities were well recognised by all concerned with the project, yet the comments suggest that both individuals and communities gained a degree of self confidence and social ability through involvement in literacy classes.

Figure 12.6 Coming together to learn (1).

Teacher Education: Improving Children's Primary Education

The nomadic teacher education component of the CEP was complementary to the adult literacy initiative. Both shared the same general organisational foundations, management structures and project office. However delivery of the components involved different resource people and institutions and there was little communication between the two components.

Primary education is managed at state level by the State Primary Education Board (SPEB), which has a Nomadic Education Coordinator. There are separate nomadic primary schools. Within each state, at Local Government Area (LGA) level, there are Nomadic Education Supervisors, who are responsible for mediating between the SPEB and the individual schools and teachers. Nomadic schools are both 'fixed' and 'mobile'. Fixed schools are used seasonally, or for children who do not migrate and where the community is not migratory, whilst mobile schools move with the migrations. The teachers are typically either trained teachers employed by the State Primary Education Board (SPEB) and posted to the school from elsewhere, or untrained school-leavers from, and employed by, the nomadic community.

Figure 12.7 *Coming together to learn (2).*

A national nomadic education curriculum and a limited amount of corresponding textbooks, developed by the NCNE, are used in the schools, along with the rudiments of chalk, blackboard, exercise books and lesson planning notebooks. As with the mainstream Nigerian system, primary schooling is to Primary 7 level, after which transition to mainstream secondary school is the option for those few nomadic children who reach that stage.

There are very few trained teachers in nomadic schools. Aside from traditional Koranic schooling, most children in nomadic communities either do not go to school at all or else attend schools where the national curriculum system is poorly taught by untrained teachers. As a result, very few children from nomadic communities complete primary education, and far fewer progress through secondary or further education. The constraint this endemic low level of education imposes on their capacity for self-determination and development is seen by various stakeholders as a major problem, and improving the availability of effective teachers is seen as a key approach to addressing the problem. Opportunities for teacher training have not been adequate to meet the needs of these nomadic communities for various reasons. A training course specifically designed for teachers in nomadic schools is considered desirable, since the nomadic curriculum, teaching environment and culture are distinct from those of the mainstream primary education sector. However, few colleges offer such courses, and those courses that do exist are not perceived to be suitable.

The predominate use of Fulfulde, as well as their own cultural and educational background, are also characteristics which differentiate many teachers in nomadic primary schools from those in mainstream primary schools. However, these distinctions are not clear cut, as many non-nomadic schools are also in Fulfulde mother-tongue communities, and not all teachers in nomadic primary schools are Fulani or nomads themselves, nor are they necessarily Fulfulde speakers.

The National Certificate of Education (NCE) nomadic education course at the local Federal College of Education is for secondary school leavers – a level higher than all but a handful of nomadic youths have reached. The cost of attending a full-time course and the prospect of three years of residential training has not made it attractive even for the few who have completed secondary school. An older ('Grade II') training course for primary leavers was still run in some colleges, and many serving teachers had this level of qualification, but it was no longer officially recognised by the federal authorities, and Grade II teachers were expected either to upgrade or to be retrenched.

The project explored alternative routes to training nomadic youth as basic primary schoolteachers, including a largely school-based model with a succession of brief college-based 'sandwich' sessions interspersed with supported on-the-job training, phasing the trainees' activity progressively from classroom observation through teaching assistance to full teaching.

This model was not, in the end, adopted, except in a very much modified form, for various reasons. In particular, the trainee teachers required a great deal of basic education themselves as a foundation, and it was felt the risk of humiliation and loss of face of the under-equipped trainee teachers would be too great and devastating in the Fulani culture and setting.

The typical potential trainee for the project was expected to be a nomadic boy or girl (predominantly boys, for cultural reasons) who had completed primary school and would be willing to undertake some basic pre-service training and remain a teacher in their nomadic community, moving with it during its migrations and living the normal life of the community. A second category of potential trainee was teachers appointed by the SPEB and already serving in nomadic primary schools. These may have had Grade II or NCE training and with the benefit of in-service training would become more effective teachers, specifically in nomadic primary schools; such teachers might or might not be nomadic Fulanis.

The project initially planned to focus on the total movement group nomads as teacher trainees, as being the most disadvantaged in terms of access to education and the wider benefits of participation in civil society. However, it became apparent that split movement groups would also be included, mainly because very few children from the total movement group nomads had the basic educational background seen as necessary to participate in the kind of training envisaged. Also, the quality and availability of education provision to partial movement group communities was itself inadequate.

During the initial project design workshop, two main teacher training interventions were decided: a pre-service training for nomadic youth, to create basic primary teachers at community level; and in-service training for existing, trained primary teachers working in nomadic primary schools. As with the adult literacy component, the nomadic communities were integrally involved in the conception and design of the teacher education component of the project, and with decisions about its management, through community level committees. The project was not based within any single institution, but, key to the implementation of the training was the Federal College of Education (FCE) in Yola, from where courses were developed and delivered. The NCNE was also involved, primarily through its teacher education unit at the University of Maiduguri, and a group of five tutors undertook a study tour to the U.K. Consultancy and training support were also provided from the U.K. Not basing the project within a government institution brought benefits of freedom and accountability, but also difficulties of integration and sustainability.

Training was relatively modest in scale. During the project life span, there were two cohorts each of 30 trainees who completed the pre-service course and a third cohort enrolled (Kanu et al 2001). There were also a total of approximately 150 trainee places on a series of short (one to two week) in-service courses. The pre-service and in-service trainees were drawn from throughout the two states involved, with a slight preferential weighting in favour of the communities targeted by complementary project inputs (school building, well construction, adult literacy).

In-service Training

A curriculum was developed for in-service training, and a series of short training courses was held at FCE Yola, to strengthen teachers' grasp of subject content and teaching methods. There was a shift as the series progressed from a predominantly content-based training to more teaching skills focus (generic and subject-specific), and from knowledge transfer to more active, participatory training.

Pre-service training was the major focus of the project. The model adopted was a college-based face-to-face course, using curricula and printed course materials developed specially for the purpose, with school-based blocks of supervised teaching practice. Trainees sat an internal end-of-course examination and later the national Grade II teachers' examinations. The training period, including intermittently supervised time teaching in nomadic school, time in college and vacations, was approximately two years. Both pre- and in-service courses were delivered to plan, with high levels of retention and completion, although the level of examination success was low at Grade II level and it took longer than anticipated for trainees to complete the pre-service course. Progression from trainee to teacher, as the trainee moved from college to school, needed considerable support; and the standard required to become a Grade II qualified teacher was demanding for the majority of trainees. However, the pre-service trainees performed well once posted to schools and their communities were generally supportive and valued their presence.

One marked area of achievement was a progressive increase in female participation in the pre-service teacher training as the project continued. The first cohort included two women students from a total of 30 students; the second cohort of 30 included five women; and the third cohort of 30 included nine women (Kanu et al., 2001). This reflected a change in perceptions amongst the communities, as they came to value women's education and training more, and to overcome their initial suspicions and reluctance to engage young women in the training and expected subsequent employment.

Overall, resource demands on course providers and stakeholders were higher than anticipated. The project had expected a relatively modest expenditure on training, and had a limited budget for developing and producing course materials. Substantially increased resources were needed for this and other aspects of project implementation. Again, this was largely attributable to the lower than anticipated entry level of trainees combined with the higher than planned exit level.

Prospects for Continuing, Expanding and Developing the Training

Whether or not successive cohorts will pursue the pre-service and in-service courses depends mainly on funding and support. With the conclusion of external funding, the third cohort of pre-service trainees started training funded solely by the communities, SPEBs, LGAs and NCNE (British Council, 2002). These bodies will need to continue to meet the costs of such training if it is to continue, which may mean substantially reduced provision.

Stakeholder buy-in was mixed. There was some predictable scepticism about the ability of the relatively under-educated pre-service trainees to perform as effective teachers; but there was also a good deal of positive (and often surprised) response to their performance once they started teaching. Some communities demonstrated high levels of commitment and willingness to contribute time, money and material resources to training and then supporting the teachers. Others were less convinced and continue to expect that donors should provide. The perception that education is of limited value changed markedly for the better through the project, with some dramatic conversions – particularly in relation to the value of educating girls and having them train and work as teachers.

Other communities and states may adopt or adapt the model developed by this project. In the north of Nigeria, the Provosts of colleges of education concluded during the lifetime of the project that, contrary to federal policy, they would continue and even strengthen the training of Grade II teachers, as this was the only realistic way of filling the need for teachers in the primary schools in their states. This bodes well for such programmes, though the issue of the wide gap between the educational background level of the potential trainees and the level which would ideally enable them to take up such training remains a major hurdle to negotiate. School-based continuing support, using a combination of distance education and face-to-face support would be highly desirable and ought to be feasible. This might be, perhaps, in the form of self-study printed materials, with correspondence assignments, school-based mentoring by local colleagues, support visits by Nomadic Education Supervisors and FCE tutors, plus occasional face-to-face seminars at local LGA cluster, state or FCE level. However, it would involve costs, and financing any kind of training remains a major underpinning problem.

Lessons Learned about Teacher Training, and Challenges for the Future

The most mobile, least accessible and least well educated and resourced nomadic groups were the ones least easy to include in training: they had the weakest base levels of education among their children and youth, and in some cases lower perceived levels of interest in or commitment to education.

Yet the most 'deserving' cases were the very communities where the educational level of candidates for training was lowest. Thus some trainees were enrolled who had no more than Primary 3 or 4 level schooling (compared to some others, from more well-provided for backgrounds, who had Secondary 3 or 4 level education and were using the programme as a relatively easy means to qualification).

Qualification levels of teachers on course completion provided a corresponding problem. The requirement to convert the trainees into Grade II qualified teachers was an ambitious late addition to the project, adopted in the face of issues about recognising and employing the teachers produced by the pre-service course. The extent of support and training needed to provide adequate education and training was greater than originally provided for and greater than could be met even with extension of time and increase in resources available for the pre-service training. The costs and opportunity costs of training and education remain very significant. Whilst external funding can make such activities seem affordable, once temporary financial support is removed and the stakeholders are expected to underwrite the full cost of the training, its sustainability becomes more doubtful. Lack of state resources for nomadic education is a major part of the funding problem. When at times teachers in all primary schools in the state are months behind in receiving salaries, it is politically impossible for SPEBs to pay nomadic teachers' salaries or to fund training of fresh teachers for nomadic schools.

At the conclusion of the project period, some challenges in both areas of activity remained to be resolved. Whilst specific to the operation of this project, these challenges include some generic points which are likely to be of relevance also in other contexts.

Scepticism in the community about education, as mentioned above, remained a major issue in some cases. There are hopes and some anecdotal evidence that the experience of communities where the training was perceived favourably led to positive advocacy among other, doubting communities.

Low female participation in education remains a major feature, despite some positive instances of change of attitude and practice on the part of community leaders and thence their followers. At every level of education, and more dramatically the further up the system one goes, the discrepancy between girls and boys' participation is great. Nevertheless, real progress was made in this regard in terms of elders' willingness to have girls delay marriage until they have completed pre-service teacher training and then to work as teachers once married.

Not all the educational outcomes were fully realised. The investment in the training of nomadic women facilitators will take time. Consistent and effective supervision of the literacy classes was also difficult, largely for logistical reasons such as long and difficult distances, overlapping timing of classes, and inaccessibility of some centres during the wet season.

Communication between the project office in Kaduna and the project was also very difficult, as the distance was great and communication facilities unreliable. The project also did not ultimately reach the 'hard to reach' nomadic clans. Two clans originally selected moved away before the project started. Of the two clans the project worked with, one was partially settled with only the herders moving in the dry season for better pastures. The second clan moved regularly between a wet season and a dry season location and the project was therefore able to build a school on the land used in the dry season, to which the clan was considering laying permanent claim.

At community level the teacher training, adult literacy and community development were seen as aspects of a single project. At the professional level there was no forum through which these links could be made and therefore no opportunity for sharing professional experience across components.

There are also no guarantees of sustainability. This depends on the ability of state stakeholders (the LGAs, the State Agencies for Mass Education, the State Primary Education Boards and the NCNE) to develop a concrete plan for taking over the responsibility of running established centres and building on project gains. In an extension year to the project's original time frame, efforts focused on scaling up the positive aspects of the project, advocacy to alert state stakeholders to the urgency of their intervention and supporting stakeholders in taking over full financial and management responsibility for continuing project activities.

Inevitably, project administration also faced tensions due to the short time frame and the pressure to agree and deliver project inputs against predetermined timetables. The participatory planning process which was crucial to generating full participation and so was key to the project, meant that expertise was brought in after the event rather than to help with planning. As a result, some decisions made at that point later turned out to be unrealistic; and because it had been difficult to project accurately in advance what would be involved, budgets were insufficient, with subsequent pressures on comprehensive forward commitment.

One widely familiar issue (see Krätli and Dyer, this volume) which remained under debate was the relevant and appropriate curriculum to use in primary school, and how far separate, specifically tailored curricula should be followed. There remained a tension between the desire to maximise opportunities for learners to integrate nationally into other (non-nomadic) social groups and educational opportunities (such as secondary schools), and the need for learning to be relevant to the reality of children's experience.

The project also raised some important educational difficulties relating to the training of teachers. A major challenge was how to enable participation and success in teacher training of those with more limited educational background, specifically the total movement group communities. The proportion of teaching methods versus subject content to include in the training course was thus an issue, with a strong demand for basic subject knowledge ultimately overriding the project education adviser's assumption that teaching skills were the essential core of the training. A further related capacity challenge was language: in many instances, the English of the young teacher trainees was very limited even though English is the national language and the language of instruction. The adult literacy project component faced a similar issue – achieving the best balance between training facilitators with no experience of teaching adults in the technical aspects of reading and writing versus training them in the broader aspects of participatory, interactive learning in a community context. In both project components, differences between established teaching and training styles prevalent in the colleges, schools and adult literacy centres, on the one hand, and those desired by the project education advisers, on the other hand, remained areas to be accommodated in planning and for fully satisfactory resolution.

By the close of the project, the impact of the pre- and in-service teacher training courses on primary school enrolment and achievement had yet to be determined. However, while objectively substantiated findings and the longer-term effects remained to be confirmed, initial anecdotal evidence was positive. Institutionalising the innovation of the pre-service teacher training course, in terms of ensuring the trainees' future employment, establishing continuing professional development for newly trained teachers emerging from the course and translating an externally-funded project into a continuing programme run by the SPEBs, remained challenges which the state and education sector partners were engaged with meeting at the close of the project.

Overall Successes of the Project

A three-year project can, at best, initiate change. To have a lasting impact it needs to be sustained long after the passing of the transitory external support. The stakeholders wanted the programme to continue and though aware of its duration still expressed surprise and disappointment on realising it would in fact end. This itself suggests a degree of success. In our view a number of factors contributed to this, and we feel these again are points which are likely to have wider resonance with experiences in other contexts.

Firstly, the project was well matched to the political, social, educational and aid environment in which it took place. It had successfully identified a way to interpret positively and as supportive the overall policy context, and to create an opportunity to operate in potentially very difficult circumstances. Thus the intervention was not in isolation, but part of a programme of improvement for nomadic education initiated by concerned Nigerians, including Fulani leaders who had already taken very significant steps and successfully developed a number of initiatives. DfID was able to support and finance a programme with the full support of the NCNE.

Equally essentially, the culture and lifestyle of the nomads was respected and valued by both donor and managing agents. The project was genuinely participatory, working in all respects closely with the communities, and some decision making was effectively devolved to local communities, who in turn supported the project. The communities had already identified a need for education, and the project responded to and furthered aims already formulated; the community leaders were, at best, powerful advocates within their communities, rather than recipients to be motivated and 'sold' an idea.

Perhaps paradoxically, the power of social cohesion within the Fulani culture and social system was of major significance in the success of the participatory approach. It meant there was a high degree of deference to the decisions of elders. Thus in cases where an elder took a position, the community would follow. Their influence was particularly interesting in relation to the education of women – a specific project focus. Respect for cultural traditions in relation to female education proved to be not an inhibiting factor but to contribute to project success. The clan leaders eventually became sufficiently convinced of the value of education for women that they led by example. In one case, a leading figure in the project sent his own daughters to join the teacher training; in another, a man sent his wife to become a literacy teacher. At the end the project women comprised 44 percent of the total participating in the literacy programme.

In addition to the factors contributing positively to overall project success, the success of the adult literacy programme was also due to features of its design. It had a practical and undogmatic methodology; the model of a four-stage training process and the on-going support provided for the literacy facilitators were successful; and training was delivered in the local languages. The LOCAL approach drew on the personal, experiential and cultural resources of the community and in doing so, developed the confidence of both learners and facilitators. It assisted learners to acquire the skills they sought and which they could put to immediate use in their daily lives. It used locally generated materials, which drew on and recorded local nomadic experience and nomadic culture, which gave a sense of pride and achievement. Also, several of the facilitators were exceptionally talented and able to provide leadership.

Indeed, despite serious concerns about the often very limited educational background of those recruited as trainee teachers and adult literacy facilitators, it was found that they had the capacity to become remarkably effective primary schoolteachers and adult literacy facilitators. It was agreed towards the end of the project, for example, that selected graduates of the pre-service course should receive additional training in literacy facilitation so that they could double as teachers and adult literacy facilitators in appropriate situations.

Conclusion

Experience to date validates the belief that a holistic approach needs to be adopted in any project with nomadic pastoralist Fulani. Development agencies, government and local institutions all need to continue to rethink their attitudes and procedures if they are effectively to support the growth of an integrated lifestyle for the pastoralist and view pastoralism as a cultural and economic resource rather than a deficit. The clans' concern and disbelief at the closure of the project was not only a testimony to its success, but also to the failure of a policy based on short-term interventions. The sector-wide approach due to be adopted by DfID should avoid this problem. However, other issues in relation to the purposes and goals of education and including nomadic pastoralists' voices in determining educational policy for their people will produce different and difficult issues.

In relation to current thinking, the 1981 National Policy on Education cited earlier, could be modified with regard to the pastoralist nomadic population. The 1981 objectives may be seen as designed to integrate, not to assimilate the nomads into broader Nigerian society. These earlier objectives might be reviewed to be more effective in enabling pastoralist nomads to acquire an education suitable to their current and future circumstances and be reformulated as:

1. Awareness of the State of Nigeria and the nomads' role within it.
2. Training in critical and analytical thinking.
3. Acquisition of functional literacy and numeracy skills and occupation-related skills and knowledge.
4. Knowledge of modern medicine, veterinary medicine, health, hygiene, child spacing and nutrition.

It is now recognised that the nature and content of education for nomadic pastoralists must be related to their social and cultural patterns and their traditional and emerging economic needs. However, the education which will best give the nomads the skills for the future also has to provide for an unknown range of alternatives, whether improved cattle production or alternative means of generating income as well their present lifestyle. This debate was rarely entered into. Those involved in education need to engage to a much greater degree than apparent during the project on the nature of the environment, grazing capacity and changing weather patterns, all of which impact directly on the nomads' traditional way of life. Interdisciplinary dialogue is essential.

Educationalists should be aware of the successes and failures of settlement resulting from coercion or encouragement through education. In Nigeria the issues remain problematic. There is increased pressure on land, conflict between pastoralists and farmers and harassment by the police. Moreover, many of the initiatives to assist the nomads such as seasonal grazing reserves and grazing routes during migration have not been enacted, and nomadic pastoralists rarely have legal entitlement to land they regularly occupy annually for six months of the year.

Assisting the Fulani pastoralists to acquire the skills to continue their traditional way of life, which currently provides 90 percent of Nigeria's meat supply and uses up a minimum of the earth's resources, takes us beyond the success or failure of the immediate project into the world of the future. The environmental and economic consequences of settlement, both for the nomadic clans themselves, but also for the environment and the economy, need to be fully considered in determining educational policy. However, a contribution of education in all communities should be to promote the acceptance of difference, of different ways of life, different traditions and different values as fundamental to a peaceful society. If retaining bio-diversity among animals and plants is crucial to the earth's survival, so surely is accommodating and valuing different lifestyles and values crucial to human survival.

Notes

1. The objectives are reproduced from the original document in which the masculine pronoun is used.
2. Regenerated Freirean Literacy through Empowering Community Techniques.
3. The term LOCAL was first used by adult literacy consultants on the ODA-supported Adult Literacy Training Project in Egypt (1995–98) when participatory methods were used to broaden and deepen the national curriculum.
4. The component on attitude change was developed by one of the national trainers, Felix Obanubi, who drew on his experience in training for community development.

References

Abadzi, H. (1994) *What We Know about Acquisition of Literacy – Is there Hope?* World Bank Discussion Paper 245.

Abba, M. and S.G. Bakari (1999) 'Empowering the Socially Deprived through the Curriculum: the Case of Fulbe Nomads in Nigeria', (mimeo) paper prepared for postponed conference 'Re-thinking the curricula for schools' effectiveness in the next millennium', the Nigeria Chapter of the World Council for the Curriculum and Instruction, scheduled for September 1999, Lagos State University.

Adepetu, A.A. (1993) 'School and Community Relationship in Mobile Setting'. In: C. Ezeomah (ed.) *Handbook for Teachers in Nomadic Schools*. Kaduna: National Commission for Nomadic Education.

Agwu, S.N. (1998) 'Education Curriculum for Nomads'. In: G. Tahir and N.D. Muhammad (eds) *Readings on Distance Education for the Pastoral Nomads of Nigeria*. Zaria: Ahmadu Bello University Press.

Aminu, J. (1991) 'The Evolution of Nomadic Education Policy in Nigeria'. In: G. Tahir (ed.) *Education and Pastoralism in Nigeria*. Zaria: Ahmadu Bello University Press.

Anyanwu, C.N. (1998) 'Transformative Research for the Promotion of Nomadic Education in Nigeria'. *Journal of Nomadic Studies* 1 (1): 44–51.

Archer, D. and S. Cottingham (1996) *The REFLECT Mother Manual: a New Approach to Adult Literacy*. London: ActionAid.

Ardo, G.V. (1991) 'Planning for Minority Education with Particular Reference to Pastoralists of Nigeria'. In: G. Tahir (ed.) *Education and Pastoralism in Nigeria*. Zaria: Ahmadu Bello University Press.

Awogbade, M. (1991) 'Nomadism and Pastoralism: a Conceptual Framework'. In: G. Tahir (ed.) *Education and Pastoralism in Nigeria*. Zaria: Ahmadu Bello University Press.

Barton, D. (1991) 'The Social Nature of Writing'. In: D. Barton and R. Ivanic (eds) *Writing in the Community*. London: Sage.

British Council (2002) *Nigeria Community Education Project*. Abuja: The British Council, Nigeria.

Charnley, A.H. and H.A. Jones (1979) *The Concept of Success in Adult Literacy*. Cambridge: Huntington.

Ezeomah, C. (1983) *The Education of Nomadic People: the Fulani of Northern Nigeria*, Driffield, Stoke-on-Trent: Nafferton Books and Deanhouse Centre.

––––– (1987) *The Settlement Patterns of Nomadic Fulbe in Nigeria: Implications for Educational Development*. Betley: Deanhouse.

––––– (ed.) (1988) *The Education of Nomadic Families in Bauchi, Gongola and Plateau States*. UNESCO/UNDP Projects Reports, Vol. 1–3, Breda.

––––– (1993) 'The Aims and Objectives of Nomadic Education'. In: C. Ezeomah (ed.) *Handbook for Teachers in Nomadic Schools*. Kaduna: National Commission for Nomadic Education.

––––– (1995a) *Educational Provision for Nomads in Lau (Taraba State), Numan (Adamawa State) and Cham (Bauchi State)*. Abuja: The British Council, Nigeria.

––––– (ed.) (1995b) *The Education of Nomadic Populations in Africa: Papers Presented at the UNESCO (Breda) Regional Seminar on the Education of Nomadic Populations in Africa, 11–15 December 1995*. Kaduna, Nigeria, Breda: UNESCO.

––––– (nd). *Report on Achievements in Nomadic Education by NCNE to Honorable Minister of Education (1992–3)*.

Ezewu, E.E. and G. Tahir (eds) (1997) *Ecology and Education in Nigeria: Studies on the Education of Migrant Fishermen*. Onitsha: Tabansi Publishers.

Federal Government of Nigeria/UNICEF (1993) *Situation and Policy Analysis of Education in Nigeria*.

Freire, P. (1972) *Pedagogy of the Oppressed*. London: Penguin Books.

Habermas, J. (1978) *Knowledge and Human Interest*. London: Heinemann.

Kanu, E.N., H.M. Mubi, S.I. Ateequ, M.B. Wambai and H. Muhammad (2001) *An Assessment of DFID-assisted Nomadic Pre-service Teacher Education Programme*. Yola: FCE Yola.

Kolb, D.A. (1993) 'The Process of Experiential Learning'. In: M. Thorpe, R. Edwards and A. Hanson (eds) *Culture and Processes of Adult Learning.* London: Routledge.

Mace, J. (1979) *Working with Words.* Readers and Writers Publishing Co-operative/ Chameleon.

McCaffery, J., F. Obanubi and K. Sanni (1997) *Initial Instructor 4 Stage Training Workshop, Biu and the Nomadic Education Project.* Abuja: The British Council, Nigeria.

McCaffery, J., F. Obanubi and K. Sanni (1998) *Review of Initial Instructor 4 Stage Training and Adult Literacy Training Programme 1997–1998.* Report for The British Council, Nigeria.

——— , ——— and ——— (2000) *A Guide for Training Literacy Instructors: Learner Oriented Community Adult Literacy.* Community Education Programme: Nigeria, Abuja: The British Council, Nigeria.

Monbiot, G. (1994) *No Man's Land.* London: Picador.

Muhammad, N. (1991) 'The Viability and Justifications for the Use of Fulfulde in Primary Schools'. In: G. Tahir (ed.) *Education and Pastoralism in Nigeria.* Zaria: Ahmadu Bello University Press.

National Commission for Nomadic Education (1998) *Annual Report 1998.* Kaduna: National Commission for Nomadic Education.

Nwoke, A. (1993) 'The English Language Curriculum for Nomadic Schools'. In: C. Ezeomah (ed.) *Handbook for Teachers in Nomadic Schools.* Kaduna: National Commission for Nomadic Education.

Overseas Development Administration, West and North Africa Department 1996. *Nigeria Community Education Programme.*

Pennells, J. (2000) 'Teacher Education for Nomads: a Cautious Approach to Adopting Distance Education in a Project in Adamawa and Taraba States', in *Open Praxis*, Volume 2.

——— and C. Ezeomah (2000) 'Basic Education for Refugees and Nomads'. In: C. Yates and J. Bradley (eds) *Basic Education at a Distance.* London and New York: Routledge Falmer.

Rogers, A. (1994) *Women, Literacy and Income Generation.* Reading: Education for Development.

——— (1996) *Teaching Adults.* Buckingham: Open University Press.

Rogers, C. (1974) *On Becoming a Person.* London: Constable.

Sa'ad, A. (2000) *Nomadic Fulani and Family Life Education in Nigeria: the Case of the Southern Borno Nomads*, paper presented at 'Voices for Change' conference, Cambridge: IEC.

Sanni, K., J. McCaffery, J. Olatunji-Hughes and F. Obanubi (1998) 'Training as Experiential Learning and Shared Experience'. In: *Literacy and Development*, BALID Bulletin Autumn 1998.

Street, B.V. (1984) *Literacy in Theory and Practice.* Cambridge: Cambridge University Press.

——— (ed.) (1993) *Cross Cultural Approaches to Literacy.* Cambridge: Cambridge University Press.

Street, B.V. (1995) *Social Literacies.* London: Longman.

Tahir, G. (1991) *Education and Pastoralism in Nigeria.* Zaria, Nigeria: ABU Press.

—— (1997) 'Nomadic Education in Nigeria'. In: Ezeomah, C. (ed) *The Education of Nomadic Populations in Africa: Papers Presented at the UNESCO (Breda) Regional Seminar on the Education of Nomadic Populations in Africa, 11–15 December 1995, Kaduna, Nigeria*, Breda: UNESCO.

—— (1998) 'Nomadic Education in Nigeria: Issues, Problems and Prospects' *Journal of Nomadic Studies* 1 (1): 10–26.

—— and N.D. Muhammad (eds) (1998) *Readings on Distance Education for the Pastoral Nomads of Nigeria*. Zaria: Ahmadu Bello University Press.

Umar, A. and A. Ardo (1998) *Report on Animal Husbandry to NCNE Committee*. Kaduna: National Commission for Nomadic Education.

VanEcke, C. (1991) 'Pulaaku: an Empowering Symbol among the Pastoral Fulbe People in Nigeria'. In: G. Tahir (ed.) *Education and Pastoralism in Nigeria*. Zaria: Ahmadu Bello University Press.

AFTERWORD

Caroline Dyer

The chapters presented in this collection have provided a rich menu of information, analysis and critique. Perhaps it is pertinent just briefly to note that had we had more space, we would have sought to include further aspects. While a couple of papers have considered adult literacy, the collection as a whole has primarily focused on formal educational systems. It has thus not paid explicit attention to the non-formal sector, and the work of local and international non-governmental organisations who are often working with governments to augment existing provision, or provide alternatives. Their non-appearance here should not be taken to negate their value, and readers who seek more information may like, for example, to look at the work of Oxfam and Save the Children Fund as just two of several organisations that are heavily engaged in educating nomadic groups. Other than brief mentions in the opening chapter, the collection has also not included in its purview either formalised early childhood education, or distance education, two promising areas where exploratory work is being done. Nor does it have a clearly defined gender focus, through which closer attention might have be paid to how changing contexts impact on gender roles – such as, for instance, how sedentarisation impacts on women's productivity.

These omissions nothwithstanding, authors have problematised from a wide range of country and community contexts the relationship between nomads and the state, and suggested that how each constructs the 'other' is fundamental to the successes or failures of state educational services. The agenda of formal education – to produce modern citizens that conform with the state's notion of contemporary development – has been thoroughly exposed as the ideological project that it is. Particularly interesting in this respect have been the reports of how groups who do use an educational system that is antagonistic to their cultural values are adroit at extracting from it what they need, and resisting what they do not. Every author, whether implicitly and explicitly, has questioned whose purpose formal schooling actually serves – and the collection as a whole demonstrates there is no single, easy, or even stable, answer. Each chapter has added further evidence of the need to articulate the often implicit kinds of 'knowledge' of 'the other' that present barriers to the emergence of educational services that support and validate nomads' choices in relation to their social and occupational identities. There is also no support, on the basis of the body of evidence presented here, for any suggestion that nomadic peoples do not care about education. Quite the contrary, indeed – every paper demonstrates that they do, and that non-indigenous 'education' has, in some shape or form, a place in their future. The extent to which nomadic groups themselves are given the space to shape the form and content of that education varies, as these accounts show, but is clearly crucial to their presence, participation and achievement in educational programmes.

The thematic anchors for this collection of papers have been the consistent issues that come up from a wide variety of country contexts. Every chapter has highlighted the need for 'development' itself, not simply the education sector, to be re-imagined in ways that are appropriate for nomadic peoples. Evidently, this is not going to be possible unless governments accept the legitimacy of nomadic peoples's way of life and occupation; comprehend that their livelihood systems are appropriate and technically adapted to their environment, rather than an anachronistic relic from the past; and honour nomads' right to being seen and treated as equal citizens with equal rights. Some basic attention to what are clearly 'common problems' with known solutions can lead to somewhat improved policy and planning for nomadic groups' development and these chapters highlight many useful points in this respect. A major challenge confronting this endeavour, on which several authors here comment, is the low visibility of nomadic groups to policy communities. This does little to help the emergence of sound macro policies, across different sectors and levels of government, and agencies; and nor does it augur well for the development of policy and practice at the micro level.

Encouragingly, some chapters have shown that appropriate educational provision for nomadic peoples is possible, providing that considerable time and energy is put into in making their needs visible through consultation, ensuring full nomadic participation in planning, decision-making and execution of jointly conceived educational programmes. Stories of success, just as much as stories of failure, point up the fallacy of schooling systems' hegemonic notion that 'one size fits all' – and an important contribution they all make is to highlight the specificity of context, and how that shapes nomads' engagement with formal education. It is perhaps particularly encouraging that, while the failures for nomads of formal schooling are manifest in every context discussed here, several chapters discuss innovation within this very system, as testimony to the possibility of reform of what is likely to remain the mainstream provider of education for the foreseeable future.

There seems to be a wide-ranging consensus that nomadic families opt for formal schooling as a means of becoming equipped for life in other livelihood systems. The patterns of take-up of schooling, where perhaps one or two children attend while others continue to work within pastoralism illustrates, however, that nomads do not see education is seen as a good *per se*, or share the discourse of individual rights that underlies the Millennium Development Goal for primary education. Rather, nomads use schools as an opportunity to develop multi-resource household economies; and this rationale for education presents strong challenges to the legitimacy or even desirability of including all children in primary education. For nomadic families, schooling for some appears a more sensitive aspiration than schooling for all.

The demand for education for adults is less in evidence, although again, this is highly context-sensitive; but it consistently appears to take second place in parents' minds to formal education for children. Insofar as there is adult provision, it has been largely envisaged in terms of literacy; an agenda for the future is to consider adult education in a fuller sense, which allows inclusion of life skills envisaged in the Education For All promises – such as how to achieve political representation and other life skills outside traditional knowledge systems that support successful adaptation in changing livelihood contexts. Much work has yet to be done on developing contextually sensitive resolutions of how forms of education and nomadic livelihoods should mutually interact, now and in the future. Implicated in this discussion, too, is the need to consider practical consequences of the fact that knowledge is constructed in different ways: can the abstract knowledge that is the preserve of formal education embrace rather than negate the situated knowledge of nomadic groups, to create synergy rather than antipathy?

A final call then, at the end of this volume, is for closer links between communities of educational policymakers, non-governmental and civil society organisers, and researchers to facilitate the generation and exchange of knowledge and information. Further case- and context-specific data is a prerequisite for deepening understandings of how best educational services should relate to nomads' cultural values and livelihood strategies, as they are now, and as they change over time; how knowledge is constructed, and applied; and what different forms of knowledge have to offer each other. Possible modes of engaging with that specificity have been a sub-text of several chapters. An intensified effort to link policy, practitioner and research communities must be framed by the intention of developing detailed and nuanced understandings of the intersection of development policies, rural livelihoods, poverty, and educational needs. It will be resource and time intensive, involving much trial (and, inevitably, error), given the unanimity among contributors to this collection that nothing much can be learned or achieved without engaging at first hand through participatory approaches.

Only then can the crucial role that 'education' plays be re-imagined for each context at an adequate level of detail and relevance. Whether governments, non-government and civil society organisations and research communities have the will and necessary capacity to commit their joint resources to doing so will significantly shape the future prospects of education for nomadic peoples.

Notes on Contributors

Ismael Abu-Saad is a member of the indigenous Negev Bedouin Arab community. He is an Associate Professor in the Department of Education, and founding director of the Center for Bedouin Studies and Development at Ben-Gurion University of the Negev in Beer-Sheva, Israel. His research interests include education and development among indigenous peoples, school management in developing societies, social identity in pluralistic societies, the impact of urbanisation on the Negev Bedouin, and organisational behaviour in multicultural contexts.

Roy Carr-Hill is Research Professor of Education in Developing Countries at the Institute of Education in London, U.K. His main interests are in understanding the demand for, and the delivery and outcomes of, basic education in the poorer of the developing countries in order to be able to give useful advice to the corresponding Ministries. He lived and worked in Mozambique for three years and since then has been a consultant in over twenty countries. He acted as technical advisor to the International Institute for Educational Planning, Paris to describe and understand attitudes to education among, and the provision of schooling to, nomadic groups in six of the countries in the Horn of Africa.

Dawn Chatty is Deputy Director of the Refugee Studies Centre, Queen Elizabeth House, and University Reader in Forced Migration, University of Oxford. She is a social anthropologist with long experience in the Middle East as a university teacher, and development practitioner. Her research interests include nomadic pastoralism and conservation, gender and development, health, illness and culture, children and adolescents in prolonged conflict and forced migration, and development-induced displacement. Her recent publications include *Conservation and Mobile Indigenous People: Displacement, Forced Settlement and Sustainable Development*. Oxford: Berghahn, 2002.

Archana Choksi is an ethnoarchaelogist by training, with interests in nomadic movements over 6000 years of the archaelogical record. After completing her work with the Rabaris, she migrated to England, where she became Policy Officer for Manchester Drugs and Race Unit. She now works in Leeds as community liason officer for Leeds Asylum Seeker Support Network (LASSN) and maintains her research and practitioner interests in diversity, equality, inclusion and strategic policy development.

Demberel came from a nomadic family and herded animals on the mountainside in Gobi Altai district in Mongolia until he was seven. He progressed through the education system, winning prizes en route, and became a physicist, spending some time in Russia. He returned to the Gobi Altai Region, first as a headteacher, then as Director of Education in the Region. He died in a jeep accident in 2000.

Caroline Dyer is Senior Lecturer, Development Practice at the Institute for Politics and International Studies, University of Leeds, U.K. A linguist by training, she has research interests in mobility and educational inclusion, working children, adult literacy, and policy implementation. She has specialised in Basic Education in South Asia for the last twelve years, and is currently also researching elective home education among Gypsy Travellers in North West England. She recently co-edited a special issue of *Compare* entitled 'Decentralisation for Educational Development?'.

Bill Edwards is an Adjunct Academic in the Unaipon School of Indigenous Studies at the University of South Australia. He was Superintendent of Ernabella Mission from 1958–72, Superintendent of Mowanjum Mission, Western Australia (1972–73) and Minister of the Pitjantjatjara Parish (1958–72, 1976–80). He lectured in Aboriginal Studies at the South Australian College of Advanced Education and the University of South Australia (1981–96). In retirement he conducts Pitjantjatjara language Summer Schools, interprets in Pitjantjatjara in hospitals and courts and continues to write. He is the author of *An Introduction to Aboriginal Societies*, 2nd revised edition, Social Science Press, 2004.

Chimah Ezeomah, former Dean of the School of Education at University of Jos, Nigeria, was the first Executive Secretary of the National Commission for Nomadic Education (NCNE). Professor Ezeomah has spent his career working in nomadic education and has published extensively on nomadic education and Fulani culture. An Igbo, he has been granted the title of *Ardo* by nomadic Fulani. He has worked as a consultant on many projects, including those managed by the British Council and UNESCO.

Michael de Jongh has research interests in ethnicity, identity and human mobility in particular. He is Professor, Anthropology and Chair of the Department of Anthropology and Archaeology, University of South Africa. His current fieldwork takes him to the Buysdorp community, Limpopo Province and the Griqua and Karretjie People of the Great Karoo of South Africa. Recent publications include: 'No Fixed Abode: the Poorest of the Poor and Elusive Identities in Rural South Africa' (*Journal of Southern African Studies* 28 (2) 2002) and 'The Buysdorp Conundrum: Constructing and Articulating Community and Identity in Soutpansberg, Limpopo Province' (*Anthropology Southern Africa*, 27 (3&4), 2004).

Saverio Krätli is a researcher at the Institute of Development Studies (IDS), University of Sussex, U.K., specialising in pastoral economy and livelihood. He has worked in Uganda, Kenya, Mongolia and Niger on pastoral conflict and education provision to nomadic people; his main research interest is the perceptions of mobile pastoralism in mainstream society and their links with pastoral development policies and practices. He is completing a Ph.D. on cattle breed selection and the management of genetic resources among the WoDaaBe of Niger.

Juliet McCaffery runs U.K.-based Consultancy and Training Services, specialising in gender, adult non-formal education and social development. She has over twenty five years experience of work in the Middle East, Africa and the Indian sub-continent. Among her various publications, the most recent is 'Closing the Gap: issues in gender integrated training of adult literacy facilitators' In *Women, Literacy and Development* (2004), edited by Anna Robinson-Pant. She is currently working on her doctoral thesis, a comparative study of the education of Gypsies and Travellers of Southern England and the nomadic Fulani of Northern Nigeria.

Helen Penn is Professor of Early Childhood at the University of East London, U.K. She has worked for a number of major donors and agencies including the Asian Development Bank, the EU Development Fund and UNICEF. Her work in Mongolia was funded by Save the Children-U.K. She evaluated the contribution of kindergarten and other early childhood projects as part of a poverty alleviation strategy by the Ministry of Education and Science. She worked with Demberel in Gobi Altai Region. Her book '*Unequal Childhoods: Young Children's Lives in Poor Countries*' has just been published by Routledge.

Jason Pennells is an education adviser with the International Extension Centre, Cambridge, U.K. He has worked on various projects concerned with education for nomadic pastoralists, in eastern Ethiopia, Somaliland, Sudan (Darfur), Kenya (Samburu) and Nigeria, where he has been engaged with basic teacher training for nomadic Fulani, a research project and conference on education for nomads and migrant fishing communities and, with NCNE, developing interactive radio instruction for nomadic primary schools.

Aparna Rao was research fellow at the Department of Social Anthropology, University of Cologne, Germany. She had extensive research experience among nomadic populations in South and Southeast Asia; had been co-editor of the journal Nomadic Peoples; and was a former co-chairperson on the 'Commission on Nomadic Peoples' of the 'International Union of Anthropological and Ethnological Sciences (IUAES).

Kayode Sanni is currently Education Specialist with the British Council, Nigeria, where he is responsible for grant-funded education programmes and provides technical support to the DfID-funded Capacity for Universal Basic Education (CUBE) project. He has considerable experience of informal approaches to basic education in Nigeria, having worked in participatory research and training as a consultant and civil society advocate, and also in literacy and community development at community level.

Mohammed Shahbazi, a Qashqa'i tribesman himself, was born into a non-literate family and was the only one of nine siblings to complete formal elementary education. He has a degree in engineering; a Master's in computer education; a Master's and Ph.D. in Cultural Anthropology; postdoctoral training in public health and is also a Certified Health Education Specialist. Currently associate professor of public health, and Interim Chair, Department of Behavioural and Environmental Health, MS (U.S.A.), he is working on several medical anthropological research and collaborative projects in North America, China and Iran.

Riana Steyn is Junior Lecturer in Anthropology in the Department of Anthropology and Archaeology, University of South Africa. She has conducted fieldwork among the Karretjie (donkey cart) children of the South African Karoo and is currently completing a dissertation on the subject. Her research interests include patterns of itinerancy and domestic fluidity, and the anthropology of childhood.

Bruce Underwood is an experienced educator who has spent many years working with indigenous people as an adult educator and classroom teacher. He is currently located in Adelaide, South Australia, from where he co-ordinates the AnTEP programme, a community based remote area tertiary education programme for people living in the Anangu Pitjantjatjara Yankunytjatjara Lands (APY Lands) in the north-west corner of South Australia. He travels extensively to the APY Lands. His main interests are in remote area indigenous education and the use of technology in remote areas.

INDEX

breed selection 265
camps 163
complex 12, 124
farming activities 242
herders 128
herds 123
industry 106, 109, 111
production 254
rearing 232
ritual attachment to 124
rustling 44, 124
station 106, 109, 110, 116
census 39, 62, 86, 160–61
CHANCE 45
Chengis Khan 202, 207
child
care 97, 100
labour 11, 22, 25, 26, 43, 48, 64
mortality 135
childhood
absence during 195
anthropology of 266
conceptions of 209
context of 54
early education in 259
education and 91–92
Karretje children's 4
knowledge for 53–54
phases of 57–58
traditional Mongolian 199, 210
China 17, 266
circumcision 59
citizen
educated 9
notions of 4, 20, 53, 69, 72, 182, 259, 260
rights of 5, 11
status of 142, 145, 150
Citizenship
benefits of 142
Mongolian 201
Omani 6, 214
state views of 2, 212
clan 102, 104–105, 108, 233, 235–37, 241–44, 251, 253–55
co-educational 68, 178
colonial countries 12
communism 187, 193–94, 196–97, 202, 205, 207, 209
Community Education Programme (CEP) 7, 231, 234–36, 242, 254
cost
benefit calculations 49, 127

of education 199, 205
of food 200
of health care 135
of high school education 147
market 243
of minority language materials 19
of moving structures 17
opportunity 26
of training 246, 249, 250
of using middle men 164
of water transport 42
cultural
antagonism 27
identity 6, 16, 28, 228
symbols 178
curriculum
adaptation of 27
agrarian 6
Bedouin schools, of 149
distinctive nomadic 246, 248
document 114
going beyond the 27
informal 145
kuttab schools 146
literacy 93
Mongolian 201
national 93, 213
negotiated 113
relevance 19–21, 109, 114, 117, 151, 207–209, 213, 214, 225, 232, 238, 251
school 68, 88, 246
as a tool for social regulation 149
Western 146

D
Dakar Conference 35–36
Danaid project 193
date garden 219
demarcation 163
Democratic Revolution 200
democracy 92, 200
demographic 201, 217, 233
dera 58
desert-based 214
development
economic 8, 12, 155, 237
human 9, 35, 39–40, 172
international/national 2, 8, 10, 24, 126, 231, 234
pastoral 8, 11–14, 21, 126–27, 132, 136–37, 265
social 10, 236, 265